# Business Ethics

**Collection Editor:**
William Frey

# Business Ethics

**Collection Editor:**
William Frey

**Authors:**
Jose A. Cruz-Cruz
William Frey

**Online:**
<http://cnx.org/content/col10491/1.9/ >

# C O N N E X I O N S

Rice University, Houston, Texas

# Table of Contents

# Chapter 1

# Ethical Leadership

## 1.1 Theory Building Activities: Mountain Terrorist Exercise[1]

### 1.1.1 Module Introduction

This module poses an ethical dilemma, that is, a forced choice between two bad alternatives. Your job is to read the scenario and choose between the two horns of the dilemma. You will make your choice and then justify it in the first activity. In the second activity, you will discuss your choice with others. Here, the objective is to reach consensus on a course of action or describe the point at which your group's progress toward consensus stopped. The Mountain Terrorist Exercise almost always generates lively discussion and helps us to reflect on of our moral beliefs. Don't expect to reach agreement with your fellow classmates quickly or effortlessly. (If you do, then your instructor will find ways of throwing a monkey wrench into the whole process.) What is more important here is that we learn how to state our positions clearly, how to listen to others, how to justify our positions, and how to assess the justifications offered by others. In other words, we will all have a chance to practice the virtue of reasonableness. And we will learn reasonableness not when it's easy (as it is when we agree) but when it becomes difficult (as it is when we disagree).

The second half of this module requires that you reflect carefully on your moral reasoning and that of your classmates. The Mountain Terrorist Exercise triggers the different moral schemas that make up our psychological capacity for moral judgment. Choosing one horn of the dilemma means that you tend to favor one kind of schema while choosing the other horn generally indicates that your favor another. The dominant moral theories that we will study this semester provide detailed articulations and justifications of these moral schemas. Reflecting on your choice, the reasons for your choice, and how your choice differs from that of your classmates will help you get started on the path of studying and effectively utilizing moral theory.

The following scenario comes originally from the philosopher, Bernard Williams. It is also presented in introductory ethics textbooks (such as Geoffrey Thomas' An Introduction to Ethics). The first time this module's author became aware of its use in the classroom was in a workshop on Agriculture Ethics led by Paul Thompson, then of Texas A&M University, in 1992.

### 1.1.2 Moral Theories Highlighted

1. Utilitarianism: the moral value of an action lies in its consequences or results
2. Deontology: the moral value of an action lies, not in its consequences, but in the formal characteristics of the action itself.
3. Virtue Ethics: Actions sort themselves out into virtuous or vicious actions. Virtuous actions stem from a virtuous character while vicious actions stem from a vicious or morally flawed character. Who we are is reveals through what we do.

---

[1]This content is available online at <http://cnx.org/content/m13764/1.11/>.

1

### 1.1.3 Mountain Terrorist Scenario

You are in a remote mountain village. A group of terrorists has lined up 20 people from the village; they plan on shooting them for collaborating with the enemy. Since you are not from the village, you will not be killed. Taking advantage of your position, you plead with the terrorists not to carry out their plan. Finally, you convince the leader that it is not necessary to kill all 20. He takes a gun, empties it of all its bullets except one, and then hands it to you. He has decided to kill only one villager to set an example to the rest. As an honored guest and outsider, you will decide who will be killed, and you will carry out the deed. The terrorists conclude with a warning; if you refuse to kill the villager, then they will revert back to the original plan of killing all 20. And if you try any "funny business," they will kill the 20 villagers and then kill you. What should you do?

**Your Options**

1. Take the gun, select a villager, and kill him or her.
2. Refuse the terrorists' offer and walk away from the situation.

**Spanish Translation by Dr. Halley Sanchez**

El Terrorista de la Montaña Tú eres un antropólogo que por un mes ha estado viviendo con y observando (o sea, estudiando) a los residents de una aldea en una area remota montañoza de un pais en América Latina. El día que te dispone irte de la aldea, aprece un grupo de hombres armados que reúnen a los aldeanos y les anuncian que se han enterado de que ellos han estado cooperando con el gobierno represivo y que, como lección, han de ejecutar viente de ellos. El líder de los terroristas te mira y te dice que tú te puedes ir, ya que no estás involucardo en la lucha patriótica y que ellos no están en la costumbre de tomar rehénes extranjeros. Debido a que te da la impresión de que el líder de los supuestos patriótas (terroristas?) es un hombre educado, tú te atreves tratar de razonar con él. Le explica que llevas un mes en la aldea y que los aldeanos no han cooperado de forma volutaria con el gobierno. Sí, por supuesto, las tropas del gobierno pasaron por la aldea y confiscaron algunas provisiones, pero los aldeanos no se las dieron libremente sino que estaban indefenso y no podieron prevenir que le confiscaran las mismas. El líder piensa un tiempo y te dice que por tú ser forastero y obviamente un antropólogo estudioso, te va a dar el benificio de la duda, y que por tanto no van a ejecutar viente aldeanos. Pero dado que la lucha patriótica está en un proceso crítico y que la aldea sí le proveyó provisiones al gobierno, por el bien de la lucha patriótica y el bien de la humanidad, es menester darle una lección a la aldea. Así que tan sólo han de ejecutar un aldeano. Más, como huesped, tú has de escoger quién ha de morir y tú has de matarlo tú mismo. Te da una pistola con una sola bala y te dice que proceda, mientras que a la vez te advierte que de tratar algo heroico, te ejecutarán inmediatamente y procederán a ejecutar a los viente aldeanos como dijeron al comienzo. Tú eres el antropólogo. ¿Qué harás?

**Activity 1**

In a short essay of 1 to 2 pages describe what you would do if you were in the position of the tourist. Then justify your choice.

**Activity 2**

Bring your essay to class. You will be divided into small groups. Present your choice and justification to the others in your group. Then listen to their choices and justifications. Try to reach a group consensus on choice and justification. (You will be given 10-15 minutes.) If you succeed present your results to the rest of the class. If you fail, present to the class the disagreement that blocked consensus and what you did (within the time limit) to overcome it.

### 1.1.4 Taxonomy of Ethical Approaches

There are many ethical approaches that can be used in decision making. The Mountain Terrorist Exercise is based on an artificial scenario designed to separate these theoretical approaches along the lines of the different "horns" of a dilemma. Utilitarians tend to choose to shoot a villager "in order to save 19." In other words they focus their analysis on the consequences of an action alternative and choose the one that produces the least harm. Deontologists generally elect to walk away from the situation. This is because they judge an action on the basis of its formal characteristics. A deontologist might argue that killing the villager violates natural law or cannot be made into a law or rule that consistently applies to everybody. A deontologist might say something like, "What right do I have to take another person's life?" A virtue ethicists might try to imagine how a person with the virtue of courage or integrity would act in this situaiton. (Williams claims that choosing to kill the villager, a duty under utilitarianism, would undermine the integrity of a person who abhorred killing.)

## Table Connecting Theory to Domain

1. Row 1: Utilitarianism concerns itself with the domain of consequences which tells us that the moral value of an action is "colored" by its results. The harm/beneficence test, which asks us to choose the least harmful alternative, encapsulates or summarizes this theoretical approach. The basic principle of utilitarianism is the principle of utility: choose that action that produces the greatest good for the greatest number. Cost/benefits analysis, the Pareto criterion, the Kalder/Hicks criterion, risk/benefits analysis all represent different frameworks for balancing positive and negative consequences under utilitarianism or consequentialism.

2. Row 2: Deontology helps us to identify and justify rights and their correlative duties The reversibility test summarizes deontology by asking the question, "Does your action still work if you switch (=reverse) roles with those on the receiving end? "Treat others always as ends, never merely as means," the Formula of End, represents deontology's basic principle. The rights that represent special cases of treating people as ends and not merely as means include (a) informed consent, (b) privacy, (c) due process, (d) property, (e) free speech, and (f) conscientious objection.

3. Row 3: Virtue ethics turns away from the action and focuses on the agent, the person performing the action. The word, "Virtue," refers to different sets of skills and habits cultivated by agents. These skills and habits, consistently and widely performed, support, sustain, and advance different occupational, social, and professional practices. (See MacIntyre, After Virtue, and Solomon, Ethics and Excellence, for more on the relation of virtues to practices.) The public identification test summarizes this approach: an action is morally acceptable if it is one with which I would willingly be publicly associated given my moral convictions. Individual virtues that we will use this semester include integrity, justice, responsibility, reasonableness, honesty, trustworthiness, and loyalty.

| Covering All the Bases | | | | |
|---|---|---|---|---|
| Ethical Dimension | Covering Ethical Approach | Encapsulating Ethical Test | Basic Principles | Application or Bridging Tools |
| Consequences | Utilitarianism | Harm/Beneficence (weigh harms against benefits) | Principle of Utility: greatest good for greatest number | Benefit & cost comparisonUtility Maximization |
| Formal Characteristics of Act | Deontology (Duty-based, rights-based, natural law, social contract) | Reversibility (test by reversing roles between agent and object of action) | Categorical ImperativeFormula of EndAutonomy | Free & Informed Consent, Privacy, Property, Due Process, Free Speech, Conscientious objection |
| *continued on next page* | | | | |

| Skills and habits cultivated by agent | Virtue Ethics | Public Identification (impute moral import of action to person of agent) | Virtues are means between extremes with regard to agent and action Virtues are cultivated dispositions that promote central community values | Integrity, justice, responsibility, reasonableness, honesty, trustworthiness, loyalty |
|---|---|---|---|---|

**Table 1.1**

### 1.1.5 Comments on the Relation Between Ethical Approaches

The Mountain Terrorist Exercise has, in the past, given students the erroneous idea that ethical approaches are necessarily opposed to one another. As one student put it, "If deontology tells us to walk away from the village, then utilitarianism must tell us to stay and kill a villager because deontology and utilitarianism, as different and opposed theories, always reach different and opposed conclusions on the actions they recommend." The Mountain Terrorist dilemma was specially constructed by Bernard Williams to produce a situation that offered only a limited number of alternatives. He then tied these alternatives to different ethical approaches to separate them precisely because in most real world situations they are not so readily distinguishable. Later this semester, we will turn from these philosophical puzzles to real world cases where ethical approaches function in a very different and mostly complimentary way. As we will see, ethical approaches, for the most part, converge on the same solutions. For this reason, this module concludes with 3 meta-tests. When approaches converge on a solution, this strengthens the solution's moral validity. When approaches diverge on a solution, this weakens their moral validity. A third meta-test tells us to avoid framing all ethical problems as dilemmas (=forced choices between undesirable alternatives) or what Carolyn Whitbeck calls "multiple-choice" problems. You will soon learn that effective moral problem solving requires moral imagination and moral creativity. We do not "find" solutions "out there" ready made but design them to harmonize and realize ethical and practical values.

**Meta-Tests**

- Divergence Test: When two ethical approaches differ on a given solution, then that difference counts against the strength of the solution. Solutions on which ethical theories diverge must be revised towards convergence.
- Convergence Test: Convergence represents a meta-test that attests to solution strength. Solutions on which different theoretical approaches converge are, by this fact, strengthened. Convergence demonstrates that a solution is strong, not just over one domain, but over multiple domains.
- Avoid Framing a Problem as a Dilemma. A dilemma is a no-win situation that offers only two alternatives of action both of which are equally bad. (A trilemma offers three bad alternatives, etc.) Dilemmas are better dissolved than solved. Reframe the dilemma into something that admits of more than two no-win alternatives. Dilemma framing (framing a situation as an ethical dilemma) discourages us from designing creative solutions that integrate the conflicting values that the dilemma poses as incompatible.

### 1.1.6 Module Wrap-Up

1. **Reasonableness and the Mountain Terrorist Exercise.** It may seem that this scenario is the last place where the virtue of reasonableness should prevail, but look back on how you responded to those of your classmates who chose differently in this exercise and who offered arguments that you had not initially thought of. Did you "listen and respond thoughtfully" to them? Were you "open to new ideas"

even if these challenged your own? Did you "give reasons for" your views, modifying and shaping them to respond to your classmates' arguments? Did you "acknowledge mistakes and misunderstandings" such as responding critically and personally to a classmate who put forth a different view? Finally, when you turned to working with your group, were you able to "compromise (without compromising personal integrity)"? If you did any or all of these things, then you practiced the virtue of reasonableness as characterized by Michael Pritchard in his book, Reasonable Children: Moral Education and Moral Learning (1996, University of Kansas Press, p. 11). Congratulate yourself on exercising reasonableness in an exercise designed to challenge this virtue. You passed the test.

2. **Recognizing that we are already making ethical arguments.** In the past, students have made the following arguments on this exercise: (a) I would take the gun and kill a villager in order to save nineteen; (b) I would walk away because I don't have the right to take another's life; (c) While walking away might appear cowardly it is the responsible thing to do because staying and killing a villager would make me complicit in the terrorists' project. As we discussed in class, these and other arguments make use of modes of thought captured by ethical theories or approaches. The first employs the consequentialist approach of utilitarianism while the second makes use of the principle of respect that forms the basis of our rights and duties. The third works through a conflict between two virtues, courage and responsibility. This relies on the virtue approach. One accomplishment of this exercise is to make you aware of the fact that you are already using ethical arguments, i.e., arguments that appeal to ethical theory. Learning about the theories behind these arguments will help you to makes these arguments more effectively.

3. **Results from Muddy Point Exercises** The Muddy Point Exercises you contributed kept coming back to two points. (a) Many of you pointed out that you needed more information to make a decision in this situation. For example, who were these terrorists, what causes were they fighting for, and were they correct in accusing the village of collaborating with the enemy? Your request for more information was quite appropriate. But many of the cases we will be studying this semester require decisions in the face of uncertainty and ignorance. These are unavoidable in some situations because of factors such as the cost and time of gathering more information. Moral imagination skillfully exercised can do a lot to compensate when all of the facts are not in. (b) Second, many of you felt overly constrained by the dilemma framing of the scenario. Those of you who entered the realm of "funny business" (anything beyond the two alternatives of killing the villager or walking away) took a big step toward effective moral problem solving. By rejecting the dilemma framing of this scenario, you were trying to reframe the situation to allow for more–and more ethically viable–alternatives. Trying to negotiate with the Terrorists is a good example of reframing the scenario to admit of more ethical alternatives of action than killing or walking away.

4. Congratulations on completing your first ethics module! You have begun recognizing and practicing skills that will help you to tackle real life ethical problems. (Notice that we are going to work with "problems" not "dilemmas".) We will now turn, in the next module, to look at those who managed to do good in the face of difficulty. Studying moral exemplars will provide the necessary corrective to the "no–win" Mountain Terrorist Exercise.

# 1.2 Theory-Building Activities: Virtue Ethics[2]

Based on material presented by Chuck Huff (St. Olaf College) and William Frey at the Association for Practical and Professional Ethics in 2005 at San Antonio, TX. Preliminary versions were distributed during this presentation.

---

[2]This content is available online at <http://cnx.org/content/m13755/1.11/>.

## 1.2.1 Module Introduction

This module uses materials being prepared for Good Computing: A Virtue Approach to Computer Ethics, to set up an exercise in which you will identify and spell out virtues relevant to your professional discipline. After identifying these virtues, you will work to contextualize them in everyday practice. Emphasis will be placed on the Aristotelian approach to virtues which describes a virtue as the disposition toward the mean located between the extremes of excess and defect. You will also be asked to identify common obstacles that prevent professionals from realizing a given virtue and moral exemplars who demonstrate consistent success in realizing these virtues and responding to obstacles that stand in the way of their realization. In a variation on this module you could be asked to compare the virtues you have identified for your profession with virtues that belong to other moral ecologies such as those of the Homeric warrier.

## 1.2.2 Three Versions of Virtue Ethics: Virtue 1, Virtue 2, and Virtue 3

Virtue ethics has gone through three historical versions. The first, Virtue 1, was set forth by Aristotle in ancient Greece. While tied closely to practices in ancient Greece that no longer exist today, Aristotle's version still has a lot to say to us in this day and age. In the second half of the twentieth century, British philosophical ethicists put forth a related but different theory of virtue ethics (virtue 2) as an alternative to the dominant ethical theories of utilitarianism and deontology. Virtue 2 promised a new foundation of ethics consistent with work going on at that time in the philosophy of mind. Proponents felt that turning from the action to the agent promised to free ethical theory from the intractable debate between utilitarianism and deontology and offered a way to expand scope and relevance of ethics. Virtue 3 reconnects with Aristotle and virtue 1 even though it drops the doctrine of the mean and Aristotle's emphasis on character. Using recent advances in moral psychology and moral pedagogy, it seeks to rework key Aristotelian concepts in modern terms. In the following, we will provide short characterizations of each of these three versions of virtue ethics.

## 1.2.3 Virtue 1: Aristotle's Virtue Ethics

- **Eudaimonia.** Happiness, for Aristotle, consists of a life spent fulfilling the intellectual and moral virtues. These modes of action are auto-telic, that is, they are self-justifying and contain their own ends. By carrying out the moral and intellectual virtues for a lifetime, we realize ourselves fully as humans. Because we are doing what we were meant to do, we are happy in this special sense of eudaimonia.
- **Arete.** Arete is the Greek word we usually translate as "virtue". But arete is more faithfully translated as excellence. For Aristotle, the moral and intellectual virtues represent excellences. So the moral life is more than just staying out of trouble. Under Aristotle, it is centered in pursuing and achieving excellence for a lifetime.
- **Virtue as the Mean.** Aristotle also characterizes virtue as a settled disposition to choose the **mean** between the extremes of excess and defect, all relative to person and situation. Courage (the virtue) is the mean between the extremes of excess (too much courage or recklessness) and defect (too little courage or cowardice). Aristotle's claim that most or all of the virtues can be specified as the mean between extremes is controversial. While the doctrine of the mean is dropped in Virtue 2 and Virtue 3, we will still use it in developing virtue tables. (See exercise 1 below.) You may not find both extremes for the virtues you have been assigned but make the effort nonetheless.
- **Ethos.** "Ethos" translates as character which, for Aristotle, composes the seat of the virtues. Virtues are well settled dispositions or habits that have been incorporated into our characters. Because our characters are manifested in our actions, the patterns formed by these over time reveal who we are. This can be formulated as a decision-making test, the **public identification test**. Because we reveal who we are through our actions we can ask, when considering an action, whether we would care to be publicly identified with this action. "Would I want to be publicly known as the kind of person who would perform that kind of action? Would I, through my cowardly action, want to be publicly

identified as a coward? Would I, through my responsible action, want to be publicly identified as a responsible person? Because actions provide others with a window into our characters, we must make sure be sure that they portray us as we want to be portrayed.

- **Aisthesis of the Phronimos.** This Greek phrase, roughly translated as the perception of the morally experienced agent, reveals how important practice and experience are to Aristotle in his conception of moral development. One major difference between Aristotle and other ethicists (utilitarians and deontologists) is the emphasis that Aristotle places on developing into or becoming a moral person. For Aristotle, one becomes good by first repeatedly performing good actions. So morality is more like an acquired skill than a mechanical process. Through practice we develop sensitivities to what is morally relevant in a situation, we learn how to structure our situations to see moral problems and possibilities, and we develop the skill of "hitting" consistently on the mean between the extremes. All of these are skills that are cultivated in much the same way as a basketball player develops through practice the skill of shooting the ball through the hoop.

- **Bouleusis.** This word translates as "deliberation." For Aristotle, moral skill is not the product of extensive deliberation (careful, exhaustive thinking about reasons, actions, principles, concepts, etc.) but of practice. Those who have developed the skill to find the mean can do so with very little thought and effort. Virtuous individuals, for Aristotle, are surprisingly unreflective. They act virtuously without thought because it has become second nature to them.

- **Akrasia.** Ross translates this word as "incontinence" which is outmoded. A better translation is weakness of will. For Aristotle, knowing where virtue lies is not the same as doing what virtue demands. There are those who are unable to translate knowledge into resolution and then into action. Because akrasis (weakness of will) is very real for Aristotle, he also places emphasis in his theory of moral development on the cultivation of proper emotions to help motivate virtuous action. Later ethicists seek to oppose emotion and right action; Aristotle sees properly trained and cultivated emotions as strong motives to doing what virtue requires.

- **Logos** Aristotle's full definition of virtue is "a state of character concerned with choice, lying in a mean, i.e. the mean relative to us, this being determined by a rational principle, and by that principle by which [a person] of practical wisdom would determine it." (Ross's translation in **Nichomachean Ethics**, 1106b, 36.) We have talked about character, the mean, and the person of practical wisdom. The last key term is "logos" which in this definition is translated by reason. This is a good translation if we take reason in its fullest sense so that it is not just the capacity to construct valid arguments but also includes the practical wisdom to assess the truth of the premises used in constructing these arguments. In this way, Aristotle expands reason beyond logic to include a fuller set of intellectual, practical, emotional, and perceptual skills that together form a practical kind of wisdom.

## 1.2.4 Virtue 2

- The following summary of Virtue 2 is taken largely from Rosalind Hursthouse. While she extensively qualifies each of these theses in her own version of virtue ethics, these points comprise an excellent summary of Virtue 2 which starts with G.E.M. Anscombe's article, "Modern Moral Philosophy," and continues on into the present. Hursthouse presents this characterization of Virtue 2 in her book, **On Virtue Ethics** (2001) U.K.: Oxford University Press: 17.

- **Virtue 2 is agent centered.** Contrary to deontology and utilitarianism which focus on whether actions are good or right, V2 is agent centered in that it sees the action as an expression of the goodness or badness of the agent. Utilitarianism focuses on actions which bring about the greatest happiness for the greatest number; deontology seeks those actions that respect the autonomy of individuals and carry out moral obligations, especially duties. These theories emphasize **doing** what is good or right. Virtue 2, on the other hand, focuses on the agent's becoming or **being** good.

- **Can Virtue 2 tell us how to act?** Because V2 is agent-centered, critics claim that it cannot provide insight into how to act in a given situation. All it can say is, "Act the way a moral exemplar would act." But what moral standards do moral exemplars use or embody in their actions? And what moral standards do we use to pick out the moral exemplars themselves? Hursthouse acknowledges that this criticism hits home. However, she points out that the moral standards come from the moral concepts that we apply to moral exemplars; they are individuals who act **courageously**, exercise **justice**, and realize **honesty**. The moral concepts "courage," "justice," and "honesty" all have independent content that helps guide us. She also calls this criticism unfair: while virtue 2 may not provide any more guidance than deontology or utilitarianism, it doesn't provide any less. Virtue 2 may not provide perfect guidance, but what it does provide is favorably comparable to what utilitarianism and deontology provide.

- **Virtue 2 replaces Deontic concepts (right, duty, obligation) with Aretaic concepts (good, virtue).** This greatly changes the scope of ethics. Deontic concepts serve to establish our minimum obligations. On the other hand, aretaic concepts bring the pursuit of excellence within the purview of ethics. Virtue ethics produces a change in our moral language that makes the pursuit of excellence an essential part of moral inquiry.

- Finally, there is a somewhat different account of virtue 2 (call it virtue 2a) that can be attributed to Alisdair MacIntyre. This version "historicizes" the virtues, that is, looks at how our concepts of key virtues have changed over time. (MacIntyre argues that the concept of justice, for example, varies greatly depending on whether one views justice in Homeric Greece, Aristotle's Greece, or Medieval Europe.) Because he argues that skills and actions are considered virtuous only in relation to a particular historical and community context, he redefines virtues as those skill sets necessary to realize the goods or values around which social practices are built and maintained. This notion fits in well with professional ethics because virtues can be derived from the habits, attitudes, and skills needed to maintain the cardinal ideals of the profession.

## 1.2.5 Virtue 3

**Virtue 3 can best be outlined by showing how the basic concepts of Virtue 1 can be reformulated to reflect current research in moral psychology.**

1. **Reformulating Happiness (Eudaimonia).** Mihaly Csikcszentmihalyi has described flow experiences (see text box below) in which autotelic activities play a central role. For Aristotle, the virtues also are autotelic. They represent faculties whose exercise is key to realizing our fullest potentialities as human beings. Thus, virtues are self-validating activities carried out for themselves as well as for the ends they bring about. Flow experiences are also important in helping us to conceptualize the virtues in a professional context because they represent a well practiced integration of skill, knowledge, and moral sensitivity.

2. **Reformulating Values (Into Arete or Excellence).** To carry out the full project set forth by virtue 3, it is necessary to reinterpret as excellence key moral values such as honesty, justice, responsibility, reasonableness, and integrity. For example, moral responsibility has often been described as carrying out basic, minimal moral obligations. As an excellence, responsibility becomes refocused on extending knowledge and power to expand our range of effective, moral action. Responsibility reformulated as an excellence also implies a high level of care that goes well beyond what is minimally required.

3. **De-emphasizing Character.** The notion of character drops out to be replaced by more or less enduring and integrated skills sets such as moral imagination, moral creativity, reasonableness, and perseverance. Character emerges from the activities of integrating personality traits, acquired skills, and deepening knowledge around situational demands. The unity character represents is always complex and changing.

4. **Practical Skill Replaces Deliberation.** Moral exemplars develop skills which, through practice, become second nature. These skills obviate the need for extensive moral deliberation. Moral exemplars resemble more skillful athletes who quickly develop responses to dynamic situations than Hamlets stepping back from action for prolonged and agonizing deliberation.

5. **Greater Role for Emotions.** Nancy Sherman discusses how, for Aristotle, emotion is not treated as an irrational force but as an effective tool for moral action once it has been shaped and cultivated through proper moral education. To step beyond the controvery of what Aristotle did and did not say about the emotions (and where he said it) we place this enhanced role for emotions within virtue 3. Emotions carry out four essential functions: (a) they serve as modes of attention; (b) they also serve as modes of responding to or signaling value; (c) they fulfill a revelatory function; and (d) they provide strong motives to moral action. Nancy Sherman, **Making a Necessity of Virtue: Aristotle and Kant on Virtue** (1997), U.K.: Cambridge University Press: 39-50.

## 1.2.6 Flow Experiences

- The psychologist, Mihaly Csikszentmihalyi, has carried out fascinating research on what he terms "flow experiences." Mike Martin in **Meaningful Work** (2000) U.K.: Oxford,: 24, summarizes these in the following bullets:
- "clear goals as one proceeds"
- "immediate feedback about progress"
- "a balance between challenges and our skills to respond to them"
- "immersion of awareness in the activity without disruptive distractions"
- "lack of worry about failure"
- loss of anxious self-consciousness"
- time distortions (either time flying or timeslowing pleasurably)"
- the activity becomes **autotelic**: an end in itself, enjoyed as such"

## 1.2.7 Virtue Tables

The table just below provides a format for spelling out individual virtues through (1) a general description, (2) the correlative vices of excess and defect, (3) the skills and mental states that accompany and support it, and (4) real and fictional individuals who embody it. Following the table are hints on how to identify and characterize virtues. We start with the virtue of integrity:

| Virtue | Description | Excess | Defect | Obstacles to realizing the virtue in professional practices | Moral Exemplar |
|---|---|---|---|---|---|
| Integrity | A meta-virtue in which the holder exhibits unity of character manifested in holding together even in the face of strong disruptive pressures or temptations | Excess: Rigidity– sticking to one´s guns even when one is obviously wrong(2,3) | Defect: Wantonness. A condition where one exhibits no stability or consistency in character | Individual corruption: Individuals can be tempted by greed toward the vice of defect. Lack of moral courage can also move one to both extremes | Saint Thomas More as portrayed in Robert Bolt´s A Man for All Seasons. More refuses to take an oath that goes against the core beliefs in terms of which he defines himself. |
|  |  |  |  | Institutional Corruption: One may work in an organization where corruption is the norm. This generates dilemmas like following an illegal order or getting fired. |  |
| | | | | *continued on next page* | |

Table 1.2

## 1.2.8 Exercise 1: Construct Virtue Tables for Professional Virtues

1. Discuss in your group why the virtue you have been assigned is important for the practice of your profession. What goods or values does the consistent employment of this virtue produce?
2. Use the discussion in #1 to develop a general description of your virtue. Think along the following lines: people who have virtue X tend to exhibit certain characteristics (or do certain things) in certain kinds of situations. Try to think of these situations in terms of what is common and important to your profession or practice.
3. Identify the corresponding vices. What characterizes the points of excess and defect between which your virtue as the mean lies?
4. What obstacles arise that prevent professionals from practicing your virtue? Do well-meaning professionals lack power or technical skill? Can virtues interfere with the realization of non-moral values like financial values? See if you can think of a supporting scenario or case here.
5. Identify a moral exemplar for your virtue. Make use of the exemplars described in the **Moral Exemplars in Business and Professional Ethics** module.
6. Go back to task #2. Redefine your description of your virtue in light of the subsequent tasks, especially the moral exemplar you identified. Check for coherence.
7. Finally, does your virtue stand alone or does it need support from other virtues or skills? For example, integrity might also require moral courage.

## 1.2.9 Exercise 2: Reflect on these Concluding Issues

- Did you have trouble identifying a moral exemplar? Many turn to popular figures for their moral exemplars. Movies and fiction also offer powerful models. Why do you think that it is hard to find moral exemplars in your profession? Is it because your profession is a den of corruption? (Probably not.) Do we focus more on villains than on heroes? Why or why not?
- What did you think about the moral leaders portrayed in the **Moral Exemplars in Business and Professional Ethics** module?
- Did you have trouble identifying both vices, i.e., vices of excess and defect? If so, do you think this because some virtues may not have vices of excess and defect? What do you think about Aristotle's doctrine of the mean?
- Did you notice that the virtue profiles given by your group and the other groups in the class overlapped? Is this a problem for virtue theory? Why do our conceptions of the key moral values and virtues overlap?
- Did you find the virtues difficult to apply? What do you think about the utilitarian and deontological criticism of virtue ethics, namely, that it cannot provide us with guidelines on how to act in difficult situations? Should ethical theories emphasize the act or the person? Or both?
- The most tenacious obstacle to working with virtue ethics is to change focus from the morally minimal to the morally exemplary. "Virtue" is the translation of the Greek word, arête. But "excellence" is, perhaps, a better word. Understanding virtue ethics requires seeing that virtue is concerned with the exemplary, not the barely passable. (Again, looking at moral exemplars helps.) Arête transforms our understanding of common moral values like justice and responsibility by moving from minimally acceptable to exemplary models.

Moral Leaders[3] The profiles of several moral leaders in practical and professional ethics. Computer Ethics Cases[4] This link provides several computer ethics cases and also has a description of decision making and

---

[3]http://www.onlineethics.org
[4]http://www.computingcases.org

socio-technical systems frameworks. Moral Exemplars in Business and Professional Ethics[5] Profiles of several moral leaders in practical and professional ethics.

# 1.3 Moral Exemplars in Business and Professional Ethics[6]

## 1.3.1 Module Introduction

Through the activities of this module you will learn to balance cautionary tales in business and professional ethics with new stories about those who consistently act in a morally exemplary way. While cautionary tales teach us what to avoid, narratives from the lives of moral exemplars show us how to be good. A study of moral best practices in business and professional ethics shows that moral exemplars exhibit positive and learnable skills. This module, then, looks at moral exemplars in business and the professions, outlines their outstanding accomplishments, and helps you to unpack the strategies they use to overcome obstacles to doing good.

You will begin by identifying outstanding individuals in business and associated practices who have developed moral "best practices." Your task is look at these individuals, retell their stories, identify the skills that help them do good, and build a foundation for a more comprehensive study of virtue in occupational and professional ethics.

## 1.3.2 Exercise 1: Choose a moral exemplar

- Identify a moral exemplar and provide a narrative description of his or her life story.
- To get this process started, look at the list of moral exemplars provided in this module. The links in the upper left hand corner of this module will help you to explore their accomplishments in detail. Feel free to choose your own exemplar. Make sure you identify someone in the occupational and professional areas such as business and engineering. These areas have more than their share of exemplars, but they tend to escape publicity because their actions avoid publicity generating disasters rather than bring them about.

## 1.3.3 Moral Exemplars

- 1. William LeMesseur. LeMesseur designed the Citicorp Building in New York. When a student identified a critical design flaw in the building during a routine class exercise, LeMesseur responded, not by shooting the messenger, but by developing an intricate and effective plan for correcting the problem before it issued in drastic real world consequences. Check out LeMesseur's profile at onlineethics and see how he turned a potential disaster into a good deed.
- 2. Fred Cuny, starting in 1969 with Biafra, carried out a series of increasingly effective interventions in international disasters. He brought effective methods to disaster relief such as engineering know-how, political savvy, good business sense, and aggressive advocacy. His timely interventions saved thousands of Kurdish refugees in the aftermath of the Persian Gulf War in 1991. He also helped design and implement an innovative water filtration system in Sarajevo during the Bosnia-Serb conflict in 1993. For more details, consult the biographical sketch at onlineethics.
- 3. Roger Boisjoly worked on a team responsible for developing o-ring seals for fuel tanks used in the Challenger Shuttle. When his team noticed evidence of gas leaks he made an emergency presentation before officials of Morton Thiokol and NASA recommending postponing the launch scheduled for the next day. When decision makers refused to change the launch date, Boisjoly watched in horror the next day as the Challenger exploded seconds into its flight. Find out about the courageous stand Boisjoly took in the aftermath of the Challenger explosion by reading the biographical sketch at onlineethics.

---

[5]http://cnx.org/content/m14256/latest
[6]This content is available online at <http://cnx.org/content/m14256/1.8/>.

- 4. Muhammad Yunus won the Nobel Prize for Peace in 2006. His effort in setting up "micro-businesses" funded through "micro-lending" has completely changed the paradigm on how to extend business practices to individuals at the bottom of the pyramid. Learn about his strategies for creating micro-businesses and how those strategies have been extended throughout the world, including Latin America, by listening to an interview with him broadcast by the Online News Hour. (See link included in this module.)
- 5. Bill Gates has often been portrayed as a villain, especially during the anti-trust suit against Mircosoft in the mid 1990's. Certainly his aggressive and often ruthless business practices need to be evaluated openly and critically. But recently Gates stopped participating in the day-to-day management of his company, Microsoft, and has set up a charitable foundation to oversee international good works projects. Click on the link included in this module to listen to and read an interview recently conducted with him and his wife, Melinda, on their charitable efforts.
- 6. Jeffrey Skilling, former CEO of Enron, can hardly be called a moral exemplar. Yet when Enron was at its peak, its CEO, Jeffrey Skilling, was considered among the most innovative, creative, and brilliant of contemporary corporate CEOs. View the documentary, The Smartest Guys in the Room, read the book of the same title, and learn about the configuration of character traits that led to Skilling's initial successes and ultimate failure. A link included in this module will lead you to an interview with Skilling conducted on March 28, 2001.
- Inez Austin worked to prevent contamination from nuclear wastes produced by a plutonium production facility. Visit Online Ethics by clicking on the link above to find out more about her heroic stand.
- Rachael Carson's book, The Silent Spring, was one of the key events inaugurating the environmental movement in the United States. For more on the content of her life and her own personal act of courage, visit the biographical profile at Online Ethics. You can click on the Supplimental Link provided above.

## 1.3.4 Exercise Two: Moral Exemplar Profiles

- What are the positive and negative influences you can identify for your moral exemplar?
- What good deeds did your exemplar carry out?
- What obstacles did your moral exemplar face and how did he or she overcome them?
- What skills, attitudes, beliefs, and emotions helped to orient and motivate your moral exemplar.?

## 1.3.5 Exercise Three

Prepare a short dramatization of a key moment in the life of your group's moral exemplar.

## 1.3.6 Textbox: Two different Types of Moral Exemplar

- Studies carried out by Chuck Huff into moral exemplars in computing suggest that moral exemplars can operate as craftspersons or reformers. (Sometimes they can combine both these modes.)
- Craftspersons (1) draw on pre-existing values in computing, (2) focus on users or customers who have needs, (3) take on the role of providers of a service/product, (4) view barriers as inert obstacles or puzzles to be solved, and (5) believe they are effective in their role.
- Reformers (1) attempt to change organizations and their values, (2) take on the role of moral crusaders, (3) view barriers as active opposition, and (4) believe in the necessity of systemic reform
- These descriptions of moral exemplars have been taken from a presentation by Huff at the STS colloquium at the University of Virginia on October 2006. Huff's presentation can be found at the link provided in the upper left hand corner of this module.

### 1.3.7 Textbox: Characteristics and Skills Exhibited by Moral Exemplars

- Moral exemplars have succeeded in integrating moral and professional attitudes and beliefs into their core identity. Going against these considerations for moral exemplars is tantamount to acting against self.
- Moral exemplars are able to carry out their goals due to surrounding, supportive communities. They do not act alone but within support groups.
- Moral exemplars often do not go through periods of intensive and prolonged deliberation in order to hit upon the correct action. If we want a literary example, we need to replace the tortured deliberations of a Hamlet with the quick and intuitive insight of an Esther Summerson. (Summerson is a character in Charles Dickens' novel, Bleak House. See both William Shakespeare and Charles Dickens for more examples of villains and exemplars.) This confirms Aristotle's view that virtues are dispositions that have been carefully cultivated through moral education into habits that become "second nature" in moral exemplars.
- Huff has identified four skill sets that aid moral exemplars in the expression of their virtues: (1) moral imagination which consists of projecting oneself into the perspective of others, (2) moral creativity or the ability to generate solutions to moral challenges while responding to multiple constraints, (3) reasonableness which consists of gathering relevant evidence, listening to others, giving reasons, changing plans/positions based on reasons, and (4) perseverance or planning moral action and responding to unforeseen circumstances while keeping moral goals intact.
- For more detail on these items consult Huff's presentation found by clicking on the link above.

## 1.4 Ethics of Team Work[7]

- Ethics of Team Work
- William J. Frey (working with material developed by Chuck Huff at St. Olaf College
- Centro de la Etica en las Profesiones
- University of Puerto Rico - Mayaguez

### 1.4.1 Module Introduction

Much of your future work will be organized around group or team activities. This module is designed to prepare you for this by getting you to reflect on ethical and practical problems that arise in small groups like work teams. Four issues, based on well-known ethical values, are especially important. How do groups achieve justice (in the distribution of work), responsibility (in specifying tasks, assigning blame, and awarding credit), reasonableness (ensuring participation, resolving conflict, and reaching consensus), and honesty (avoiding deception, corruption, and impropriety)? This module asks that you develop plans for realizing these moral values in your group work this semester. Furthermore, you are provided with a list of some of the more common pitfalls of group work and then asked to devise strategies for avoiding them. Finally, at the end of the semester, you will review your goals and strategies, reflect on your successes and problems, and carry out an overall assessment of the experience.

### 1.4.2 Module Activities

1. Groups are provided with key ethical values that they describe and seek to realize thorugh group activity.
2. Groups also study various obstacles that arise in collective activity: the Abilene Paradox, Groupthink, and Group Polarization.

---

[7]This content is available online at <http://cnx.org/content/m13760/1.7/>.

3. Groups prepare initial reports consisting of plans for realizing key values in their collective activity. They also develop strategies for avoiding associated obstacles.

4. At the end of the semester, groups prepare a self-evaluation that assesses success in realizing ethical values and avoiding obstacles.

5. Textboxes in this module describe pitfalls in groups activities and offer general strategies for preventing or mitigating them. There is also a textbox that provides an introductory orientation on key ethical values or virtues.

## 1.4.3 Value Profiles for Professional Ethics

1. Definition - A value "refers to a claim about what is worthwhile, what is good. A value is a single word or phrase that identifies something as being desirable for human beings." Brincat and Wike, Morality and the Professional Life: Values at Work

2. Reasonableness - Defusing disagreement and resolving conflicts through integration. Characteristics include seeking relevant information, listening and responding thoughtfully to others, being open to new ideas, giving reasons for views held, and acknowledging mistakes and misunderstandings. (From Michael Pritchard, Reasonable Children)

3. Responsibility - The ability to develop moral responses appropriate to the moral issues and problems that arise in one's day-to-day experience. Characteristics include avoiding blame shifting, designing overlapping role reponsibilities to fill responsibility "gaps", expanding the scope and depth of general and situation-specific knowledge, and working to expand control and power.

4. Respect - Recognizing and working not to circumvent the capacity of autonomy in each individual. Characteristics include honoring rights such as privacy, property, free speech, due process, and participatory rights such as informed consent. Disrespect circumvents autonomy by deception, force, or manipulation.

5. Justice - Giving each his or her due. Justice breaks down into kinds such as distributive (dividing benefits and burdens fairly), retributive (fair and impartial administration of punishments), administrative (fair and impartial administration of rules), and compensatory (how to fairly recompense those who have been wrongfully harmed by others).

6. Trust - According to Solomon, trust is the expectation of moral behavior from others.

7. Honesty - Truthfulness as a mean between too much honesty (bluntness which harms) and dishonesty (deceptiveness, misleading acts, and mendaciousness).

8. Integrity - A meta-value that refers to the relation between particular values. These values are integrated with one another to form a coherent, cohesive and smoothly functioning whole. This resembles Solomon's account of the virtue of integrity.

## 1.4.4 Exercise 1: Developing Strategies for Value Realization

- Design a plan for realizing key moral values of team work. Your plan should address the following value-based tasks

- How does your group plan on realizing justice? For example, how will you assign tasks within the group that represent a fair distribution of the work load and, at the same time, recognize differences in individual strengths and weaknesses? How does your group plan on dealing with members who fail to do their fair share?

- How does your group plan on realizing responsibility? For example, what are the responsibilities that members will take on in the context of collective work? Who will be the leader? Who will play devil's advocate to avoid groupthink? Who will be the spokesperson for the group? How does your group plan to make clear to each individual his or her task or role responsibilities?

- How does your group plan on implementing the value of reasonableness? How will you guarantee that each individual participates fully in group decisions and activities? How will you deal with the differences, non-agreements, and disagreements that arise within the group? What process will your group use to reach agreement? How will your group insure that every individual has input, that each opinion will be heard and considered, and that each individual will be respected?

- How does your group plan on implementing the value of (academic) honesty? For example, how will you avoid cheating or plagiarism? How will you detect plagiarism from group members, and how will you respond to it?
- Note: Use your imagination here and be specific on how you plan to realize each value. Think preventively (how you plan on avoiding injustice, irresponsibility, injustice, and dishonesty) and proactively (how you can enhance these values). Don't be afraid to outline specific commitments. Expect some of your commitments to need reformulation. At the end of the semester, this will help you write the final report. Describe what worked, what did not work, and what you did to fix the latter.

## 1.4.5 Obstacles to Group Work (Developed by Chuck Huff for Good Computing: A Virtue Approach to Computer Ethics)

1. The Abilene Paradox. The story involves a family who would all rather have been at home that ends up having a bad dinner in a lousy restaurant in Abilene, Texas. Each believes the others want to go to Abilene and never questions this by giving their own view that doing so is a bad idea. In the Abilene paradox, the group winds up doing something that no individual wants to do because of a breakdown of intra-group communication.
2. Groupthink. The tendency for very cohesive groups with strong leaders to disregard and defend against information that goes against their plans and beliefs. The group collectively and the members individually remain loyal to the party line while happily marching off the cliff, all the while blaming "them" (i.e., outsiders) for the height and situation of the cliff.
3. Group Polarization. Here, individuals within the group choose to frame their differences as disagreements. Framing a difference as non-agreement leaves open the possibility of working toward agreement by integrating the differences or by developing a more comprehensive standpoint that dialectally synthesizes the differences. Framing a difference as disagreement makes it a zero sum game; one's particular side is good, all the others bad, and the only resolution is for the good (one's own position) to win out over the bad (everything else).
4. Note: All of these are instances of a social psychological phenomenon called conformity. But there are other processes at work too, like group identification, self-serving biases, self-esteem enhancement, self-fulfilling prophecies, etc.

### Best Practices for Avoiding Abilene Paradox

- At the end of the solution generating process, carry out an anonymous survey asking participants if anything was left out they were reluctant to put before group.
- Designate a Devil's Advocate charged with criticizing the group's decision.
- Ask participants to reaffirm group decision–perhaps anonymously.

### Best Practices for Avoiding Groupthink (Taken from Janis, 262-271)

- "The leader of a policy-forming group should assign the role of critical evaluator to each member, encouraging the group to give high priority to airing objections and doubts."
- "The leaders in an organization's hierarchy, when assigning a policy-planning mission to a group, should be impartial instead of stating preferences and expectations at the outset."
- "Throughout the period when the feasibility and effectiveness of policy alternatives are being surveyed, the policy-making group should from time to time divide into two or more subgroups to meet separately...."

- One or more outside experts or qualified colleagues within the organization who are not core members of the policy-making group should be invited to each meeting ...and should be encouraged to challenge the views of the core members."
- "At every meeting devoted to evaluating policy alternatives, at least one member should be assigned the role of devil's advocate."

**Best Practices for Avoiding Polarizatoin (Items taken from "Good Computing: A Virtue Approach to Computer Ethics" by Chuck Huff, William Frey and Jose Cruz (Unpublished Manuscript)**

- **Set Quotas.** When brainstorming, set a quota and postpone criticism until after quota has been met.
- **Negotiate Interests, not Positions.** Since it is usually easier to integrate basic interests than specific positions, try to frame the problem in terms of interests.
- **Expanding the Pie.** Conficts that arise from situational constraints can be resolved by pushing back those constraints through negotiation or innovation..
- **Nonspecific Compensation.** One side makes a concession to the other but is compensated for that concession by some other coin.
- **Logrolling.** Each party lowers their aspirations on items that are of less interest to them, thus trading off a concession on a less important item for a concession from the other on a more important item.
- **Cost-Cutting.** One party makes an agreement to reduce its aspirations on a particular thing, and the other party agrees to compensate the party for the specific costs that reduction in aspirations involves.
- **Bridging.** Finding a higher order interest on which both parties agree, and then constructing a solution that serves that agreed-upon interest.

## 1.4.6 Exercise 2 - Avoiding the Pitfalls of Group Work

- Design a plan for avoiding the pitfalls of group work enumerated in the textbox above.
- How does your group plan on avoiding the Abilene Paradox?
- How does your group plan on avoiding Group Polarization?
- How does your group plan on avoiding Groupthink?
- Note: Use imagination and creativity here. Think of specific scenarios where these obstacles may arise, and what your group can do to prevent them or minimize their impact.

## 1.4.7 Exercise 3: Prepare a Final, Group Self-Evaluation

- Due Date: One week after the last class of the semester when your group turns in all its materials.
- Length: A minimum of five pages not including Team Member Evaluation Forms
- Contents:
- 1. Restate the Ethical and Practical Goals that your group developed at the beginning of its formation.
- 2. Provide a careful, documented assessment of your group's success in meeting these goals. (Don't just assert that "Our group successfully realized justice in all its activities this semester." How did your group characterize justice in the context of its work? What specific activities did the group carry out to realize this value? What, among these activities, worked and what did not work?)
- 3. Identify obstacles, shortcomings or failures that you group experienced during the semester. How did these arise? Why did they arise? How did you respond to them? Did your response work? What did you learn from this experience?
- 4. Assess the plans you set forth in your initial report on how you intended to realize values and avoid pitfalls. How did these work? Did you stick to your plans or did you find it necessary to change or abandon them in the face of challenges?
- 5. Discuss your group's procedures and practices? How did you divide and allocate work tasks? How did you reach consensus on difficult issues? How did you ensure that all members were respected and

allowed significant and meaningful participation? What worked and what did not work with respect to these procedures? Will you repeat them in the future? Would you recommend these procedures as best practices to future groups?

- 6. What did you learn from your experience working as a team this semester? What will require further reflection and thought? In other words, conclude your self-evaluation with a statement that summarizes your experience working together as a team this semester.

### 1.4.8 Wrap Up: Some further points to consider...

1. Don't gloss over your work with generalizations like, "Our group was successful and achieved all of its ethical and practical goals this semester." Provide evidence for success claims. Detail the procedures designed by your group to bring about these results. Are they "best practices"? What makes them best practices?

2. Sometimes—especially if difficulties arose—it is difficult to reflect on your group's activities for the semester. Make the effort. Schedule a meeting after the end of the semester to finalize this reflection. If things worked well, what can you do to repeat these successes in the future? If things didn't work out, what can you do to avoid similar problems in the future? Be honest, be descriptive and avoid blame language.

3. This may sound harsh but get used to it. Self-evaluations—group and individual—are an integral part of professional life. They are not easy to carry out, but properly done they help to secure success and avoid future problems.

4. Student groups—perhaps yours—often have problems. This self-evaluation exercise is designed to help you face them rather than push them aside. Look at your goals. Look at the strategies you set forth for avoiding Abilene, groupthink, and group polarization. Can you modify them to deal with problems? Do you need to design new procedures?

# Chapter 2

# Ethical Decision-Making

## 2.1 Ethical Rights for Working Engineers and Other Professionals[1]

### 2.1.1 Module Introduction

Preliminary Draft distributed at APPE, 2005 in San Antonio, TX

Engineers and other professionals work in large corporations under the supervision of managers who may lack their expertise, skills, and commitment to professional standards. This creates communication and ethical challenges. At the very least, professionals are put in the position of having to advocate their ethical and professional standards to those who, while not being opposed to them, may not share their understanding of and commitment to them.

This module is designed to give you the tools and the practice using them necessary to prevail in situations that require advocacy of ethical and professional standards. In this module you carry out several activities. (1) You will study the philosophical and ethical foundations of modern rights theory through a brief look at Kantian Formalism. (2) You will learn a framework for examining the legitimacy of rights claims. (3) You will practice this framework by examining several rights claims that engineers make over their supervisors. This examination will require that you reject certain elements, rephrase others, and generally recast the claim to satisfy the requirments of the rights justification framework. (4) Finally, in small groups you will build tables around your reformulation of these rights claims and present the results to the class. This module will help you to put your results together with the rest of your classmates and collectively assemble a toolkit consisting of the legitimate rights claims that engineers and other professionals can make over their managers and supervisors.

For more background on rights theory and the relation of rights and duties see (1) Henry Shue, **Basic Rights: Subsistence, Affluence, and U.S. Foreign Policy**, 2nd edition, Princeton, 1980 and (2) Thomas Donaldson, **The Ethics of International Business**, Oxford, 1989. This exercise has been used in computer and engineering ethics classes at the University of Puerto Rico at Mayaguez from 2002 on to the present. It is being incorporated into the textbook, Good Computing: A Virtue Approach to Computer Ethics by Chuck Huff, William Frey, and Jose Cruz.

### 2.1.2 What you need to know...

**Problematic Right Claims**

1. El derecho para actuar de acuerdo a la conciencia etica y rechazar trabajos en los cuales exista una variacion de opinones morales.
2. El derecho de expresar juicio profesional, y hacer pronunciamientos publicos que sean consistentes con restricciones corporativas sobre la informacion propietaria.

---

[1]This content is available online at <http://cnx.org/content/m15554/1.1/>.

3. El derecho a la lealtad corporativa y la libertad de que sea hecho un chivo expiatorio para catastrofes naturales, ineptitud de administracion u otras fuerzas mas alla del control del ingeniero.

4. El derecho a buscar el mejoramiento personal mediante estudios postgraduados y envolverse en asociaciones profesionales.

5. .El derecho a participar en actividades de partidos politicos fuera de las horas de trabajo.

6. El derecho a solicitar posiciones superiores con otras companias sin que la companis en la que trabaje tome represalias contra el ingeniero.

7. El derecho al debido proceso de ley y la libertad de que se le apliquen penalidades arbitrarias o despidos.

8. El derecho a apelar por revision ante una asociacion profesional, ombudsman o arbitro independiente.

9. El derecho a la privacidad personal.

10. These rights are taken from Etica en la Practica Profesional de la Ingenieria by Wilfredo Munoz Roman published in 1998 by the Colegio de Ingenieros y Agrimensores de Puerto Rico and Universidad Politecnica de Puerto Rico

## Problematic Rights Claims (translated)

1. The right to act in accordance with one's ethical conscience and to refuse to work on projects that go against one's conscience or personal or professional moral views.

2. The right to express one's professional judgment and to make public declarations as long as these do not violate a corporation's rights to proprietary information.

3. The right to corporate loyalty and freedom from being made a scapegoat for natural catastrophes, administrative ineptitude, and other forces that are beyond the control of the individual engineer.

4. The right to better oneself through postgraduate studies and through participation in one's professional society.

5. The right to participate in political activities outside of work hours.

6. The right not to suffer retaliation from one's current employer when one seeks better employment elsewhere.

7. The right to due process under the law and freedom from the application of artibrary penalties including being fired at will without just cause.

8. The right to appeal judgments made against one before a professional association, ombudsman, or independent arbitrator.

9. The right to personal privacy.

## Kantian Formalism, Part I: Aligning the moral motive and the moral act

- Kant's moral philosophy has exercised substantial influence over our notions of right and duty. We begin with a brief summary of this theory based on the work, **The Foundations of the Metaphysics of Morals**.

- Kant states that the only thing in this world that is good without qualification is a good will. He characterizes this will in terms of its motive, "duty for duty's sake."

- Consider the following example. You see a boy drowning. Even though the water is rough and the current strong you are a good enough swimmer to save him. So while your inclination may be to give way to fear and walk away, you are duty-bound to save the drowning boy.

- An action (saving or not saving the drowning boy) has moral worth depending on the the correct correlation of right action and right motive. The following table shows this.

### Duty for Duty's Sake

|  | Motive = Inclination (desire for reward or fear) | Motive = Duty |
|---|---|---|
| Act Conforms to Duty | You save the drowning boy for the reward. Act conforms to duty but is motivated by inclination. Has no moral worth. | You save the drowning boy because it is your duty. Act conforms to duty and is for the sake of duty. Your act has moral worth. |
| Act violates a duty. | You don't save the drowning boy because you are too lazy to jump in. Act violates duty motivated by inclination. | You drown trying to save the drowning boy. He also dies. Act fails to carry out duty but is motivated by duty anyway. The act miscarries but since the motive is duty it still has moral worth. |

**Table 2.1**

## Part II of Kantian Formalism: Giving content to Duty for Duty's Sake

- Kant sees morality as the expression and realization of the rational will. The first formulation of this rational will is to will consistently and universally.
- This leads to the Categorical Imperative: **I should act only on that maxim (=personal rule or rule that I give to myself) that can be converted into a universal law (a rule that applies to everybody) without self-contradiction.**
- This formulation is an imperative because it commands the will of all reasonable beings. It is categorical because it commands without exceptions or conditions. The CI tells me unconditionally not to lie. It does not say, do not like unless it promotes your self interest to do so.
- The following table shows how to use the Categorical Imperative to determine whether I have a duty not to lie.

### Applying the Categorical Imperative

| 1. Formulate your maxim (=personal rule) | Whenever I am in a difficult situation, I should tell a lie. |
|---|---|
| 2. Universalize your maxim. | Whenever anybody is in a difficult situation, he or she should tell a lie. |
| 3. Check for a contradiction (logical or practical) | When I lie, I will the opposite for the universal law. Put differently, I will that everybody (but me) be a truth-teller and that everybody believe me a truth-teller. I then make myself the exception to this universal law. Thus my maxim (I am a liar) contradicts the law (everybody else is a truth-teller) |

**Table 2.2**

## Kantian Formalism, Part III: The Formula of the End

- When I will one thing as universal law and make myself the exection in difficult circumstances, I am treating others, in Kantian terms, merely as means.
- This implies that I subordinate or bend them to my interests and projects without their consent. I do this by circumventing their autonomy through (1) force, (2) fraud (often deception), or (3) manipulation. Treating them with respect would involve telling them what I want (what are my plans and projects) and on this basis asking them to consent to particpate and help me. The extreme case for treating others merely as means is enslaving them.

- We do on occasion treat others as means (and not as mere means) when we hire them as employees. But this is consistent with their autonomy and rational consent because we explain to them what is expected (we give them a job description) and compensate them for their efforts. For this reason there is a world of difference between hiring others and enslaving them.
- **The Formula of the End = Act so as to treat others (yourself included) always as ends and never merely as means.**

## Some Key Definitions for a Rights Framework

- Kantian formalism provides a foundation for respect for the intrinsic value of humans as autonomous rational beings. Using this as a point of departure, we can develop a method for identifying, spelling out, and justifying the rights and duties that go with professionalism. This framework can be summarized in four general propositions:
- 1. Definition: A **right** is an essential capacity of action that others are obliged to recognize and respect. This definition follows from autonomy. Autonomy can be broken down into a series of specific capacities. Rights claims arise when we identify these capacities and take social action to protect them. Rights are inviolable and cannot be overridden even when overriding would bring about substantial public utility.
- 2. All rights claims must satisfy three requirements. They must be (1) **essential to the autonomy** of individuals and (2) **vulnerable** so that they require special recognition and protection (on the part of both individuals and society). Moreover, the burden of recognizing and respecting a claim as a right must not deprive others of something essential. In other words, it must be (3) **feasible** for both individuals and social groups to recognize and respect legitimate rights claims.
- 3. Definition: A **duty** is a rule or principle requiring that we both recognize and respect the legitimate rights claims of others. Duties attendant on a given right fall into three general forms: (a) duties not to deprive, (b) duties to prevent deprivation, and (c) duties to aid the deprived.
- 4. **Rights and duties are correlative**; for every right there is a correlative series of duties to recognize and respect that right.
- These four summary points together form a system of professional and occupational rights and correlative duties.

## Right Claim Justification Framework

- **Essential**: To say that a right is essential to autonomy is to say that it highlights a capacity whose exercise is necessary to the general exercise of autonomy. For example, autonomy is based on certain knowledge skills. Hence, we have a right to an education to develop the knowledge required by autonomy, or we have a right to the knowledge that produces informed consent. In general, rights are devices for recognizing certain capacities as essential to autonomy and respecting individuals in their exercise of these capacities.
- **Vulnerable**: The exercise of the capacity protected under the right needs protection. Individuals may interfere with us in our attempt to exercise our rights. Groups, corporations, and governments might overwhelm us and prevent us from exercising our essential capacities. In short, the exercise of the capacity requires some sort of protection. For example, an individual's privacy is vulnerable to violation. People can gain access to our computers without our authorization and view the information we have stored. They can even use this information to harm us in some way. The right to privacy, thus, protects certain capacities of action that are vulnerable to interference from others. Individual and social energy needs to be expended to protect our privacy.
- **Feasible**: Rights make claims over others; they imply duties that others have. These claims must not deprive the correlative duty-holders of anything essential. In other words, my rights claims over you are not so extensive as to deprive you of your rights. My right to life should not deprive you of your right to self-protection were I to attack you. Thus, the scope of my right claims over you and the rest of society are limited by your ability to reciprocate. I cannot push my claims over you to recognize and respect my rights to the point where you are deprived of something essential.

## Types of Duty Correlative to a Right

- **Duty not to deprive**: We have a basic duty not to violate the rights of others. This entails that we must both recognize and respect these rights. For example, computing specialists have the duty not to deprive others of their rights to privacy by hacking into private files.
- **Duty to prevent deprivation**: Professionals, because of their knowledge, are often in the position to prevent others from depriving third parties of their rights. For example, a computing specialist may find that a client is not taking sufficient pains to protect the confidentiality of information about customers. Outsiders could access this information and use it without the consent of the customers. The computing specialist could prevent this violation of privacy by advising the client on ways to protect this information, say, through encryption. The computing specialist is not about to violate the customers' rights to privacy. But because of special knowledge and skill, the computing specialist may be in a position to prevent others from violating this right.
- **Duty to aid the deprived**: Finally, when others have their rights violated, we have the duty to aid them in their recovery from damages. For example, a computing specialist might have a duty to serve as an expert witness in a lawsuit in which the plaintiff seeks to recover damages suffered from having her right to privacy violated. Part of this duty would include accurate, impartial, and expert testimony.

## Application of Right/Duty Framework

1. We can identify and define specific rights such as due process. Moreover, we can set forth some of the conditions involved in recognizing and respecting this right.
2. Due Process can be justified by showing that it is essential to autonomy, vulnerable, and feasible.
3. Right holders can be specified.
4. Correlative duties and duty holders can be specified.
5. Finally, the correlative duty-levels can be specified as the duties not to violate rights, duties to prevent rights violations (whenever feasible), and the duties to aid the deprived (whenever is feasible).

**Example Rights Table: Due Process**

| Right: Due Process | Justification | Right-Holder:Engineer as employee and member of professional society. | Correlative Duty-Holder: Engineer's Supervisor, officials in professional society. | Duty Level |
|---|---|---|---|---|
| Definition: The right to respond to organizational decisions that may harm one in terms of a serious organizational grievance procedure.Necessary Conditions:1. Several levels of appeal.2. Time limits to each level of appeal.3. Written notice of grievance.4. Peer representation.5. Outside arbitration. | Essential: Due Process is essential in organizations to prevent the deprivation of other rights or to provide aid in the case of their deprivation. | Professionals who are subject to professional codes of ethics. Supports professionals who are ordered to violate professional standards. | Human Resources, Management, Personnel Department.(Individuals with duty to design, implement, and enforce a due process policy)Corporate directors have the duty to make sure this is being done. | Not to Deprive:Individuals cannot be fired, transferred, or demoted without due process |
| | Vulnerable: Rights in general are not recognized in the economic sphere, especially in organizations. | | | Prevent Deprivation: Organizations can prevent deprivation by designing and implementing a comprehensive due process policy. |
| | Feasible: Organizations, have successfully implemented due process procedures. | | | Aid the DeprivedBinding arbitration and legal measures must exist to aid those deprived of due process rights |

**Table 2.3**

## 2.1.3 What you are going to do...

**Exercise: Develop a Rights Table**

1. You will be divided into small groups and each will be assigned a right claim taken from the above list.
2. Describe the claim (essential capacity of action) made by the right. For example, due process claims the right to a serious organizational grievance procedure that will enable the right-holder to respond to a decision that has an adverse impact on his or her interests. It may also be necessary in some situations to specify the claim's necessary conditions.
3. Justify the right claim using the rights justification framework. In other words show that the right claim is essential, vulnerable, and feasible.
4. Be sure to show that the right is essential to **autonomy**. If it is vulnerable be sure to identify the **standard threat**. (A standard threat is an existing condition that threatens autonomy.)
5. Provide an example of a situation in which the right claim becomes operative. For example, an engineer may claim a right to due process in order to appeal what he or she considers an unfair dismissal, transfer, or performance evaluation.
6. Identify the correlative duty-holder(s) that need to take steps to recognize and respect the right. For example, private and government organizations may be duty-bound to create due process procedures to recognize and respect this right.

7. Further spell out the right by showing what actions the correlative duties involve. For example, a manager should not violate an employee's due process right by firing him or her without just cause. The organization's human resources department might carry out a training program to help managers avoid depriving employees of this right. The organization could aid the deprived by designing and implementing binding arbitration involving an impartial third party.

Be prepared to debrief on your right claim to the rest of the class. When other groups are debriefing, you are free to challenge them on whether their claim is essential to autonomy, whether they have identified a valid "standard threat," and whether the correlative duties are feasible or deprive others of something essential. Your goal as a class is to have a short but effective list of rights that professionals take with them to the workplace.

## 2.1.4 Conclusion

**Conclusion: Topics for Further Reflection**

- Not every claim to a right is a legitimate or justifiable claim. The purpose of this framework is to get you into the habit of thinking critically and skeptically about the rights claims that you and others make. Every legitimate right claim is essential, vulnerable, and feasible. Correlative duties are sorted out according to different levels (not to deprive, prevent deprivation, and aid the deprived); this, in turn, is based on the capacity of the correlative duty holder to carry them out. Finally, duties correlative to rights cannot deprive the duty-holder of something essential.
- Unless you integrate your right and its correlative duties into the context of your professional or practical domain, it will remain abstract and irrelevant. Think about your right in the context of the real world. Think of everyday situations in which the right and its correlative duties will arise. Invent cases and scenarios. If you are an engineering student, think of informed consent in terms of the public's right to understand and consent to the risks associated with engineering projects. If you are a computing student think of what you can do with computing knowledge and skills to respect or violate privacy rights. Don't stop with an abstract accounting of the right and its correlative duties.
- Rights and duties underlie professional codes of ethics. But this is not always obvious. For example, the right of free and informed consent underlies much of the engineer's interaction with the public, especially the code responsibility to hold paramount public health, safety, and welfare. Look at the different stakeholder relations covered in a code of ethics. (In engineering this would include public, client, profession, and peer.) What are the rights and duties outlined in these stakeholder relations? How are they covered in codes of ethics?
- This module is effective in counter-acting the tendency to invent rights and use them to rationalize dubious actions and intentions. Think of rights claims as credit backed by a promise to pay at a later time. If you make a right claim, be ready to justify it. If someone else makes a right claim, make them back it up with the justification framework presented in this module.

# 2.2 Three Frameworks for Ethical Decision Making and Good Computing Reports[2]

## 2.2.1 Module Introduction

In this module you will learn and practice three frameworks designed to integrate ethics into decision making in the areas of practical and occupational ethics. The first framework divides the decision making process into four stages: problem specification, solution generation, solution testing, and solution implementation. It is based on an analogy between ethics and design problems that is detailed in a table presented below.

---

[2]This content is available online at <http://cnx.org/content/m13757/1.12/>.

The second framework focuses on the process of solution testing by providing four tests that will help you to evaluate and rank alternative courses of action. The reversibility, harm/beneficence, and public identification tests each "encapsulate" or summarize an important ethical theory. A value realization test assesses courses of action in terms of their ability to realize or harmonize different moral and nonmoral values. Finally, a feasibility test will help you to uncover interest, resource, and technical constraints that will affect and possibly impede the realization of your solution or decision. Taken together, these three frameworks will help steer you toward designing and implementing ethical decisions the professional and occupational areas.

Two online resources provide more extensive background information. The first, www.computingcases.org, provides background information on the ethics tests, socio-technical analysis, and intermediate moral concepts. The second, http://onlineethics.org/essays/education/teaching.html, explores in more detail the analogy between ethics and design problems. Much of this information will be published in Good Computing: A Virtue Approach to Computer Ethics, a textbook of cases and decision making techniques in computer ethics that is being authored by Chuck Huff, William Frey, and Jose A. Cruz-Cruz.

### 2.2.2 Problem-Solving or Decision-Making Framework: Analogy between ethics and design

Traditionally, decision making frameworks in professional and occupational ethics have been taken from rational decision procedures used in economics. While these are useful, they lead one to think that ethical decisions are already "out there" waiting to be discovered. In contrast, taking a design approach to ethical decision making emphasizes that ethical decisions must be created, not discovered. This, in turn, emphasizes the importance of moral imagination and moral creativity. Carolyn Whitbeck in Ethics in Engineering Practice and Research describes this aspect of ethical decision making through the analogy she draws between ethics and design problems in chapter one. Here she rejects the idea that ethical problems are multiple choice problems. We solve ethical problems not by choosing between ready made solutions given with the situation; rather we use our moral creativity and moral imagination to design these solutions. Chuck Huff builds on this by modifying the design method used in software engineering so that it can help structure the process of framing ethical situations and creating actions to bring these situations to a successful and ethical conclusion. The key points in the analogy between ethical and design problems are summarized in the table presented just below.

| Analogy between design and ethics problem-solving | |
| --- | --- |
| Design Problem | Ethical Problem |
| Construct a prototype that optimizes (or satisfices) designated specifications | Construct a solution that integrates and realizes ethical values (justice, responsibility, reasonableness, respect, and safety) |
| Resolve conflicts between different specifications by means of integration | Resolve conflicts between values (moral vs. moral or moral vs. non-moral) by integration |
| Test prototype over the different specifications | Test solution over different ethical considerations encapsulated in ethics tests |
| | *continued on next page* |

| Implement tested design over background constraints | Implement ethically tested solution over resource, interest, and technical constraints |
|---|---|

**Table 2.4**

### 2.2.3 Software Development Cycle: Four Stages

(1) problem specification, (2) solution generation, (3) solution testing, and (4) solution implementation.

### 2.2.4 Problem specification

Problem specification involves exercising moral imagination to specify the socio-technical system (including the stakeholders) that will influence and will be influenced by the decision we are about to make. Stating the problem clearly and concisely is essential to design problems; getting the problem right helps structure and channel the process of designing and implementing the solution. There is no algorithm available to crank out effective problem specification. Instead, we offer a series of guidelines or rules of thumb to get you started in a process that is accomplished by the skillful exercise of moral imagination.

For a broader problem framing model see Harris, Pritchard, and Rabins, **Engineering Ethics: Concepts and Cases,** 2nd Edition, Belmont, CA: Wadsworth, 2000, pp. 30-56. See also Cynthia Brincat and Victoria Wike, **Morality and Professional Life: Values at Work**, New Jersey: Prentice Hall, 1999.

**Different Ways of Specifying the Problem**

- Many problems can be specified as disagreements. For example, you disagree with your supervisor over the safety of the manufacturing environment. Disagreements over facts can be resolved by gathering more information. Disagreements over concepts (you and your supervisor have different ideas of what safety means) require working toward a common definition.
- Other problems involve conflicting values. You advocate installing pollution control technology because you value environmental quality and safety. Your supervisor resists this course of action because she values maintaining a solid profit margin. This is a conflict between a moral value (safety and environmental quality) and a nonmoral value (solid profits). Moral values can also conflict with one another in a given situation. Using John Doe lawsuits to force Internet Service Providers to reveal the real identities of defamers certainly protects the privacy and reputations of potential targets of defamation. But it also places restrictions on legitimate free speech by making it possible for powerful wrongdoers to intimidate those who would publicize their wrongdoing. Here the moral values of privacy and free speech are in conflict. Value conflicts can be addressed by harmonizing the conflicting values, compromising on conflicting values by partially realizing them, or setting one value aside while realizing the other (=value trade offs).
- If you specify your problem as a disagreement, you need to describe the facts or concepts about which there is disagreement.
- If you specify your problem as a conflict, you need to describe the values that conflict in the situation.
- One useful way of specifying a problem is to carry out a stakeholder analysis. A stakeholder is any group or individual that has a vital interest at risk in the situation. Stakeholder interests frequently come into conflict and solving these conflicts requires developing strategies to reconcile and realize the conflicting stakes.
- Another way of identifying and specifying problems is to carry out a socio-technical analysis. Socio-technical systems (STS) embody values. Problems can be anticipated and prevented by specifying possible value conflicts. Integrating a new technology, procedure, or policy into a socio-technical system can create three kinds of problem. (1) Conflict between values in the technology and those in the STS. For example, when an attempt is made to integrate an information system into the STS of a small business, the values present in an information system can conflict with those in the socio-technical system. (Workers may feel that the new information system invades their privacy.) (2) Amplification

of existing value conflicts in the STS. The introduction of a new technology may magnify an existing value conflict. Digitalizing textbooks may undermine copyrights because digital media is easy to copy and disseminate on the Internet. (3) Harmful consequences. Introducing something new into a socio-technical system may set in motion a chain of events that will eventually harm stakeholders in the socio-technical system. For example, giving laptop computers to public school students may produce long term environmental harm when careless disposal of spent laptops releases toxic materials into the environment.

- The following table helps summarize some of these problem categories and then outlines generic solutions.

| Problem Type | Sub-Type | Solution Outline | | |
|---|---|---|---|---|
| Disagreement | Factual | | Type and mode of gathering information | |
| | Conceptual | | Concept in dispute and method for agreeing on its definition | |
| Conflict | Moral vs. Moral | Value Integrative | Partially Value Integrative | Trade Off |
| | Non-moral vs. moral | | | |
| | Non-moral vs. non-moral | | | |
| Framing | Corruption | Strategy for maintaining integrity | Strategy for restoring justice | Value integrative, design strategy |
| | Social Justice | | | |
| | Value Realization | | | |
| Intermediate Moral Value | Public Welfare, Faithful Agency, Professional Integrity, Peer Collegiality | Realizing Value | Removing value conflicts | Prioritizing values for trade offs |

**Table 2.5**

## 2.2.5 Solution Generation

In solution generation, agents exercise moral creativity by brainstorming to come up with solution options designed to resolve the disagreements and value conflicts identified in the problem specification stage. Brainstorming is crucial to generating nonobvious solutions to difficult, intractable problems. This process must take place within a non-polarized environment where the members of the group respect and trust one another. (See the module on the Ethics of Group Work for more information on how groups can be successful and pitfalls that commonly trip up groups.) Groups effectively initiate the brainstorming process by suspending criticism and analysis. After the process is completed (say, by meeting a quota), then participants can refine the solutions generated by combining them, eliminating those that don't fit the problem, and ranking them in terms of their ethics and feasibility. If a problem can't be solved, perhaps it can be dissolved through reformulation. If an entire problem can't be solve, perhaps the problem can be broken down into parts some of which can be readily solved.

## 2.2.6 Solution Testing: The solutions developed in the second stage must be tested in various ways.

1. Reversibility: Are they reversible between the agent and key stakeholders?

2. Harm/Beneficence: Do they minimize harm? Do they produce benefits that are justly distributed among stakeholders?
3. Public Identification: Are these actions with which I am willing to be publicly identified? Does these actions identify me as a moral person?
4. Value: Do these actions realize key moral values and instantiate moral virtues?
5. Code: A code test can be added that refers to a professional or occupational code of ethics. Do the solutions comply with the professional's or practitioner's code of ethics?
6. The solution evaluation matrix presented just below provides a nice way of modeling and summarizing the process of solution testing.

| Solution/Test | Reversibility | Harm/ Beneficence | Virtue | Value | Code |
|---|---|---|---|---|---|
| Descrip-tion | Is the solution reversible with stakeholders? Does it honor basic rights? | Does the solution produce the best benefit/harm ratio? Does the solution maximize utility? | Does the solution express and integrate key virtues? | Moral values realized? Moral values frustrated? Value conflicts resolved or exacerbated? | Does the solution violate any code provisions? |
| Best solution | | | | | |
| Second Best | | | | | |
| Worst | | | | | |

**Table 2.6**

## 2.2.7 Solution Implementation

The chosen solution must be examined in terms of how well it responds to various situational constraints that could impede its implementation. What will be its costs? Can it be implemented within necessary time constraints? Does it honor recognized technical limitations or does it require pushing these back through innovation and discovery? Does it comply with legal and regulatory requirements? Finally, could the surrounding organizational, political, and social environments give rise to obstacles to the implementation of the solution? In general this phase requires looking at interest, technical, and resource constraints or limitations. A Feasibility Matrix helps to guide this process.

The Feasibility Tests focuses on situational constraints. How could these hinder the implementation of the solution? Should the solution be modified to ease implementation? Can the constraints be removed or remodeled by negotiation, compromise, or education? Can implementation be facilitated by modifying both the solution and changing the constraints?

| Feasibility Matrix | | |
|---|---|---|
| Resource Constraints | Technical Constraints | Interest Constraints |
| | | Personalities |
| Time | | Organizational |
| Cost | Applicable Technology | Legal |
| Materials | Manufacturability | Social, Political, Cultural |

**Table 2.7**

**Different Feasibility Constraints**

1. The Feasibility Test identifies the constraints that could interfere with realizing a solution. This test also sorts out these constraints into **resource** (time, cost, materials), **interest** (individuals, organizations, legal, social, political), and **technical** limitations. By identifying situational constraints, problem-solvers can anticipate implementation problems and take early steps to prevent or mitigate them.

2. **Time.** Is there a deadline within which the solution has to be enacted? Is this deadline fixed or negotiable?

3. **Financial.** Are there cost constraints on implementing the ethical solution? Can these be extended by raising more funds? Can they be extended by cutting existing costs? Can agents negotiate for more money for implementation?

4. **Technical.** Technical limits constrain the ability to implement solutions. What, then, are the technical limitations to realizing and implementing the solution? Could these be moved back by modifying the solution or by adopting new technologies?

5. **Manufacturability.** Are there manufacturing constraints on the solution at hand? Given time, cost, and technical feasibility, what are the manufacturing limits to implementing the solution? Once again, are these limits fixed or flexible, rigid or negotiable?

6. **Legal.** How does the proposed solution stand with respect to existing laws, legal structures, and regulations? Does it create disposal problems addressed in existing regulations? Does it respond to and minimize the possibility of adverse legal action? Are there legal constraints that go against the ethical values embodied in the solution? Again, are these legal constraints fixed or negotiable?

7. **Individual Interest Constraints.** Individuals with conflicting interests may oppose the implementation of the solution. For example, an insecure supervisor may oppose the solution because he fears it will undermine his authority. Are these individual interest constraints fixed or negotiable?

8. **Organizational.** Inconsistencies between the solution and the formal or informal rules of an organization may give rise to implementation obstacles. Implementing the solution may require support of those higher up in the management hierarchy. The solution may conflict with organization rules, management structures, traditions, or financial objectives. Once again, are these constraints fixed or flexible?

9. **Social, Cultural, or Political.** The socio-technical system within which the solution is to be implemented contains certain social structures, cultural traditions, and political ideologies. How do these stand with respect to the solution? For example, does a climate of suspicion of high technology threaten to create political opposition to the solution? What kinds of social, cultural, or political problems could arise? Are these fixed or can they be altered through negotiation, education, or persuasion?

## 2.2.8 Ethics Tests For Solution Evaluation

Three ethics tests (reversibility, harm/beneficence, and public identification) encapsulate three ethical approaches (deontology, utilitarianism, and virtue ethics) and form the basis of stage three of the SDC, solution testing. A fourth test (a value realization test) builds upon the public identification/virtue ethics test by evaluating a solution in terms of the values it harmonizes, promotes, protects, or realizes. Finally a code test provides an independent check on the ethics tests and also highlights intermediate moral concepts such as safety, health, welfare, faithful agency, conflict of interest, confidentiality, professional integrity, collegiality, privacy, property, free speech, and equity/access). The following section provides advice on how to use these tests. More information can be found at www.computingcases.org.

## 2.2.9 Setting Up the Ethics Tests: Pitfalls to avoid

Set-Up Pitfalls: Mistakes in this area lead to the analysis becoming unfocused and getting lost in irrelevancies. (a) Agent-switching where the analysis falls prey to irrelevancies that crop up when the test application is not grounded in the standpoint of a single agent, (b) Sloppy action-description where the analysis fails because no specific action has been tested, (c) Test-switching where the analysis fails because one test is substituted for another. (For example, the public identification and reversibility tests are often reduced to the harm/beneficence test where harmful consequences are listed but not associated with the agent or stakeholders.)

**Set up the test**

1. Identify the agent (the person who is going to perform the action)
2. Describe the action or solution that is being tested (what the agent is going to do or perform)
3. Identify the stakeholders (those individuals or groups who are going to be affected by the action), and their stakes (interests, values, goods, rights, needs, etc.
4. Identify, sort out, and weigh the consequences (the results the action is likely to bring about)

## 2.2.10 Harm/Beneficence Test

- What harms would accompany the action under consideration? Would it produce physical or mental suffering, impose financial or non-financial costs, or deprive others of important or essential goods?
- What benefits would this action bring about? Would it increase safety, quality of life, health, security, or other goods both moral and non-moral?
- What is the magnitude of each these consequences? Magnitude includes likelihood it will occur (probability), the severity of its impact (minor or major harm) and the range of people affected.
- Identify one or two other viable alternatives and repeat these steps for them. Some of these may be modifications of the basic action that attempt to minimize some of the likely harms. These alternatives will establish a basis for assessing your alternative by comparing it with others.
- Decide on the basis of the test which alternative produces the best ratio of benefits to harms?
- Check for inequities in the distribution of harms and benefits. Do all the harms fall on one individual (or group)? Do all of the benefits fall on another? If harms and benefits are inequitably distributed, can they be redistributed? What is the impact of redistribution on the original solution imposed?

**Pitfalls of the Harm/Beneficence Test**

1. "Paralysis of Analysis" comes from considering too many consequences and not focusing only on those relevant to your decision.
2. Incomplete Analysis results from considering too few consequences. Often it indicates a failure of moral imagination which, in this case, is the ability to envision the consequences of each action alternative.
3. Failure to compare different alternatives can lead to a decision that is too limited and one-sided.
4. Failure to weigh harms against benefits occurs when decision makers lack the experience to make the qualitative comparisons required in ethical decision making.
5. Finally, justice failures result from ignoring the fairness of the distribution of harms and benefits. This leads to a solution which may maximize benefits and minimize harms but still give rise to serious injustices in the distribution of these benefits and harms.

## 2.2.11 Reversibility Test

1. Set up the test by (i) identifying the agent, (ii) describing the action, and (iii) identifying the stakeholders and their stakes.
2. Use the stakeholder analysis to identify the relations to be reversed.
3. Reverse roles between the agent (you) and each stakeholder: put them in your place (as the agent) and yourself in their place (as the one subjected to the action).
4. If you were in their place, would you still find the action acceptable?

**Cross Checks for Reversibility Test (These questions help you to check if you have carried out the reversibility test properly.)**

- Does the proposed action treat others with respect? (Does it recognize their autonomy or circumvent it?)
- Does the action violate the rights of others? (Examples of rights: free and informed consent, privacy, freedom of conscience, due process, property, freedom of expression)
- Would you recommend that this action become a universal rule?
- Are you, through your action, treating others merely as means?

**Pitfalls of the Reversibility Test**

- Leaving out a key stakeholder relation
- Failing to recognize and address conflicts between stakeholders and their conflicting stakes
- Confusing treating others with respect with capitulating to their demands ("Reversing with Hitler")
- Failing to reach closure, i.e., an overall, global reversal assessment that takes into account all the stakeholders the agent has reversed with.

## 2.2.12 Steps in Applying the Public Identification Test

- Set up the analysis by identifying the agent, describing the action, and listing the key values or virtues at play in the situation.
- Association the action with the agent.
- Describe what the action says about the agent as a person. Does it reveal him or her as someone associated with a virtue or a vice?

**Alternative Version of Public Identification**

- Does the action under consideration realize justice or does it pose an excess or defect of justice?
- Does the action realize responsibility or pose an excess or defect of responsibility?
- Does the action realize reasonableness or pose too much or too little reasonableness?
- Does the action realize honesty or pose too much or too little honesty?
- Does the action realize integrity or pose too much or too little integrity?

**Pitfalls of Public Identification**

- Action not associated with agent. The most common pitfall is failure to associate the agent and the action. The action may have bad consequences and it may treat individuals with respect but these points are not as important in the context of this test as what they imply about the agent as a person who deliberately performs such an action.
- Failure to specify moral quality, virtue, or value. Another pitfall is to associate the action and agent but only ascribe a vague or ambiguous moral quality to the agent. To say, for example, that willfully harming the public is bad fails to zero in on precisely what moral quality this ascribes to the agent. Does it render him or her unjust, irresponsible, corrupt, dishonest, or unreasonable? The virtue list given above will help to specify this moral quality.

## 2.2.13 Code of Ethics Test

- Does the action hold paramount the health, safety, and welfare of the public, i.e., those affected by the action but not able to participate in its design or execution?
- Does the action maintain faithful agency with the client by not abusing trust, avoiding conflicts of interest, and maintaining confidences?
- Is the action consistent with the reputation, honor, dignity, and integrity of the profession?
- Does the action serve to maintain collegial relations with professional peers?

## 2.2.14 Meta Tests

- The ethics and feasibility tests will not always converge on the same solution. There is a complicated answer for why this is the case but the simple version is that the tests do not always agree on a given solution because each test (and the ethical theory it encapsulates) covers a different domain or dimension of the action situation. Meta tests turn this disadvantage to your advantage by feeding the interaction between the tests on a given solution back into the evaluation of that solution.
- When the ethics tests converge on a given solution, this convergence is a sign of the strength and robustness of the solution and counts in its favor.
- When a given solution responds well to one test but does poorly under another, this is a sign that the solution needs further development and revision. It is not a sign that one test is relevant while the others are not. Divergence between test results is a sign that the solution is weak.

## 2.2.15 Application Exercise

You will now practice the four stages of decision making with a real world case. This case, Risk Assessment, came from a retreat on Business, Science, and Engineering Ethics held in Puerto Rico in December 1998. It was funded by the National Science Foundation, Grant SBR 9810253.

**Risk Assessment Scenario**

Case Scenario: You supervise a group of engineers working for a private laboratory with expertise in nuclear waste disposal and risk assessment. The DOE (Department of Energy) awarded a contract to your laboratory six years ago to do a risk assessment of various nuclear waste disposal sites. During the six years in which your team has been doing the study, new and more accurate calculations in risk assessment have become available. Your laboratory's study, however, began with the older, simpler calculations and cannot integrate the newer without substantially delaying completion. You, as the leader of the team, propose a delay to the DOE on the grounds that it is necessary to use the more advanced calculations. Your position is that the laboratory needs more time because of the extensive calculations required; you argue that your group must use state of the art science in doing its risk assessment. The DOE says you are using overly high standards of risk assessment to prolong the process, extend the contract, and get more money for your company. They want you to use simpler calculations and finish the project; if you are unwilling to do so, they plan to find another company that thinks differently. Meanwhile, back at the laboratory, your supervisor (a high level company manager) expresses to you the concern that while good science is important in an academic setting, this is the real world and the contract with the DOE is in jeopardy. What should you do?

**Part One: Problem Specification**

1. Specify the problem in the above scenario. Be as concise and specific as possible
2. Is your problem best specifiable as a disagreement? Between whom? Over what?
3. Can your problem be specified as a value conflict? What are the values in conflict? Are the moral, nonmoral, or both?

**Part Two: Solution Generation**

1. Quickly and without analysis or criticism brainstorm 5 to ten solutions
2. Refine your solution list. Can solutions be eliminated? (On what basis?) Can solutions be combined? Can solutions be combined as plan a and plan b?
3. If you specified your problem as a disagreement, how do your solutions resolve the disagreement? Can you negotiate interests over positions? What if your plan of action doesn't work?
4. If you formulated your problem as a value conflict, how do your solutions resolve this conflict? By integrating the conflicting values? By partially realizing them through a value compromise? By trading one value off for another?

**Part Three: Solution Testing**

1. Construct a solution evaluation matrix to compare two to three solution alternatives.
2. Choose a bad solution and then compare to it the two strongest solutions you have.
3. Be sure to avoid the pitfalls described above and set up each test carefully.

**Part Four: Solution Implementation**

1. Develop an implementation plan for your best solution. This plan should anticipate obstacles and offer means for overcoming them.
2. Prepare a feasibility table outlining these issues using the table presented above.
3. Remember that each of these feasibility constraints is negotiable and therefore flexible. If you choose to set aside a feasibility constraint then you need to outline how you would negotiate the extension of that constraint.

---

**Decision-Making Presentation**

---

This is an unsupported media type. To view, please see http://cnx.org/content/m13757/latest/Decision Making Manual V3.ppt

---

**Figure 2.1:** Clicking on this figure will allow you to open a presentation designed to introduce problem solving in ethics as analogous to that in design, summarize the concept of a socio-technical system, and provide an orientation in the four stages of problem solving. This presentation was given February 28, 2008 at UPRM for ADMI 6005 students, Special Topics in Research Ethics.

---

**Decision Making Worksheet**

---

This is an unsupported media type. To view, please see http://cnx.org/content/m13757/latest/Decision Making Worksheet.docx

---

**Figure 2.2:** This exercise is designed to give you practice with the three frameworks described in this module. It is based on the case, "When in Aguadilla."

## 2.3 Values-Based Decision-Making in Gilbane Gold[3]

### 2.3.1 Module Introduction

The Federal Sentencing Guidelines introduced in the early 1990's have transformed the way businesses respond to ethics. Formerly, corporations relied on compliance measures which became activated only after wrongdoing occurred. Violations occurred and compliance responses consisted of identifying and punishing

---

[3]This content is available online at <http://cnx.org/content/m15783/1.4/>.

those responsible. But the Federal Sentencing Guidelines push corporations toward a much more proactive stance; if a corporation is found guilty of law violation, its punishment is determined by the measures the corporation has already implemented to prevent the crime as well as the measures the corporation develops in response to the crime to mitigate it and prevent future reoccurrences. Working to prevent crime, accepting responsibility for crimes that could not be prevented, and learning from past mistakes all serve to "flag" corporate intention. In other words, corporations can demonstrate good intentions by documenting measures implemented to prevent crime and by showing a "responsive adjustment" to crimes they could not prevent.

It is in this new corporate context that corporations have begun to adopt values-based decision making. Instead of setting forth rules that outline minimum levels of forced compliance, they now ask employees to work beyond the moral minimum and seek occasions to actually realize or enhance moral value. In the decision making context, employees ask: (1) What can I do to make this a more just environment? (2) How do I go about respecting my co-workers? and (3) How do I identify and carry out my responsibilities, including social responsibilities, in my daily work?" These questions, representing instances of values-based decision-making, serve to change your focus from getting by with the moral minimum to realigning your moral and workplace efforts toward moral excellence.

In this module you will learn about ethical leadership, ethical decision-making, corporate social responsibility, and corporate governance. The occasion for this learning is the classical ethics video, "Gilbane Gold." You will view the video and practice values-based decision-making from within the role of David Jackson, the young engineer around whom the narrative of this video is built. To get you started, you will use the values portrayed in the University of Puerto Rico's College of Business Administration Statement of Values. Module sections will outline what you will be doing and what you need to know as well as provide opportunities for you to reflect on what you have learned upon completion of this module.

## 2.3.2 What you need to know...

### Value-Based Decision Making

In value-based decision-making, you use moral values to pose problems and solutions. For example, problems can be posed as conflicts between values (moral vs. non-moral or moral vs. moral), lack of information about how to realize or maintain values, and situations where key values need to be defended. The point in value-based decision making is to design solutions that realize the maximum number of values possible by integrating them, drawing successful compromises between them, or choosing to act upon the most important value given the situation. In this module, you will be working from within David Jackson's position to design a solution to his problem that best responds to the value needs in his situation.

### Gilbane Gold

- You are David Jackson a young engineer working for the computer manufacturer, Z-Corp. Your studies into the waste emissions of Z-Corp indicate that they are a little bit over the boarderline of what is legally acceptable in the Gilbane metropolitan area. Two further issues complicate your findings. (1) Gilbane draws sludge from the river and sells it to farmers to cover their fields; if heavy metals are present in this sludge, they will be passed on to consumers who eat the vegetables grown in fields covered with this "Gilbane Gold." This could produce long and short term health problems for the Gilbane community. (2) Z-Corp has just entered into a new agreement with a Japanese company that will produce a five-fold increase in demand for their product. While this will also increase their emissions of heavy metals into the water supply by the same amount, it will not violate city regulations because these regulations only take into account the concentration of heavy metals in each discharge. Z-Corp merely dilutes the heavy metals dumped into Gilbane's water supply to reflect acceptable concentration levels. David Jackson holds that this loophole in environmental regulations could endanger the health and safety of the citizens in the Gilbane. But he has trouble sharing these concerns with his supervisors, Diane Collins, Phil Port, and Frank Seeders.
- David (you) has made several efforts to make his concerns known to Z-Corp officials, including Phil Port, Frank Seeders, and Diane Collins. Their response is that spending money on increased pollution

control measures will threaten Z-Corp's thin profit margin. Diane puts the issue even more strongly when she says that Z-Corp's social responsibility is to provide the Gilbane community with good jobs and to obey local environmental regulations. If the city wants stricter regulations, then **they** need to pass them through the legislative process. But taking proactive measures on this count goes far beyond Z-Corp's ethical and social responsibilities to the Gilbane community.

- You are David. What values do you see involved in this situation? Design a solution that best preserves and integrates them.

## Partial List of Characters

1. **David Jackson**: Young engineer whose measurements show that Z-Corp's emissions into the Gilbane water supply barely exceed local standards. He expresses concern to his supervisors on the impact on the safety and health of the local community.
2. **Diane Collins**: David's supervisor who is under strong pressure to maintain the Z-Corp Gilbane plant's thin profit levels. She is concerned about environment responsibility but defines it as staying within the limits of the law as put forth by the Gilbane community. Gilbane sets for the law and Z-Corp is responsible for staying within its limits. If the law is inadequate, then Gilbane is responsible for changing it.
3. **Tom Richards**: Environmental engineer hired to measure Z-Corp's heavy metal emissions into the Gilbane water supply. Richards warns David that he bears ultimate responsibility for Z-Corp's emisions into the Gilbane water supply.
4. **Phil Port**: Z-Corp's official in charge of the company's compliance with environmental regulations. He calls David during the TV documentary to claim that it portrays him as an "environmental rapist."
5. **Frank Seeders**: Frank is the point man on helping to gear up Z-Corp's operations to meet the new demand created by their recent venture with a Japanese company. He asks David to help him streamline Z-Corp's manufacturing process.
6. **Maria Renato**: Local reporter who produces documentary exposing Z-Corp's potentially dangerous emissions. She has prepared her report based on documentation provided by David Jackson.

## Statement of Values List

1. **Justice / Fairness**: Be impartial, objective and refrain from discrimination or preferential treatment in the administration of rules and policies and in its dealings with students, faculty, staff, administration, and other stakeholders.
2. **Responsibility**: Recognize and fulfill its obligations to its constituents by caring for their essential interests, by honoring its commitments, and by balancing and integrating conflicting interests. As responsible agents, the faculty, employees, and students of the college of business Administration are committed to the pursuit of excellence, devotion to the community's welfare, and professionalism.
3. **Respect**: Acknowledge the inherent dignity present in its diverse constituents by recognizing and respecting their fundamental rights. these include rights to property, privacy, free exchange of ideas, academic freedom, due process, and meaningful participation in decision making and policy formation.
4. **Trust**: Recognize that trust solidifies communities by creating an environment where each can expect ethically justifiable behavior from all others. While trust is tolerant of and even thrives in an environment of diversity, it also must operate within the parameters set by established personal and community standards.
5. **Integrity**: Promote integrity as characterized by sincerity, honesty, authenticity, and the pursuit of excellence. Integrity shall permeate and color all its decisions, actions and expressions. It is most clearly exhibited in intellectual and personal honesty in learning, teaching, mentoring and research.

## 2.3.3 What you are going to do...

1. Watch the video and make sure you understand the situation from David's point of view. At the end David makes his decision. You should be open to the possibility that there may be other decisions that

can be taken in this situation that may be better from a moral point of view.

2. What is David's problem? Try formulating it in terms of values that are under threat and conflicts between values. You may even want to identify information needs relevant to solving this problem?

3. What solutions do different individuals in the video recommend to David? How good are they in terms of realizing or protecting key moral values? Does David (and the video) pay sufficient attention to these different recommendations? Does he miss better value-integrative solutions?

4. Make your decision. Defend it in terms of key moral values. Use the values provided above in the UPRM College of Business Administration's Statement of Values.

5. Give special attention to the links provided in this module. Are there solutions to David's problem not mentioned in the video?

### 2.3.4 Conclusion

More and more, business ethics is concentrating on four general themes or issues. In this section, you will use the video, "Gilbane Gold," to reflect on these different themes. Consider this your first incursion into business ethics. Most important, remember that ethics forms a central part of everyday business practice and is essential to good business.

**Ethical Leadership: In terms of the values mentioned in the SOV, discuss and rate the following characters in terms of the leadership skills and qualities they exhibit:**

- Diane Collins
- David Jackson
- Phil Port
- Tom Richards
- Frank Seeders

**Social Responsibility:**
David reminds Diane that corporations like Z-Corp are responsible for the health and safety impacts of their operations. Diane disagrees placing more emphasis on following the law and serving the community by creating economic opportunity and jobs. Who sets for the better argument? Using these positions as a springboard, set forth your own conception of corporate social responsibility.

**Corporate Governance:**
Toward the end of the video, David goes to local reporter, Maria Renato, and provides her with inside information on his and Tom Richards's environmental and safety concerns. Was this a necessary action? Did David have other options which would have allowed him to work within Z–Corp for an effective response to his concerns? How do engineers advocate within for-profit corporations for including ethical values into corporate decisions? What do real world corporations do to recognize and respond to dissenting professional opinions held by their employees?

---

**Values in Gilbane Gold Handout**

---

This is an unsupported media type. To view, please see http://cnx.org/content/m15783/latest/Values in Gilbane Gold Handout.doc

---

**Figure 2.3:** This handout for students provides exercises based on Gilbane Gold that introduces the three AACSB business ethics themes: ethical leadership, ethical decision-making, and social responsibility.

---

**Virtues for ADMI 3405**

---

This is an unsupported media type. To view, please see http://cnx.org/content/m15783/latest/Virtues for ADMI 3405.pptx

---

**Figure 2.4:** Clicking on this file are the virtues worked out in the previous module. Use these to carry out the values-based decision making exercise in Gilbane Gold.

## 2.4 Socio-Technical Systems in Professional Decision Making[4]

### 2.4.1 Module Introduction

**Milagro Beanfield War**

Joe Mondragon has created quite a stir in Milagro, a small village in New Mexico. He has illegally diverted water from the irrigation ditch to his field to grow beans. Access to scarce water in New Mexico has created sharp political and social disputes which have reached a crises point in Milagro. Competing with traditional subsistence farmers like Joe is the profitable recreation industry. Ladd Devine, a wealthy developer, has joined with the state government in New Mexico to build a large recreational center consisting of a restaurant, travel lodge, individual cabins and a lavish golf course. Since there is not enough water to cover both recreational and agricultural uses and since Ladd Devine's project promises large tax revenues and new jobs, the state government has fallen behind him and has promised to give to the recreational facilities all the water it needs. Hence, the problem created by Mondragon's illegal act. You work for Ladd Devine. He has asked you to look into local opposition to the recreational facility. Along these lines, you attend the town meeting scheduled by Ruby Archuleta in the town's church. You are concerned about Charlie Bloom's presentation and the impact it may have on the local community. Prepare a STS analysis to test Bloom's assertions and better prepare Ladd Devine for local opposition to his facility.

**Incident at Morales**

Fred is a chemical engineer hired by Phaust Corporation to design and make operational a new chemical plant for the manufacture of their newly redesigned paint thinner. Under financial pressure from the parent French

---

[4]This content is available online at <http://cnx.org/content/m14025/1.9/>.

company, Chemistre, they have decided to locate their new plant in Morales, Mexico to take advantage of lower costs and more flexible government regulations. You are well on the way toward designing this new plant when news comes from Chemistre that all budgets are being cut 20% to finance Chemistre's latest takeover acquisition. You are Fred and are now faced with a series of difficult financial-engineering decisions. Should you hold out for the more expensive Lutz and Lutz controls or use the cheaper ones produced locally? Should you continue with the current plant size or cut plant size and capacity to keep within budgetary constraints? You have also been made aware of the environmental and health risks associated with not lining the waste ponds used by the plant. Do you advocate lining the ponds or not, the latter being within compliance for Mexican environmental and health regulations. Prepare a STS analysis to help you make and justify these decisions. Make a series of recommendations to your supervisors based on this study.

**Puerto Rican Projects**

- Your company, Cogentrix, proposes a cogeneration plant that uses coal, produces electricity, and creates steam as a by-product of electricity generation process. Because the steam can be sold to nearby tuna canning plants, your company wishes to study the feasibility of locating its plant in or near Mayaguez, Puerto Rico. (Co-generation technology has become very popular and useful in some places.) Carry out a STS analysis to identify potential problems. Make a recommendation to your company. If your recommendation is positive, discuss how the plant should be modified to fit into the Mayaguez, Puerto Rico STS.

- Your company, Southern Gold Resources, is interested in mining different regions in central Puerto Rico for copper and gold. But you know that twenty years earlier, two proposals by two international mining companies were turned down by the PR government. Carry out a STS study to examine the feasibility of designing a different project that may be more acceptable to local groups. What does your STS analysis tell you about social and ethical impacts, financial promise, and likely local opposition. Can profitable mining operations be developed that respect the concerns of opposed groups? What is your recommendation based on your STS analysis?

- Windmar, a company that manufactures and operates windmills for electricity generation has proposed to locate a windmill farm in a location adjacent to the Bosque Seco de Guanica. They have encountered considerable local opposition. Carry out a STS analysis to understand and clarify this opposition. Can the concerns of local stakeholders be addressed and the windmill farm still remain profitable? How should the windmill project be modified to improve its chances of implementation?

## 2.4.2 Things to Know about STSs

**What is a Socio-Technical System? (STS)**

A socio-technical system (=STS) is a tool to help a business anticipate and successfully resolve interdisciplinary business problems. "Interdisciplinary business problems" refer to problems where financial values are intertwined with technical, ethical, social, political, and cultural values. (Reference: Chuck Huff, Good Computing: A Virtue Approach to Computer Ethics, draft manuscript for Jones and Bartlett Publishers)

**Four Things to Know About STSs**

1. **Socio-Technical Systems are first and foremost systems: their components are interrelated and interact so that a change in one component often produces changes in the other components and in the system as a whole.** Bringing about good changes and preventing bad ones requires adjusting the different elements in relation to one another to maintain or strengthen key values embedded in the system.

2. **STS have different components which interact with one another.** Some of these are described just below. They include business projects/processes, physical surroundings, stakeholders, procedures, laws and regulations, financial and market systems, information systems, and environmental systems. The first part of a STS analysis is to identify these components and further describe them so as to include what makes each system special and unique.

3. **Socio-Technical systems embody values which can be located in the system's components and throughout the system as a whole.** (a) These values may be vulnerable, under attack, or at risk. For example, the way a company stores employee data makes make it vulnerable to unauthorized access. This would endanger the value of privacy. (b) These values may come into conflict with one another so that resolving these conflicts may require adjusting the entire system. (c) The system and its components may change in such a way as to produce significant risks or harms.

4. STSs change, and this change displays a **trajectory** or path. Frequently this trajectory is brought about by the power exercised by entrenched interests. Ladd Devine, as a wealthy business person, is able to exercise considerable over state policies regarding the distribution of water. His exercise of this power sets the community of Milagro on a trajectory of change away from agriculture and more toward the recreation industry.

## 2.4.3 Constituents

1. **Technology** including hardware, software, designs, prototypes, products, or services. Examples of engineering projects in Puerto Rico are provided in the PR STS grid. In the Therac-25 case, the hardware is the double pass accelerator, in Hughes the analogue-to-digital integrated circuits, and in Machado the UNIX software system and the computers in the UCI laboratories that are configured by this system. Because technologies are structured to carry out the intentions of their designers, they embed values.

2. **Physical Surroundings**. Physical surroundings can also embed values. Doors, by their weight, strength, material, size, and attachments (such as locks) can promote values such as security. Physical surroundings promote, maintain, or diminish other values in that they can permit or deny access, facilitate or hinder speech, promote privacy or transparency, isolate or disseminate property, and promote equality or privilege.

3. **People, Groups, and Roles**. This component of a STS has been the focus of traditional stakeholder analyses. A stakeholder is any group or individual which has an essential or vital interest in the situation at hand. Any decision made or design implemented can enhance, maintain, or diminish this interest or stake. So if we consider Frank Saia a decision-maker in the Hughes case, then the Hughes corporation, the U.S. Air Force, the Hughes sub-group that runs environmental tests on integrated circuits, and Hughes customers would all be considered stakeholders.

4. **Procedures**. How does a company deal with dissenting professional opinions manifested by employees? What kind of due process procedures are in place in your university for contesting what you consider to be unfair grades? How do researchers go about getting the informed consent of those who will be the subjects of their experiments? Procedures set forth ends which embody values and legitimize means which also embody values.

5. **Laws, statutes, and regulations** all form essential parts of STSs. This would include engineering codes as well as the state or professional organizations charged with developing and enforcing them

6. The final category can be formulated in a variety of ways depending on the specific context. Computing systems gather, store, and disseminate information. Hence, this could be labeled **data and data storage structure**. (Consider using data mining software to collect information and encrypted and isolated files for storing it securely.) In engineering, this might include the information generated as a device is implemented, operates, and is decommissioned. This information, if fed back into refining the technology or improving the design of next generation prototypes, could lead to uncovering and preventing potential accidents. Electrical engineers have elected to rename this category, in the context of power systems, rates and rate structures.

## 2.4.4

**Ethics of STS Research**

- **Right of Free and Informed Consent**: This is the right of participants in a research project to know the harms and benefits of the research. It also includes the right not to be forced to participate in a project but, instead, offer or withdraw voluntarily their consent to participate. When preparing a STS analysis, it is mandatory to take active measures to facilitate participants's free and informed consent.
- Any STS analysis must take active measures to recognize potential harms and minimize or eliminate them. This is especially the case regarding the information that may be collected about different individuals. Special provisions must be taken to maintain confidentiality in collecting, storing, and using sensitive information. This includes careful disposal of information after it is no longer needed.

## 2.4.5 Participatory Observation

- As we said above, a socio-technical system (STS) is "an intellectual tool to help us recognize patterns in the way technology is used and produced." Constructing these tools requires combining modes of analysis that are ordinarily kept separate. Because STSs embed values, they are normative. These values can help to chart out trajectories of change and development because they outline values that the system needs to realize, maintain, or even enhance. In this way, the study of STSs is normative and a legitimate inquiry for practical and professional ethics. On the other hand, STS analysis requires finding out what is already there and describing it. So STS analysis is descriptive as well. In this textbox, we will talk briefly about the descriptive or empirical components of STS analysis. This material is taken from the draft manuscript of Good Computing: A Virtue Approach to Computer Ethics and has been developed by Chuck Huff.
- **Interviews**: Semi-Structured and Structured Interviews conducted with those familiar with a given STS provide an excellent source of information on the constituents of a given STS and how these fit together into an interrelated whole. For example, the STS grid on power systems was put together by experts in this area who were able to provide detailed information on power rates and protocols, software used to distribute energy through the gridlines, and different sources (representing both hard and soft technologies) of power generation.
- **Field Observation**: Those constructing a STS analysis go directly to the system and describe it in its day-to-day operation. Two books provide more information on the types and techniques of field observation: 1. David M. Fetterman, Ethnography: 2nd Edition, Applied Social Research Methods Series, Vol 17. London, UK.: Sage Publishers, 1998 and 2. James P. Spradley, Participant Observation. New York, Harcourt, 1980. The data collected in this method can also be used to construct day-in-the-life scenarios that describe how a given technology functions on a typical day. These scenarios are useful for uncovering value conflicts and latent accidents. See James T. Reason, Human Error, Cambridge, UK.: Cambridge University Press, 1990 for information on latent accidents, how they are detected, and how they are prevented.
- **Questionnaires**: Questionnaires are useful for gathering general information from large numbers of people about a STS. Constructing good questionnaires is a difficult process that requires patience as well as trial and error. (Trying out questions on classmates and friends is the best way to identify unclear or misleading questions.) Avoiding complex, overly leading, and loaded questions represent a few of the challenges facing those who would construct useful questionnaires.
- **Archival and physical trace methods**: Looking at user manuals provides insight into how a system has been designed and how it works. Studying which keys are worn down on computer keyboards provides information on the kind of work being done. Comparing how a system is intended to work with how it is in fact being used is also illuminating, especially when one is interested in tracing the trajectory of a STS. Working with archival and physical trace methods requires critical thought and detective work.
- None of the above methods, taken in isolation, provides complete information on a STS. Triangulation represents the best way to verify data and to reconcile conflicting data. Here we generate evidence and data from a variety of sources then compare and collate. Claims made by interviewees that match direct

on-site observations confirm one another and indicate data strength and veracity. Evidence collected through questionnaires that conflicts with evidence gathered through archival research highlights the need for detective work that involves further observation, comparison, interpretation, and criticism.

- Developing STS analyses bears a striking resemblance to requirements analysis. In both cases, data is collected, refined, and put together to provide an analysis. A key to success in both is the proper combination of normative and descriptive procedures.

### 2.4.6 Exercise 1: Make a Table that Describes the Socio-Technical System

**Directions: Identify the constituents of the Socio-Technical System. Use the broad categories to prompt you.**

1. What are the major hardware and software components?
2. Describe the physical surroundings.
3. What are the major people groups or roles involved?
4. Describe any procedures in the STS.
5. Itemize the laws, statutes, and regulations.
6. Describe the data and data structures in your STS. Use the two templates below that fill in this table for energy generation systems and for engineering ethics in Puerto Rico.

**Socio Technical System Table**

|  | Hard-ware | Software | Physical Sur-round-ings | People, Groups, Roles | Procedures | Laws | Data and Data Struc-tures |
|---|---|---|---|---|---|---|---|
|  |  |  |  |  |  |  |  |
|  |  |  |  |  |  |  |  |
|  |  |  |  |  |  |  |  |

Table 2.8

### 2.4.7 Exercise 2: Identify Value Mismatches in the STS

**Directions: identify the values embedded in the STS. Use the table below to suggest possible values as well as the locations in which they are embedded.**

1. **Integrity**: "Integrity refers to the attributes exhibited by those who have incorporated moral values into the core of their identities. Such integration is evident through the way values denoting moral excellence permeate and color their expressions, actions, and decisions. Characteristics include wholeness, stability, sincerity, honesty to self and others, suthenticity, and striving for excellence.

2. **Justice**: Justice as fairness focuses on giving each individual what is his or her due. Three senses of justice are (1) the proper, fair, and proportionate use of sanctions, punishments and disciplinary measures to enforce ethical standards (retributive justice), (2) the objective, dispassionate, and impartial distribution of the benefits and burdens associated with a system of social cooperation (distributive justice), (3) an objectively determined and fairly administered compensation for harms and injustices suffered by individuals (compensatory justice), and (4) a fair and impartial formulation and administration of rules within a given group.

3. **Respect**: Respecting persons lies essentially in recognizing their capacity to make and execute decisions as well as to set forth their own ends and goals and integrate them into life plans and identities. Respects underlies rights essential to autonomy such as property, privacy, due process, free speech, and free and informed consent.

4. **Responsibility**: (Moral) Responsibility lies in the ability to identify the morally salient features of a situation and then develop actions and attitudes that answer to these features by bringing into play moral and professional values. Responsibility includes several senses: (1) individuals are responsible in that they can be called upon to answer for what they do; (2) individuals have responsibilities because of commitments they make to carrying out the tasks associated with social and professional roles; (3) responsibility also refers to the way in which one carries out one's obligations (This can range from indifference to others that leads to minimal effort to high care for others and commitment to excellence)

5. **Free Speech**: Free Speech is not an unlimited right. Perhaps the best place to start is Mill's argument in **On Liberty**. Completely true, partially true, and even false speech cannot be censored, the latter because censoring false speech deprives the truth of the opportunity to clarify and invigorate itself by defending itself. Mill only allows for a limitation of free speech based on harm to those at which the speech is directed. Speech that harms an individual (defamatory speech or shouting "fire" in a crowded theatre) can be censored out of a consideration of self-defense, not of the speaker, but of those who stand to be harmed by the speech.

6. **Privacy**: If an item of information is irrelevant to the relation between the person who has the information and the person sho seeks it, then that information is private. Privacy is necessary to autonomy because control over information about oneself helps one to structure and shape one's relations with others.

7. **Property**: According to Locke, we own as property that with which we have mixed our labor. Thomas Jefferson argues that ideas are problematic as property because, by their very nature, they are shared once they are expressed. They are also nonrivalrous and nonexclusive.

## Drawing Problems from Embedded Values

- Changes in a STS (e.g., the integration of a new technology) produce value mismatches as the values in the new component conflict with those already existing within the STS. Giving laptops to children produces a conflict between children's safety requirements and the safety features embedded in laptops as designed for adults.

- Changes within a STS can exaggerate existing value conflicts. Using digitalized textbooks on laptop computers magnifies the existing conflict concerning intellectual property; the balance between copyrights and educational dissemination is disrupted by the ease of copying and distributing digitalized media.

- Changes in STS can also lead to long term harms. Giving laptops to children threatens environmental harm as the laptops become obsolete and need to be safely disposed of.

**Values Embedded in STS**

| | Hard-ware | Software | Physical Sur-round-ings | People, Groups, Roles | Procedures Laws | | Data and Data Struc-tures |
|---|---|---|---|---|---|---|---|
| **Integrity** | | | | | | | |
| **Justice** | | | | | | | |
| **Respect** | | | | | | | |
| **Responsibility for Safety** | | | | | | | |
| **Free Speech** | | | | | | | |
| **Privacy** | | | | | | | |
| **Intellectual Property** | | | | | | | |

**Table 2.9**

## 2.4.8 Using Socio-Technical System Grids for Problem Specification

The activity of framing is a central component of moral imagination. Framing a situation structures its elements into a meaningful whole. This activity of structuring suggests both problems and solutions. Framing a situation in different ways offers alternative problem specifications and solution possibilities. Since skillful framing requires practice, this part of the module suggests how socio-technical system tables can help provide different frames for problem specification and solution generation.

**Different Problem Frames**

- **Technical Frame**: Engineers frame problems technically, that is, they specify a problem as raising a technical issue and requiring a technical design for its resolution. For example, in the STS grid appended below, the Burger Man corporation wishes to make its food preparation areas more safe. Framing this technically, it would be necessary to change the designs of ovens so they are more accident-proof.
- **Physical Frame**: How can the Burger Man corporation redesign its restaurants as physical facilities to make them more accessible? One way is to change the access points by, say, designing ramps to make restaurants wheel chair accessible. Framing this as a physical problem suggests solutions based on changing the physical structure and arrangement of the Burger Man STS.
- **Social Frame**: Burger Man as a corporation has stakeholders, that is, groups or individuals who have an essential interest at play in relation to the corporation. For example, framing the problem of making Burger Man more safe as a social problem might suggest the solution of integrating workplace safety into worker training programs and conducting regular safety audits to identify embedded risks.
- **Financial or Market-Based Frames**: Burger Man is a for-profit corporation which implies that it has certain financial responsibilities. Consequently, Burger Man should be concerned with how to provide safe, child-proof chairs and tables that do not cut unduly into corporate profits. But like the legal perspective, it is necessary to conduct ethical and social framing activities to compensate for the one-sidedness of financial framing.
- **Managerial Frame**: Many times ethical problems can be framed as managerial problems where the solution lies in changing managerial structures, reporting relations, and operating procedures. For example, Burger Man may develop a specific procedure when a cashier finishes a shift and turns over

the cash register and its contents to another cashier. Burger Man may develop cleaning procedures and routines to minimize the possibility of serving contaminated or spoiled food to customers.

- **Legal Frame**: Burger Man may choose to frame its environmental responsibilities into developing effective procedures for complying with OSHAA and EPA regulations. Framing a problem legally certainly helps to identify effective and necessary courses of action. But, because the ethical and social cannot be reduced to the legal, it is necessary to apply other frames to uncover additional risks not suggested by the legal framing.

- **Environmental Framing**: Finally, how does Burger Man look from the environmental standpoint? Does it consider environmental value (environmental health, safety, and integrity) as merely a side constraint to be addressed only insofar as it interferes with realizing supposedly more important values such as financial values? Is it a value to be traded off with other values? (For example, Burger Man may destroy the local environment by cutting down trees to make room for its latest restaurant but it offsets this destruction through its program of planting new trees in Puerto Rican tropical rain forests.) Framing a problem as an environmental problem puts the environment first and sets as a goal the integration of environmental values with other values such as worker safety and corporate profits.

### Burger Man Socio-Technical System Table

This media object is a downloadable file. Please view or download it at
&lt;Socio Technical System Grid for Business Ethics.docx&gt;

**Figure 2.5:** Clicking on this figure will open as a Word file a STS table based on the fictional corporation, Burger Man. Below are a list of problems suggested by the STS analysis.

## 2.4.9 Media File Uplinks

This module consists of two attached Media Files. The first file provides background information on STSs. The second file provides two sample STS grids or tables. These grids will help you to develop specific STSs to analyze cases in engineering, business, and computer ethics without having to construct a completely new STS for each case. Instead, using the two tables as templates, you will be able to zero in on the STS that is unique to the situation posed by the case. This module also presents background constraints to problem-solving in engineering, business, and computer ethics. These constraints do not differ absolutely from the constituents of STSs. However, they pose underlying constraints that outline the feasibility of an ethical decision and help us to identify obstacles that may arise when we attempt to implement ethical decisions.

### Socio-Technical Systems

This media object is a downloadable file. Please view or download it at
&lt;STS_Background_V3.doc&gt;

**Figure 2.6:** Socio-Technical Systems: Constituents, Values, Problems, and Constraints.

---

### STS Templates

This media object is a downloadable file. Please view or download it at
<STS_Templates.doc>

**Figure 2.7:** Two STSs, Power Engineering and the Puerto Rican Context of Engineering Practice.

---

### References

1. Brincat, Cynthia A. and Wike, Victoria S. (2000) Morality and the Professional Life: Values at Work. Upper Saddle River, NJ: Prentice Hall.
2. Huff, Chuck and Jawer, Bruce, "Toward a Design Ethics for Computing Professionals in **Social Issues in Computing: Putting Computing in its Place**, Huff, Chuck and Finholt, Thomas Eds. (1994) New York: McGraw-Hill, Inc.
3. Solomon, Robert C. (1999) A Better Way to Think About Business: How Personal INtgrity Leads to Corporate Success. Oxford, UK: Oxford University Press.
4. Wike, Victoria S. (2001) "Professional Engineering Ethics Bahavior: A Values-based Approach," **Proceedings of the 2001 American Society for Engineering Education Annual Conference and Exposition**, Session 2461.

### Bibliographical Information on Power STS

1. Acceptable Evidence: Science and Values in Risk Management, edited by Deborah G. Mayo and Rachelle D. Hollander. London, UK: Oxford University Press, 1991.
2. K. S. Shrader-Frechette. "Ethics and Energy" in Earthbound: New Introductory Essays in Environmental Ethics, 1st Edition, edited by Tom Regan. NY, NY: Random House, 1984.
3. Nancy G. Leveson. Safeware: System Safety and Computers. NY, NY: Addison-Wesley Publishing Company, 1995.
4. Charles Perrow. Normal Accidents: Living with High Risk Technologies. North America, Basic Books, 1984.
5. Malcolm Gladwell. "Blowup" in The New Yorker, January 22, 1996: 32-36.
6. James Reason. Human Error. Cambridge, UK: Cambridge University Press. 1990.
7. Mark Sagoff. The Economy of the Earth: Philosophy, Law, and the Environment. Cambridge, UK: Cambridge University Press, 1988.

# Chapter 3

# CSR (Corporate Social Responsibility)

## 3.1 A Short History of the Corporation[1]

NOTE:

---

**Word Version of this Template**

---

This is an unsupported media type. To view, please see http://cnx.org/content/m17314/latest/ EAC TK STD TEMPLATE.doc

---

**Figure 3.1:** This is an example of an embedded link. (Go to "Files" tab to delete this file and replace it with your own files.)

---

### 3.1.1 Introduction

In this module you will learn about the history of corporations. Antecedants of the modern corporation can be found in the Middle Ages, the Renaissance, and in the Industrial Revolution in Great Britain and the United States. Corporations have evolved into their present form as the synthesis of discrete solutions to specific historical problems that have arisen in the practice of business. This module has been designed for courses in (1) business, society, and government, (2) business ethics, (3) corporate governance, and (4) corporate social responsibility.

### 3.1.2 What you need to know ...

#### 3.1.2.1 The History of the Corporation

**This historical process has produced five functions that characterize the modern corporation. Corporations have emerged as...**

---

[1]This content is available online at <http://cnx.org/content/m17314/1.1/>.

1. "Passive devices" that hold property
2. Structures designed to exert monopoly control over and regulate a domain of specialized knowledge and skill
3. Means designed to pool capital and resources including human resources
4. A legal shield that protects owners and investors from liability and helps to spread and distribute financial, moral, and legal risk
5. Organizational decision-making structures that subordinate and synthesize the actions of human agents to bring about collective goals such as building a railroad, designing and manufacturing automobiles, and pursuing legitimate business ventures.

### 3.1.2.1.1 Passive Devices that hold property

When the abbot of a medieval monastery died, public officials had difficulty determining to whom its property, wealth, and resources passed. While this is hard to conceptualize from a modern standpoint, during the Middle Ages, no legal distinction could be made between (1) managing property owned by others, (2) exercising stewardship over property owned by others, and (3) owning property. Moreover, the concept and practice of owning property is complex. "Property" in its modern sense has been spelled out as a bundle of distinct rights including "the right to possess, control, use, benefit from, dispose of and exclude others from the property." (DesJardins: 37) These distinct rights are not given as entailments of a natural concept of property but represent legally endowed capacities designed to respond to specific practical problems. So, to return to the problem created by the death of the abbot, a legal entity (called the church) was created and endowed with the one of the bundled rights accompanying the notion of property, namely, the right to possess and hold property (Stone 1974: 11)

### 3.1.2.1.2 Structures that exert monopoly control and regulate a domain of specialized

Those familiar with European history know that the university came from student guilds. Students banded together to hire noted scholars willing to teach their research. Other guilds were formed around practical occupations as butchering or shoe making. Eventually, guilds evolved to address a series of practical problems: (1) how to educate individuals concerning the skills and knowledge required by the practice, (2) how to identify those responsible for the improper practice of the craft, (3) how to control who could and could not participate in (and profit from) the craft, and (4) how to regulate the craft to promote the interests of its practitioners and its beneficiaries or clients. Guilds became responsible for controlling the privileges of a trade, establishing rules and standards of practice, and holding courts to adjudicate grievances between participants. (Stone: 11-13)

### 3.1.2.1.3 A set of means specially designed to pool capital and resources including human resources.

As business ventures became more ambitious, their successful execution required raising considerable funds and capital along with the coordination of the activities of diverse human agents. Organizational structures were created slowly over time to raise money, acquire capital, and manage these complex ventures. This included creating roles that were coordinated through complex organizational systems. The distinction between the **owner** and **manager** functions, so crucial to the structure of the modern corporation, emerged slowly during this period. Owners provided money and capital and determined the overall goals pursued by the organization. Managers carried out administrative tasks concerned with day to day operations; their moral and legal duty was to remain faithful to the aims and interests of the owners. Unchartered joint stock companies served as proto-corporations that generated capital, protected monopolies of trade and craft, and managed complex ventures such as importing spices and tea from the Orient. As these structures evolved, they increasingly embodied the important distinction between the ownership and management functions.

49

### 3.1.2.1.4 Providing a legal shield to limit owner and operator liability

Scandals in 18th century Great Britain revealed another set of problems besetting the emerging corporation. When the unchartered joint stock company, the South Sea Company, went bankrupt, all the investors and owners found themselves responsible for covering the huge debt created when risky investments and questionable ventures went sour. This debt went well beyond resources of the investors destroying their personal fortunes and placing many of them in debtor's prison. (This and other fiascoes were dramatized by Charles Dickens in his novel, **Little Dorrit**.) The specter of unlimited liability scared off potential investors and set back the development of the corporation. It became necessary to endow joint stock companies with powers and devices that limited and distributed financial, moral, and legal risk. (Both owners and managers required protection although in different ways.) Individuals would invest in joint stock companies only when the associated risks became manageable and widely distributed.

### 3.1.2.1.5 Organizational structure that subordinate and synthesize the actions of human agents

**Negatively**, the development of the modern corporation was facilitated by creating a shield that limited the liability of owners and managers. Liability for owners was limited legally to the amount invested. Liability for managers required proving that they failed to remain faithful to the interests of the stockholders, the principals or originators of their actions. This broke down into demonstrating failure to exercise "sound business judgment" by, among other things, allowing outside, competing interests to corrupt their business judgment. **Positively**, the corporation emerged out of a series of legal innovations designed to establish and then control the collective power of corporate organizations. Complex organizational structures were created that designed differentiated roles filled by employees. These structures served to channel the activities of employees toward corporate ends. The investor role stabilized into that of **stockholders** who owned or held shares of the corporation. To promote their interests and to establish the cardinal or fundamental objectives of the corporation, the stockholders elected representatives to serve on a board of directors. The directors then appointed managers responsible for running the corporation and realizing the interests and objectives of the stockholders. Managers, in turn, hired and supervised employees who executed the company's day to day operations (**line** employees) and provided expert advice (**staff** employees). These roles (and the individuals who occupied them) were related to one another through complex decision-making hierarchies. Davis (1999) in his discussion of the Hitachi Report shows how many modern companies have dropped or deemphasized the staff-line distinction. Others (Stone, Nader) cite instances where managers have become so powerful that they have supplanted the directorial role. (They hand pick the directors and carefully filter the information made available to stockholders.) But these two distinctions (staff v. line and owner v. operator) remain essential for understanding and classifying modern corporations. (See Fisse, Stone, and Nader.)

### 3.1.2.1.6 Profile of the Modern Corporation

Corporations became full blown legal persons. They acquired **legal standing** (can sue and be sued), have been endowed with **legal rights** (due process, equal protection, and free speech), and have acquired **legal duties** (such as tax liabilities). (See table below for the common law decisions through which these corporate powers and rights have been established.) The powers of the corporation were regulated by the state through founding charters which served roughly the same function for a corporation as a constitution did for a state. Initially, charters limited corporate powers to specific economic activities. Railroad companies, for example, had charters that restricted their legitimate operations to building and operating railroads. When they sought to expand their operations to other activities they had to relate these to the powers authorized in the founding charter. If a charter did not specifically allow an operation or function, then it was literally **ultra vires**, i.e., beyond the power of the corporation (Stone: 21-22). This method of control gradually disappeared as states, competing to attract business concerns to incorporate within their boarders, began to loosen charter restrictions and broaden legitimate corporate powers in a process called "charter mongering." Eventually charters defined the legitimate powers of corporations so broadly that they ceased to be effective regulatory vehicles.

Given this vacuum, governments have had to resort to other measures to control and direct corporations toward the public good. The practice of punishment, effective in controlling human behavior, was extended to corporations. But Baron Thurlow (a British legal theorist) framed the central dilemma in corporate punishment with his oft quoted comment that corporations cannot be punished because they have "no soul to damn" and "no body to kick." The unique attributes of corporations has given rise to creative options for corporate control and punishment: fining, stock dilution, court-mandated changes in corporate structure, adverse publicity orders, and community service. (See Fisse) Most recently, Federal Sentencing Guidelines have sought to provide incentives for corporations to take preventive measures to avoid wrongdoing by developing ethics compliance programs. These guidelines adjust punishments in light of ethics programs that the corporations have designed and implemented to prevent wrongdoing. Corporations found guilty of wrongdoing would still be punished. But punishments can be reduced when guilty corporations show that they have developed and implemented compliance programs to promote organizational ethics and to prevent corporate wroingdoing. These include compliance codes, ethics training programs, ethics risk identification measures, and corporate ethical audits.

## History of Corporation

| Problem | Solution | Organizational Form |
|---|---|---|
| Successfully transferring stewardship over church holdings to new abbot | Create a "passive device to hold property" | Proto-corporation |
| Control over and regulation of a practice or skill | Create a device to (a) hold the privileges of some particular trade, (b) establish rules and regulations for commerce, and (c) hold courts to adjudicate grievances among members. | Medieval guilds that evolve into regulated companies. |
| Pooling capital and resources and directing complex ventures | Create a device (a) to hold privileges of trade, (b) where investors provide capital, and (c) that delegates operations to managers | Unchartered joint stock companies |
| Limiting investor liability, limiting manager liability, and balancing the two | Corporation evolves into a legal person with (a) legal rights and duties, (b) owned by shareholders, (c) run by managers, (d) regulated through state charter | Limited corporation whose operations are defined in and limited by the charter |
| | | *continued on next page* |

| Ultra Vires (charter prevents growth) and Charter Mongering | Granted broad powers through more broadly defined charters | Full Blown Corporation |
|---|---|---|
| Finding agent responsible for wrongdoing | (a) Due process, equal protection, and free speech rights, (b) legal duties, (c) legal standing, (d) Federal Sentencing Guidelines, and Sarbanes-Oxley Act | Corporation as **Legal** Person |

**Table 3.1:** Modified from Christopher Stone, Where the Law Ends

### Options for Corporate Punishment (Fisse and French)

| | Description | Example | Target of Punishment | Deterrence Trap Avoided? | Non-financial Values Addressed? | Responsive Adjustment | Interference with Corporate Black Box |
|---|---|---|---|---|---|---|---|
| **Monetary Exaction** | Fines | Pentagon Procurement Scandals | Harms innocent | Fails to Escape | Few or None Targeted | None | No interference |
| **Stock Dilution** | Dilute Stock and award to victim | | Stockholders (Not necessarily guilty) | Escapes by attacking future earnings | Few or None | Limited | No interference |
| **Probation** | Court orders internal changes (special board appointments) | SEC Voluntary Disclosure Program | Corporation and its Members | Escapes since it mandates organizational changes | Focuses on management and subgroup values | Passive adjustment since imposed from outside | Substantial entry into and interference with corporate black box |
| | | | | | | *continued on next page* | |

| Court Ordered Adverse Publicity | Court orders corporation to publicize crime | English Bread Acts (Hester Prynne shame in **Scarlet Letter**) | Targets corporate image | Escapes (although adverse publicity indirectly attacks financial values) | Loss of prestige / Corporate shame / Loss of Face/Honor | Active adjustment triggered by shame | No direct interference (corporation motived to restore itself) |
|---|---|---|---|---|---|---|---|
| Community Service Orders | Corporation performs services mandated by court | Allied chemical (James River Pollution) | Representative groups/individuals from corporation | Escapes shame, targets non-financial values | Adds value to community | Passive or no adjustment: sometimes public does recognize that cs is punishment | None |

**Table 3.2**

**Requirements of Sarbanes-Oxley (Summarized by Dyrud: 37)**

- Provide increased protection for whistle-blowers
- Adhere to an established code of ethics or explain reasons for non-compliance
- Engage in "full, fair, timely and understandable disclosure"
- Maintain "honest and ethical" behavior.
- Report ethics violations promptly
- Comply with "applicable governmental laws, rules, and regulations"
- Dyurd cites: ELT, **Ethics and Code of Conduct**, n.d.; http://www.elt-inc.com/solution/ethics_and_code_of_conduct_training_obligations.html

**Amended Federal Sentencing Guidelines (Taken from Dyrud: 37)**

1. Establishing standards and procedures to prevent and detect criminal conduct
2. Promoting responsibility at all levels of the program, together with adequate program resources and authority for its managers
3. Exercising due diligence in hiring and assigning personnel to positions with substantial authority
4. Communicating standards and procedures, including a specific requirement for training at all levels
5. Monitoring, auditing, and non-internal guidance/reporting systems
6. Promiting and enforcing of compliance and ethical conduct
7. Taking reasonable steps to respond appropriately and prevent further misconduct in detecting a violation

### 3.1.2.2 Legal Trail Toward Corporate Moral Personhood: A Table Summary

| Date | Decision | Legal Right Affirmed |
|---|---|---|
| 1889 | Minneapolis and St. L. R. Co. v. Beckwith | Right for judicial review on state legislation |
| 1893 | Noble v. Union River Logging R. Col, | Right for judicial review for rights infringement by federal legislation |
| 1906 | Hale v. Henkel | Protection "against unreasonable searches and seizures (4th) |
| 1908 | Armour Packing C. v. United States | Right to trial by jury (6th) |
| 1922 | Pennsylvania Coal Co. V. Mahon | Right to compensation for government takings |
| 1962 | Fong Foo v. United States | Right to freedom from double jeopardy (5th) |
| 1970 | Ross v. Bernhard | Right to trial by jury in civil case (7th) |
| 1976 | Virginia Pharmacy Board v. Virginia Consumer Council) | Right to free speech for purely commercial speech (1st) |
| 1978 | First National Bank of Boston v. Bellotti | Right to corporate political speech (1st) |
| 1986 | Pacific Gas and Electric Company v. Public Utility Commn of California | Right against coerced speech (1st) |

**Table 3.3**: From Ritz, Dean. (2007) "Can Corporate Personhood Be Socially Responsible?" in eds. May, S., Cheney, G., and Roper, J., Oxford, UK: Oxford University Press: 194-195.

### 3.1.2.3

## 3.1.3 What you will do ...

### 3.1.3.1 Exercise One: Other People's Money

**Watch the shareholder's meeting in the movie, " Other People's Money." Then answer the questions below. Think generally about what the manager of a corporation should do with the money its stakeholders have invested in it.**

- What is Larry the Liquidator's basic argument? What is Andrew Jorgensen's basic argument?
- What is Larry the Liquidator's conception of the nature and value of the corporation? What is Andrew Jorgensen's conception of the nature and value of the corporation?
- What is the social responsibility of a corporation according to Larry the Liquidator? What is it according to Andrew Jorgensen?
- Write a paragraph on which argument you find most persuasive, that of Larry or that of Andrew. Explain why you find it persuasive.

**3.1.3.2 Exercise Two: How to punish Arthur Andersen**

**Watch the documentary, "The Smartest Guys in the Room," paying special attention to the role played in the Enron fiasco by the accounting firm, Arthur Andersen. Then answer the following questions.**

- How important should AA's former, excellent reputation have been in determining how to punish it in the role it played in the Enron case? Explain your answer.
- Enron was only the last of a series of ethics scandals that AA had fallen into. How should it have adjusted to prior scandals? (Are the Federal Sentencing Guidelines of any help here?)
- Consider that Sarbanes-Oxley was passed largely in response to Enron. Do its provisions go far enough to prevent future Enrons? Do they go too far?.
- Using the table that summarizes punishment options provided by French and Fisse, how would you construct a punishment for Arthur Andersen? Who should be targeted? Should the company's black box be left alone? Is it better to attack financial or non-financial values? Should Arthur Andersen and other corporate offenders be encouraged to reform themselves or should those reforms be designed and directed from the outside?

**3.1.3.3**

**3.1.4 What did you learn?**

Peter French speculates on the possibility that a corporation could consist of nothing more than a sophisticated software program. He also holds forth the notion of corporate moral personhood (as opposed to natural personhood). Now that you have had an opportunity to study the history of and structure of the modern corporation, what do you think about the nature of corporations?

**3.1.5 Appendix**

**3.1.5.1 Bibliography**

1. Stone, C. D. (1975) **Where the Law Ends: The Social Control of Corporate Behavior**. Prospectr Heights, IL: Waveland Press, INC: 1-30.
2. Des Jardins, J.R. (1993) **Environmental Ethics: An Introduction to Environmental Philosophy**. Belmont, CA: Wadsworth Publishing Company: 37.
3. Clarke, T. (2004) "Introduction: Theories of Governance–Reconceptualizing Corporate Governance Theory After the Enron Experience," in **Theories of Corporate Governance: The Philosophical Foundations of Corporate Governance**, ed. Thomas Clarke. New York: Routledge: 1-30.
4. French, P.A. (1984) **Collective and Corporate Responsibility**. New York: Columbia University Press..
5. French, P.A. (1997) "Corporate Moral Agency" in Werhane, P.H., and Freeman, R.E. **Blackwell Encyclopedic Dictionary of Business Ethics**. Oxford, UK: Blackwell: 148-151.
6. May, L. (1987) **The Morality of Groups: Collective Responsibility, Group-Based Harm, and Corporate Rights**. Notre Dame, IN: University of Notre Dame Press.
7. Werhane, P. H. (2008) "Mental Models: Moral Imagination and System Thinking in the Age of Globalization," in **Journal of Business Ethics**, 78: 463–474.
8. Werhane, P. (2007) "Corporate Social Responsibility/Corporate Moral Responsibility: Is There a Difference and the Difference It Makes," in eds., May, S., Cheney, G., and Roper, J., **The Debate over Corporate Social Responsibility**. Oxford, UK: Oxford University Press: 459-474.
9. Fisse, B. and French, P.A., eds. (1985) **Corrigible Corporations and Unruly Law**. San Antonio, TX: Trinity University Press.
10. Nader, R. and Green, M.J., eds. (1973) **Corporate Power in America**. New York: Grossman.
11. Nader,, R. Green, M. and Seligman, J. (1976) **Taming the Giant Corporation**. New York: Norton.

12. Davis, M. (1998) **Thinking Like an Engineer: Studies in the Ethics of a Profession**. Oxford, UK: Oxford University Press: 119-156.
13. Jackall, R. (1988) **Moral Mazes: The World of Corporate Managers**. Oxford, UK: Oxford University Press.
14. Carol, A. B., "Social Responsibility," in Werhane, P., and Freeman, R. E., eds. (1997, 1998) **Blackwell Encyclopedic Dictionary of Business Ethics**. Oxford, UK: Blackwell Publishers, INC: 593-595.
15. Dyrud, M.A. (2007) "Ethics, Gaming, and Industrial Training," in **IEEE Technology and Society Magazine**. Winter 2007: 36-44.
16. Ritz, Dean. (2007) "Can Corporate Personhood Be Socially Responsible?" in eds. May, S., Cheney, G., and Roper, J., **Corporate Governance**. Oxford, UK: Oxford University Press: 194-195.

## 3.1.6 EAC ToolKit Project

**3.1.6.1 This module is a WORK-IN-PROGRESS; the author(s) may update the content as needed. Others are welcome to use this module or create a new derived module. You can COLLABORATE to improve this module by providing suggestions and/or feedback on your experiences with this module.**

Please see the Creative Commons License[2] regarding permission to reuse this material.

**3.1.6.2 Funded by the National Science Foundation: "Collaborative Development of Ethics Across the Curriculum Resources and Sharing of Best Practices," NSF-SES-0551779**

# 3.2 Moral Ecologies in Corporate Governance[3]

---

### Word Version of this Template

This media object is a downloadable file. Please view or download it at
< EAC TK STD TEMPLATE.doc>

**Figure 3.2:** This is an example of an embedded link. (Go to "Files" tab to delete this file and replace it with your own files.)

---

## 3.2.1 Two Thought Experiments

### The Ring of Gyges (Plato's Republic II, S359)

Gyges a poor shepherd is tending his flock when there is an earthquake. A hugh crack opens in the earth to expose a sarcopagus. Gyges reaches in and takes the ring that draws his attention. Later, when he is talking among friends, he notices that he becomes invisible when he turns the ring in toward himself. He tries this out a few times and then forms his plans. Invisible, he gains entry to the king's castle and rapes the queen. Drawing her into his nefarious plan, they kill the king and take over the kingdom. Gyges marries the queen and becomes ruler of a large and wealthy kingdom. Somehow it doesn't seem fit to say that he lives "happily ever after." But, since he is never caught, it doesn't follow that his ill-gotten gain has made him miserable.

Before finding his ring, Gyges was, at least outwardly, a well-behaved, just citizen. But the combination of vast power and no accountability drew Gyges over to the dark side. Does the human character, like that

---

[2]http://creativecommons.org/licenses/by/2.0/
[3]This content is available online at <http://cnx.org/content/m17353/1.5/>.

of Gyges, dissolve in the face of temptation and lack of accountability? Is the threat of punishment necessary to keep individuals moral? Is visibility and the threat of punishment all that stands between an individual and a life of injustice?

**The Milgram Experiments**

From 1960 until 1963, Stanley Milgram, a social psychologist, carried out a series of experiments on around 1000 subjects. Each experiment brought together three participants, a subject (or teacher), a learner, and an experimenter. In the initial orientation, the experimenter told the subject/teacher and the learner that they were about to participate in an experiment designed to measure the influence of punishment (in the form of electrical shocks) on learning. The learner was presented with information. The teacher then asked questions based on this information. If the learner answered correctly, then they went on to the next question. If the learner answered incorrectly, then he was given an electrical shock by the teacher. With each missed question the intensity of the shock increased. The experiment continued until all the questions were asked and answered.

However, these instructions constituted a deception brought upon the teacher/subject by the secret collaboration of the experimenter and the learner. The real purpose of the experiment was to determine how far individuals would go in turning against their moral views on the basis of an external authority. The learner feigned pain and suffering because there was no actual electrical shock. And the learner deliberately missed most of the questions in order to force the teacher to progress to higher and what appeared to be life-threatening levels of shock. While teachers were not physically forced to continue the experiment over the feigned protests of the learners, whenever they tried to stop it, they were told by the experimenter that they had to continue to the end.

Before the Milgram experiments were carried out, a group of psychogists were asked to predict how many teachers/subjects would go all the way to the end and give the learner what they thought were life-threatening and highly painful shocks. The consensus was that most would stop the experiment early on when the learner first began to protest. But the actual results were quite "shocking." Nearly 60 percent of the teachers went all the way and gave the learner the maximum shock. You can read more about these experiments and how they have been interpreted by reading Milgram 1974 and Flanagan 1991. You Tube has several video vignettes on the Milgram Experiments. Simply type "Milgram Experiments" in the search window and browse the results.

Can authority and environment override our everyday moral beliefs as well as the characters constructed from them? Is character robust and "trans-situational?" Or is it radically dependent on situation and environment? Can normally decent and well-behaved individuals turn into moral monsters given the right external conditions?

**From Gyges and Milgram to Moral Ecology**

Both of these thought experiments raise the question of the influence of environment on character. This module is designed to help increase the strength of moral character by identifying different organizational environments (called "moral ecologies") and having you developing strategies to resist their pressures and maintain integrity.

## 3.2.2 Introduction

Corporate governance is defined in the Blackwell Encyclopedic Dictionary of Business Ethics as "concerned with those decisions made by the senior executives of a firm and the impacts of their decisions on various stakeholder groups." (EBE 147) This module turns corporate governance inside-out and looks at it from the perspective of the governed, that is, from the directors, managers, and employees subject to the structures and strategies of corporate governance. Corporate environments function as "moral ecologies," that is, "the somewhat stable, but constantly negotiated set of values, practices, and influences within societies, organizations, professions, and work groups." (Huff et. al., 2008) The thrust of this module is to help you begin to strategize on how to develop sustainable moral careers within different moral ecologies. You will study different kinds of moral ecologies using a taxonomy developed from the research of Michael Davis in **Thinking Like an Engineer** and Robert Jackall in **Moral Mazes**. Huff (2008) provides some generic strategies for individuals to pursue within in these organizational environments. But the exercises included in this module will encourage you to expand upon this list. Working through this module will help you to view corporate governance from within from the micro perspective of the individual. Another module will allow you to see corporate governance from the outside from the macro point of view.

## 3.2.3 What you need to know ...

### 3.2.3.1 Three Moral Ecologies

**Summary Table**

| Type / Characteristics | Managers and engineers: role and participation | Centrality of ethics and values | Allocation of praise and blame | Withholding information | Treatment of dissent and DPOs |
|---|---|---|---|---|---|
| **Finance-Driven** | Managers play line role (=make decisions) Engineers provide technical information (=staff role) | Ethics and values are side constraints dealt with when they oppose financial considerations | Allocated according to hierarchical position: praise goes up and blame goes down. | Managers withhold to control and protect secrets. Engineers withhold bad news to avoid blame. | "Shoot the messenger!" Dissent = disloyalty and betrayal. |
| **Customer-Driven** | Managers make decisions on financial matters. Engineers "go to the mat" on engineering matters. | Ethics and values are not central but are still important. | Praise and blame are fairly allocated based on assigned responsibility and contribution. | Information not withheld but gaps arise because or role differences. | Differences occur but engineers are expected to advocate their perspective in decision making process. |
| **Quality-Driven** | Manager and engineering distinction drops out. Interdisciplinary work teams are empowered and responsible | Ethics and values are constitutive of the organization's identity. | Praise and blame are attributed to group and distributed to individuals within according to contribution. | Open consensus process ensures that needed information is integrated into decision making | Engineers and managers work toward consensus by gathering more information, continuing the discussion, and (as last resort) postponing the decision until consensus is reached. |

**Table 3.4**

**Breakdown of Table**

- Moral ecologies can be categorized according to a series of considerations. The table above focuses on five.

- First, managers and engineers occupy distinct roles and participate differently in the decision making process. Managers play the **line** role. They collect information to make decisions that govern the day to day operations of the corporation. Engineers are hired as **staff** employees. They provide technical information to decision makers but do not participate directly in the decision making process. This raises difficulties when engineers, for technical or ethical reasons, disagree with the decisions taken by their managers. The line and staff roles channel decision making and constrain dissent.

- Moral ecologies can also be typed according to the centrality of ethical considerations in the corporation's goals, charter, operations, and even identity. Ethical considerations can range from (1) playing a **central** role, (2) to playing an important but subordinate role, (3) to being marginalized as irrelevant **side constraints**. The importance a corporation places on ethics colors all the other categories mentioned in the table above. If ethics is central to a corporation then it plays a central role in the decision making process, guides the allocation of praise and blame, determines the nature and amount of information shared in the decision making process, and determines how an organization treats dissent and disagreement.

- A corporation's conception of responsibility is revealed through the ways in which it allocates praise and blame. Significant differences arise between the way finance companies assign praise and blame and the ways these are allocated in quality or customer driven companies. Again, this related to the roles played by engineers and managers and the centrality of ethics in the corporation's governance.

- Ethical problems arise when crucial information is withheld from the decision making process. Hence, the flow of communication and the kinds of situations in which communication flow is disrupted helps to characterize a moral ecology. For example, the Hitachi report asserts that communication between managers and engineers breaks down predictably within finance-driven companies. This breakdown is grounded in the characteristics of the finance-driven moral ecology, especially in differences between the managerial and engineering roles and the extent to which managers and engineers participate in decision making.

- Finally, moral ecologies can be classified according to how they treat dissent and dissenting professional opinions. Dissent is less likely in quality than in finance-driven companies. While finance-driven companies treat dissent as disloyalty, quality- and customer-driven driven companies treat dissent as a stage in the process of reaching consensus.

### Finance-Driven Companies

1. Finance-driven companies place financial objectives at the very heart of their constitutive objectives and corporate identity. For example, such companies are focused on maximizing returns for investors.

2. **Manager and Engineer Roles and Participation in Decision Making Process**: Managers play the line role in that they make the decisions that drive the day to day operations of the corporation. They bear responsibility for the consequences of their decisions and they are also responsible as the faithful agents of the company's directors. Being a faithful agent requires that one treat another's interests as one's own, maintain confidentialities, and avoid interests that conflict with the director. Engineers play the staff role, that is, they answer questions put to them by managers and are responsible for providing competent technical information. However, they do not participate directly in the decision making process, nor do they bear responsibility for the results of their manager's decisions.

3. **Centrality of ethics and values in the corporations decision making process**: Ethical considerations play only the role of side constraints in the setting of corporate policity and in the formulation and execution of its decisions. This means that ethical considerations are important only if they promote or interfere with the central, financial objectives. If appearing philanthropical is good for a corporation's image (and generates customers and profits) then the corporation appears philanthropic. If the corporation is likely to get caught in an ethical violation (excessive pollution) and this negative publicity will lower its prestige (and profits) then the corporation will not commit the violation. But in each case, the end is the promotion of financial objectives and the means are appearing ethical.

4. **Allocating Praise and Blame**Jackall goes into detail on how finance-driven corporations (and bureaucracies in general) assign praise and blame. The crucial factor is one's position in the corporate

hierarchy. Praise works its way up the corporate ladder. If engineer Smith saves the company from a sever financial loss, then Smith's supervisor (or his supervisor's supervisor) gets the credit. However, if Smith's supervisor messes up, the blame passes down the corporate ladder to Smith. Praise moves up the corporate hierarchy, blame down.

5. **Information Exchange between Engineers and Managers**: In finance driven companies, managers withhold information from the engineers under their supervision for a variety of reasons. For example, if it is proprietary information, the manager may withhold all or part to prevent engineers from leaving the firm and revealing its secrets to a competitor. Managers may also use information to wield power and authority. By keeping engineers in the dark (like mushrooms) they effectively maintain authority and prevent dissent. On the other hand, engineers withhold bad news from their managers to avoid blame as well as the "shoot the messenger" syndrome. (When the incompetent general receives bad news from a soldier, he shoots the soldier rather than respond to the news.)

6. **Handling Dissenting Professional Opinions**: Dissent is interpreted as disloyalty in finance-driven companies. This organizational habit (maintained by managers to hold on to their authority) will even undermine DPO (dissenting professional opinion) procedures that look good on paper. A good DPO procedure communicates the opinion to several levels of supervisor, allows for the independent investigation of the merits of the opinion, and prevents retaliation against the professional asserting the opinion. But ruthless managers find ways to undermine such a procedure at all levels. Engineers may claim the right not to be held as scape goats to administrative incompetence. (See the Theory Building Activities: Rights module) This right may be supported on paper by a detailed DPO procedure. But it also has to be implemented at all levels and continually monitored.

## Customer-Driven Companies

- Customer-driven companies focus on customer satisfaction. If the customer asks for or is satisfied with a lower quality product, then this is an acceptable result for this type of company as opposed to a quality driven company which would stand fast with the higher quality product.
- **Managers and engineers: roles and participation**: Managers make decisions on financial matters. But engineers are expected to "go to the mat" for engineering standards when these form all or part of the decision. Hence the distinction between managers (playing the line role) and engineers (playing the staff role) weakens, and engineers play a much more active role (advocates for engineering standards) in decision making. (Engineering standards include engineering ethics standards.)
- **Centrality of Ethics and Values**: While customer satisfaction plays the central role, ethical considerations are still important, especially regarding the ethical treatment of customers and reflecting the ethical values held by the customers. In many cases, it is difficult to distinguish quality and customer driven companies as the role ethical standards play gets closer to a central, constitutive one.
- **Allocation of Praise and Blame**: Responsibility in customer driven companies is tied closely to individual performance and contribution. This is because customer satisfaction is a more objective criterion than the internal political standards that dominate finance driven companies. Responsibility is closely alligned with contribution.
- **Withholding Information**: Information enhances control and responsibility. (The more you know, the more reponsibly you can act.) Since praise and blame are allocated according to contribution, there is less incentive to withhold information. If communication gaps arise between engineers and managers, these are much more likely to hinge on disciplinary differences. Engineers may have trouble communicating technical information to managers, or appear condescending by "dumbing down" the information. Managers may have difficulties communicating financial constraints to engineers who focus on quality standards. But these are minor, resolvable gaps.
- **Treatment of Dissent**: Dissent and disagreement are not only tolerated but actually expected. Managers expect engineers to advocate for issues in their sphere as they pertain to the decision making process. This process itself is adversarial because it is assumed that this is the best way to get all the information out on the table. Bad news and professional dissenting opinions are not interpreted as disloyalty; in fact, disloyalty lies in refusing to expose flaws in the choices proposed by one's supervisor.

Managers expect their engineers to "go to the mat" when advocating technical positions based on their professional judgment.

## Quality-Driven Companies

- Quality-driven companies stand out for the emphasis they place on achieving high engineering standards and on elevating the participation of the engineer in the decision making process. As is implied by the name, the central focus of these corporations is the achievement of high quality in products and services.

- **Managers and Engineers: Role and Participation**: In quality-driven companies, the distinction between the manager and engineering roles drops out. For example, while engineers play the staff role and provide expert engineering advice, they also participate fully in the decision making process. The locus of decision making moves from individual managers to small interdisciplinary groups. These groups, in turn, carry out consensus-based decision making procedures.

- **Centrality of Ethics and Values**: In quality-driven companies, ethics and values are central to the organization's objectives, charter, and identity. This has a decisive impact on the role of the engineer in the decision-making process. In customer driven companies, engineers are expected to advocate engineering and ethical standards precisely because these are not central to the organization's identity. But the centrality of ethical concerns in quality driven companies changes the engineer's role from advocacy to channeling technical expertise toward realizing ethical value.

- **Allocation of praise and blame**: In customer-driven companies, blame avoidance procedures no longer dominate the decision making process. In quality driven companies they disappear completely. Decisions are made by interdisciplinary groups in which engineers and managers participate fully and equally. Responsibility (praise and blame) then is allocated to the group. If it is distributed to members inside the group it is done so on the basis of contribution. But the primary target of responsibility ascriptions is the group, not the individual. And the response to untoward happenings is not targeting individuals and groups for blame but taking measures to learn from mistakes and avoiding them in the future.

- **Withholding Information**: The open, consensus-based decision process ensures that the needed information is brought forth and integrated into the decision. This results from removing a primary motivation to withholding information, namely, blame avoidance. Quality-driven corporations aggressively move to prevent untoward occurrences and, should prevention fail, make adjustments to ensure they do not reoccur. The motive to withhold information does not arise in this moral ecology.

- **Treatment of Dissent and DOPs (dissenting professional opinions)**: Engineers and managers work toward consensus by gathering information, discussing the problem and continuing the discussion until consensus is reached. Thus, dissent does not stand alone but is considered to be an essential and healthy component to the decision-making process. When consensus is not immediately reached, participants seek more information. If consensus is still not reached, the decision is postponed (if this is possible). The most viable strategy to reach consensus is to continue the discussion. For example, an engineer and manager might approach a supervisor; in this way they bring a new perspective into the decision-making process. They might consult other experts. The crucial point here is that disagreement (really non-agreement) is not a bad thing but a necessary stage in the process of reaching agreement and consensus.

## Skill Sets

- The four skills described below are derived from studying the moral expertise displayed by moral exemplars. Each moral ecology will require the exercise of each of the skills described below. However, each skill has to be contextualized into the moral ecology. For example, reasonableness should not be exercised in the same way in a finance-driven company as it should be exercised in a quality-driven company. The reasonable exercise of dissent is manifested differently in an environment where dissent is equated with disloyalty than in one in which dissent is embraced as a necessary part of the consensus-reaching process. So your job, in constructing your moral careers within these different moral ecologies, is to contextualize the skill, that is, describe specifically how each skill should be practiced in each particular moral ecology.

- **Moral imagination** consists of projecting oneself into the perspective of others. It also includes multiple problem definitions and the ability to distance oneself from the decision situation to gain impartiality.
- **Moral creativity** is the ability to generate non-obvious solutions to moral challenges while responding to multiple constraints.
- **Reasonableness** consists of gathering relevant evidence, listening to others, giving reasons for one's own positions (arguments and evidence), and changing plans/positions only on the basis of good reasons.
- **Perseverance** involves planning moral action and responding to unforeseen circumstances while keeping moral goals intact.

### Personality Traits

- **Extraversion**: Extraversion, which is paired with its opposite, introversion, has also been called confident self-expression, assertiveness, social extraversion, and power. An individual in whom this trait dominates tends to be assertive and out-going.
- **Conscientiousness**: Individuals with this trait are successful in carrying out tasks because they can discipline themselves to stay focused on a task. They are successful in the right moral ecology and tend to conform to the basic norms of their environment. This trait can lead to bad results if not guided by moral considerations.
- **Neuroticism**: This trait indicates a lack of emotional stability. According to Huff et al., "it is correlated with less effective coping and depression." Neuroticism has also been shown to interfere with the exercise of moral skills. Is there a particular moral ecology that can heighten the negative impacts of this personality trait?
- **Agreeableness**: According to Huff et al, this trait has also been called "social adaptability, likability, friendly compliance, and love." Again think about how this trait would operate within a finance-driven moral ecology as opposed to a quality-driven one.

### Two Kinds of Moral Expertise

- Studies carried out by Chuck Huff into moral exemplars in computing suggest that moral exemplars can operate as craftspersons or reformers. (Sometimes they can combine both these modes.)
- Craftspersons (1) draw on pre-existing values in computing, (2) focus on users or customers who have needs, (3) take on the role of providers of a service/product, (4) view barriers as inert obstacles or puzzles to be solved, and (5) believe they are effective in their role.
- Reformers (1) attempt to change organizations and their values, (2) take on the role of moral crusaders, (3) view barriers as active opposition, and (4) believe in the necessity of systemic reform
- These descriptions of moral exemplars have been taken from a presentation by Huff at the STS colloquium at the University of Virginia on October 2006.

## 3.2.4 What you will do ...

In this section, you will learn about this module's activities and/or exercises. You will also find step by step instructions on how to carry them out.

### Exercise 1: What we do when nobody is looking

- **You will be asked either to defend or criticize the following position on the nature and function of punishment**

- Entiendo que ser castigado es una manera de educar a la persona a cometió la falta y a la sociedad en general para que comprendan y entiendan que su conducta es una falta y afecta a la sociedad. En conclusión es una solución viable hasta el memento bastante efectiva siempre y cuando el castigo sea ejecutado de una manera prudente, saludable y dentro de lo que las leyes permiten.
- Restate this argument in your own words. (Try to shorten it by summarizing its key points.) Then discuss and clarify its key terms. Offer ethical and practical considerations in its defense.

### Exercise 2: Milgram and Business

- **Continuing with the task in part one, you will be asked to either defend or criticize the following position on the meaning that the results of the Milgram experiments have for business administration**
- The Milgram experiments teach us that under the right conditions, anyone is capable of committing immoral activities. If a strong, dominant boss exists and has a weak, dependable employer, then the employer will out of necessity do whatever the boss wants.
- Many people are willing to commit immoral acts even though they know it is wrong if they know they are not being watched.
- It teaches us that many employees tend to do illegal works just because their managers ask them to so they assume they will be taking full responsibility for the situation even though it is unethical.

### Exercise 3: Commentary Groups

- **Your job is to evaluate the arguments made by the teams debating in parts one and two. Be sure to focus on the argument and not the content of the position. Listen to their statements.**
- Do they base these on sound statements?
- What kind of ethical and practical principles (or values) do they use to make their case?
- Do their frame their position broadly or narrowly?

### Exercise 4: Closure Groups

- **After listening to the debate and commentary, recap what has happened and discuss whether there are any conclusions that can be drawn from this activity**
- Do people agree or disagree about these 2 issues?
- If there is agreement, why does it exist?
- If there is disagreement, why does it exist?
- Is agreement possible? Why or why not?

## 3.2.5 What did you learn?

This module was designed to help you visualize how to realize a moral career within three dominant moral ecologies. Apply these matters to yourself. Which moral ecology would be best for you? Of the two moral careers mentioned above, reformer and helper, which best fits your personality? Why? In other words, begin the process of visualizing and planning your own moral career.

## 3.2.6 Appendix

### References

1. Davis, M. (1998) **Thinking Like an Engineer: Studies in the Ethics of a Profession**. Oxford, UK: Oxford University Press: 117-156.
2. Doris, J.M. (2002) **Lack of Character: Personality and Moral Behavior**. New York: Cambridge University Press.

3. Flanagan, O. (1991) **Varieties of Moral Personality: Ethics and Psychological Realism**. Cambridge, Mass: Harvard University Press: 293-314.

4. Harris, C.E., Pritchard, M.S., and Rabins, M.J. (1999) **Engineering Ethics: Concepts and Cases, 2nd Ed**. New Jersey: Wadsworth: 181-188.

5. Huff, C., Barnard, L. and Frey, W. (2008) "Good Computing: A Pedagogically focused model of virtue in the practice of computing, Part II," in **The Journal of Information, Communication and Ethics in Society**. (Under Review)

6. Jackall,R. (1983). "Moral Mazes: Bureaucracy and Managerial Work," in **Harvard Business Review**: Sept and Oct 1983.

7. Jackall, R. (1988) **Moral Mazes: The World of Corporate Managers**. Oxford, UK: Oxford University Press.

8. Mannix, E., and Neale, M.A. (2005) "What Differences Make a Difference?: The Promise and Reality of Diverse Teams in Organizations," in **American Psychological Society**, 6(2): 31-49.

9. Milgram, S. (1974) **Obedience to Authority**. New York: Harper Perennial.

10. Solomon, R.C. (2003) "Victims of Circumstances?: A Defense of Virtue Ethics in Business," in **Business Ethics Quarterly**. Volume 13, Issue 1: 43-62.

This optional section contains additional or supplementary information related to this module. It could include: assessment, background such as supporting ethical theories and frameworks, technical information, discipline specific information, and references or links.

### 3.2.7 EAC ToolKit Project

**3.2.7.1 This module is a WORK-IN-PROGRESS; the author(s) may update the content as needed. Others are welcome to use this module or create a new derived module. You can COLLABORATE to improve this module by providing suggestions and/or feedback on your experiences with this module.**

Please see the Creative Commons License[4] regarding permission to reuse this material.

**3.2.7.2 Funded by the National Science Foundation: "Collaborative Development of Ethics Across the Curriculum Resources and Sharing of Best Practices," NSF-SES-0551779**

## 3.3 Three Views of CSR (Corporate Social Responsibility)[5]

---

**Word Version of this Template**

---

This is an unsupported media type. To view, please see http://cnx.org/content/m17318/latest/ EAC TK STD TEMPLATE.doc

---

**Figure 3.3:** This is an example of an embedded link. (Go to "Files" tab to delete this file and replace it with your own files.)

---

[4]http://creativecommons.org/licenses/by/2.0/
[5]This content is available online at <http://cnx.org/content/m17318/1.5/>.

```
   - The first two links to this module are to sample corporate social
responsibility statements put out by McDonalds and Starbucks. These
will help you to benchmark your own efforts both in the fictional
Burger Man case and in your efforts to develop CSR reports for real
companies.
```

```
- The other link is a story from reporter, Paul Solomon, that reports on
  the annual Business for Social Responsibility conference.  This story,
  first broadcast on December 23, 2004 reports on outstanding and suc-
  cessful efforts on CSR.  Its title is "Good Business Deeds" and it was
  accessed for this module on August 17, 2008 at the following URL:
  http://www.pbs.org/newshour/bb/business/july-dec04/corporate_12-23.html
```

### 3.3.1 Introduction

This module will introduce you to the theme of corporate social responsibility. Three representative cases will help to pose the central problems and basic issues of CSR. Then you will work on developing a social contract between the business corporation and society to articulate the interests, goods, and rights at stake in CSR. Three different approaches dominate this field: the shareholder approach set forth by Milton Friedman, the stakeholder approach articulated by Evan and Freeman, and Patricia Werhane's alliance model. Finally, you will work on developing a CSR program for the hypothetical corporation, Burger Man. This will be based on a shareholder meeting that consists of six or seven stakeholder presentations. (You will play the role of one of the stakeholders.) Your CSR program will address and integrate the needs and interests of the Burger Man stakeholders.

**Three CSR Challenges**

Patricia Werhane discusses how six corporate organizations deal with three CSR challenges: (1) carrying out oil drilling in a corrupt political environment, (2) working with suppliers who impose sweatshop conditions on employees, and (3) addressing the HIV/AIDS challenge in Africa. Each challenge elicits two corporate responses, one from a shareholder or stakeholder perspective, the other from an alliance perspective. Shell Oil's response to political corruption in Nigeria will be compared with Exxon/Mobile's response in Chad and Cameroon. Nike's answer to public criticism of the employment practices of its third world suppliers will be compared to Wal Mart's reputedly heavy-handed treatment of its employees and suppliers. Finally, while the pharmaceutical industry has developed an expensive drug cocktail to treat HIV/AIDS in patients in developed nations, the NGO (Non Government Organization), the Female Health Company, has designed a program to distribute of condoms to prevent infection in the first place. These paired corporate responses to CSR challenges are not provided in support of the position that the superiority of the alliance approach is a "no-brainer." Instead, they provide you with a menu of CSR strategies that you will evaluate using the CSR framework you will develop out of the social contract that between business and society. These three CSR challenges come from Werhane (2007)

**Operating in a Corrupt Environment**

- A big challenge facing multinational corporations is how they should respond to local corruption. Both Shell Oil and Exxon/Mobile sought to carry out drilling operations at sites plagued by corrupt local and national governments.
- Shell took a shareholder approach arguing that their primary CSR was to their stockholders and that involvement in corrupt local politics would be tantamount to paternalism.
- Exxon/Mobile, on the other hand, adopted a more active approach. They took expensive measures to mitigate the environmental impact of their operations. They also hired and provided technical training to local residents. Finally, they worked to ensure that the revenues they introduced into the local communities were not lost through political and business corruption.

- What are the CSRs of multinational corporations that operate in corrupt local environments? Are these fashioned around the minimal obligation of creating no additional harm? Or should they expand to preventing harm (if possible) that others are about to inflict? To move even further up the ladder of responsibility, do multinational corporations have positive, supererogatory responsibilities that consist of adding value to the communities they do business in?

## Vicarious CSR: Responding to Supplier Sweatshops

- Vicarious responsibility occurs when one agent accepts responsibility for actions executed by another. For example, under agency theory, the principal bears overall moral and legal responsibility for the action since he or she has originated it. Although the agent executes the action, he or she is responsibility only for executing the action faithfully and treating the principal's interests as his or her own.
- In this context, can we hold corporations such as Nike and Wal Mart vicariously responsible for the morally questionable actions of their suppliers? If so, then under what conditions?
- Nike fell under siege when the press found out that its suppliers based in the third world imposed harsh, sweatshop conditions on their employees, including child labor. Nike could have argued that this was beyond the scope of their repsonsibility. How could **they** be held **vicariously responsible** for the actions of another? Their job was to produce shoes at the lowest possible price to deliver an affordable quality product to customers and to maximize shareholder value. But Nike went beyond this minimal responsibility to carefully vet suppliers and to work with them to improve working conditions. Thus, they expanded the scope of their CSR to include improving working conditions for, not only their employees, but also the employees of their suppliers.
- Wal Mart has been identified by Collins and Porras (Built to Last) as a highly successful and visionary company. It has certainly led the way in providing consumers with high quality products at surprisingly low prices. But the savings it provides to customers and the high returns it guarantees investors are purchased at a high price. Wal Mart prevents its employees from joining unions which has lowered their wages and restricted their health and retirement benefits. Wal Mart employees are also expected to work long hours for the company. While it provides cheap, high quality products to its customers, Wal Mart pushes suppliers narrowing their profit margin and placing upon them the responsibility of supplying product just-in-time to meet demand.
- In its earlier days, Wal Mart targeted small towns. Their competitive practices forced less aggressive, local business to leave. While they have brought considerable benefits to these communities, they have also seriously changed established business and social structures.
- Finally, Wal Mart, like Nike initially, exercises minimal supervision over their suppliers many of whom are oversees. Wal Mart suppliers also have been known to impose harsh working conditions on their employees.

## Some CSR Questions for Nike and Wal Mart

1. From a broader CSR perspective, is Nike maximizing stakeholder value? Is it redistributing burdens and costs from customers and investors to its suppliers and their employees? Does CSR allow this redistribution of the corporate wealth form the shareholders to other stakeholders? (Think about Friedman's arguments here.
2. If it is necessary to trade off stakeholder stakes as both Wal Mart and Nike do, which trade off is more just? Nike's distribution of its wealth from its stockholders to the needy manifested in its efforts to improve the working conditions and income of the employees of its suppliers? Or Wal Mart's distribution of benefits to its stockholders and its comparatively prosperous customers?
3. Which model would Friedman prefer under the his version of the shareholder view of CSR? Explain and evaluate.
4. Which model would be preferable by Evan and Freeman under the stakeholder view? Who are Nike and Wal Mart's stakeholders? What are their stakes? How should the wealth produced by these two corporations be distributed among their stakeholders?

5. Werhane, in her alliance model, argues for the importance of a CSR model that decentralizes the corporation and facilitates morally imaginative solutions. Why does she argue that Nike's program is than Wal Mart's from this perspective? What could Wal Mart do to improve its CSR on the alliance view?

## Facing the AIDS Challenge in Africa

- The widespread and devastating effects of the AIDS epidemic in Africa are well known. But what are the responsibilities of corporations in the face of this terrible CSR challenge? Should they do business as usual and allow others who are perhaps more qualified respond to this pervasive social problem? Or should they recognize a broader responsibility to channel their wealth, knowledge and expertise toward mitigating this social problem?

- Pharmaceutical corporations invest huge amounts of money in research and development. The market place is a good place for both encouraging this necessary risk and for distributing it among several groups and interests. Developing new medicines requires costly research. So Friedman's question is highly pertinent here: does imposing CSR on a corporation do more harm than good because it interferes with the delicate mechanism of the market?

- At any point along the way, the product may not meet expectations, a competitor may beat the pharmaceutical to the market, the regulatory process may delay or even prevent sale, and so on. The rewards from patenting a successful medicine are astoundingly high. But heavy, possibly devastating losses are also possible. Adding CSR to the mixture may be the formula for corporate disaster.

- Pharmaceutical corporations also face daunting challenges from regulatory agencies such as the Food and Drug Administration. New products must be exhaustively and painstakingly tested to avoid problems that have arisen in the past such as the Dalkon Shield and Thalidomide. Again, considerable effort must be expended in exploring the middle and long term consequences accompanying product and drug use, and all of this before the product can be marketed and profits made. Government regulation also raises another problem. Is government prodding necessary to force corporations into a proper CSR posture? Or should corporations be allowed to develop voluntarily their own CSR responses?

- In the case at hand, pharmaceutical companies have invested considerable resources to carry out research into medicines that control HIV infection and prevent it from developing into full-blown AIDS. But these treatments are very expensive and bring with them considerable side effects. An anti-AIDS chemical cocktail can cost patients in developed nations between 15 and 20 thousand dollars per patient per year. This is far beyond the financial resources available to a typical HIV/AIDS patient in Africa. Some NGOs and critics of the pharmaceutical industry accuse the latter of gouging victims and drawing excess profits from the misfortune of others. A spokesperson for "Doctors Without Borders," for example, claims that the AIDS treatment "cocktail" that costs U.S. patients 15 to 20 thousand dollars could be made available to Africans at less than 300 dollars per patient per year. Pharmaceuticals, according to their critics, need to rethink their CSR, cease operating as for-profit businesses, and make these drugs available to third world sufferers at cost.

- What are the CSRs of multinational pharmaceutical corporations for making HIV/AIDS drugs available to victims in the poverty-stricken nations of Africa? Are they responsible for charging what the market will bear? Assuming they have the right to recoup their heavy investment in research, should governments, recognizing the necessity of compensating drug companies for their research, buy these drugs and redistribute them at little or no cost to those who can't afford them? Or should the pharmaceuticals charge more to those who can pay and less to those who cannot? (This redistributes the burden of cost from the haves to the have nots.)

- Many NGOs have taken the stance that their responsibility lies in pressuring drug companies to do the right thing and donate medicines to patients who cannot pay. This is their corporate social responsibility, and the pharmaceutical industry certainly has enough money to do this.

- But others have tried to reframe this issue using moral imagination. Treating individuals for HIV infection once they have contracted it is expensive no matter how you look at it. But, redefining the problem, can moderate and affordable measures be taken to prevent the spread of the disease?

- This is the imaginative approach taken by the Female Health Company which has initiated a widespread effort to distribute condoms to those at risk for contracting AIDS.
- How does the approach of the FHO exemplify Werhane's alliance model? How should pharmaceutical companies respond to this kind of initiative? Is it necessary to frame the relation between the pharmaceutical industry and NGOs as an adversarial relation or should broader alliances be formed that coordinate the efforts of these groups?

## 3.3.2 The Social Contract between Business and Society

**Every contract is built on the basis of three conditions (1) free and informed consent, (2) a quid pro quo, and (3) the rational self interest of the contracting parties.**

- **Free and Informed Consent**: No contract is legitimate that is based on force, fraud or deception. The parties must enter into this agreement freely and without compulsion. They must understand the terms of the contract which excludes deception and fraud. In short, the contract presupposes the uncoerced participation of all the parties. To enter into the contract they must understand all the key issues and consent to the constitutive exchange.
- **Quid Pro Quo**: Quid Pro Quo literally means something in exchange for something. Every contract is built around a mutually beneficial exchange. I give you my baseball cap in exchange your ice cream. Most exchanges are simultaneous. But some are what Hobbes calls "covenants." Here I give you my baseball cap with the understanding that later this afternoon you will pass by your refrigerator, get my ice cream cone and give it to me. I give you my part now and trust you to carry out your part later.
- **Rational Self Interest**: Each of us should know the value of the items to be exchanged. (That is one reason why a contract requires free and informed consent.) This knowledge is determined, in part, by the preference schedules that we have developed as rationally self-interested beings. So a legitimate contract assumes that I have interests, that I am capable of determining what promotes these interests, and that I am rational enough to determine means to promote them and avoid other means that interfere with them.

### Social Contracts

A social contract differs from other contracts because it is hypothetical. Business and Society have never sat down in a room and hammered out a contract outlining their relation. But this hypothetical contract provides a good means of making sense out of the relation that has gradually evolved between society and business. Forget for a moment the historical details of the relation between business and society. If this relation is summarized as a contract, what does society give to business? What does business give to society? Do these two institutions trust one another or do they each adopt means to monitor and control the other? What are these means? Treating the relation between business and society as a contract between two mutually consenting agents or actors does get some of the facts wrong. But it provides a useful "heuristic" device, i.e., a framework that will help us to summarize, structure, and, in a work, make sense of the relation between the two. Moving from the terms of this "contract" you will be able to develop a framework for understanding the social responsibilities of business corporations. This, in turn, will help you to understand the CSR challenges presented above and the CSRs of the fictional but realistic Burger Man corporation.

### Exercise 1: In small groups, spell out the social contract between society and business.

- How can the absence of force, deception, and fraud be guaranteed in this contract? How should each side hold the other accountable? (This is especially the case where one side delivers at one time and the other side is trusted to deliver later.)
- What benefits can busines bring to society? How can society benefit business. Develop a table with one column listing what business has to contribute to society and the other what society has to contribute to business. This table is the heart of your social contract.

- Assume that society and business are rationally self interested. How does this effect the formulation of the goods of the exchange? How does this enforce the terms of the contract? Are these self interests divergent? (Then each side must monitor the other to prevent the corruption of the contract.) Are these interests convergent? (Then the contract consists largely in building social capital and trust between the contracting parties.)
- Donaldson, 1993 uses social contract theory to account for the rights and duties of multinational corporations

### Exercise 2: CSR and STS

Choose one of the CSR challenges above and construct a socio-technical table around it

### STS Table

| Component / Embedded Value | Technology (Hardware) | Technology (Software) | Physical Surroundings | Stakeholder | Procedures | Laws | Information and Information Systems |
|---|---|---|---|---|---|---|---|
| Justice | | | | | | | |
| Free Speech | | | | | | | |
| Property | | | | | | | |
| Privacy | | | | | | | |
| Safety | | | | | | | |

Table 3.5

## 3.3.3 Three CSR Frameworks

### Shareholder View

From Milton Friedman, "The Social Responsibility of Business is to Increase Its Profits." "But the doctrine of "social responsibility" taken seriously would extend the scope of the political mechanism to every human activity. It does not differ in philosophy from the most explicitly collectivist doctrine. It differs only by professing to believe that collectivist ends can be attained without collectivist means. That is why, in my book **Capitalism and Freedom**, I have called it a "fundamentally subversive doctrine" in a free society, and have said that in such a society, "there is one and only one social responsibility of business–to use its resources and engage in activities designed to increase its profits so long as it stays wihtin the rules of the game, which is to say, engages in open and free competition without deception or fraud." 1970 by New York Times Company

### Stakeholder View

- A stakeholder must be distinguished from a stockholder. The latter owns a share of the corporation. On the other hand, a stakeholder is any group or individual that has a vital interest in the doings of the corporation. Hence the stockholder is a stakeholder of the corporation whose vital interest at play is the share owned of the corporation and the money invested in this share.
- There are several other stakeholders of the corporation. These include (1) employees, (2) customers, (3) suppliers, (4) local community, (4) surrounding governments, (5) the surrounding human and natural environment, and (6) the corporation's managers. (In some situations there are other stakeholders such as competitors.)

- Stakeholder theory requires that the corporation recognize and respect the vital interests of each of its surrounding stakeholders. This frequently issues in proposing stakeholder rights and assigning to others correlative duties to recognize and respect these rights.
- Stakeholder theory also requires that the corporation integrate interests where possible, mediate or broker conflicts between interests, and only trade off competing interests when absolutely necessary and when more conciliatory efforts have already been made and have failed.
- See Evan and Freeman 1988

**Werhane's Alliance Approach**

- Werhane's alliance approach is similar to the stakeholder approach in that it recognizes several groups that surround the corporation and have vital interests that depend on the doings of the corporation. These surrounding groups are more or less the same as those in the stakeholder approach: owners, managers, employees, customers, suppliers, local communities, governments, the environment, etc.
- But Werhane makes two significant departures from the stakeholder approach. First, she uses moral imagination to distance the corporation from the problem solving process; the lens of problem solving refocuses on each of the other stakeholders. Whereas for stakeholder theory the corporation is the center of analysis and is visualized as surrounded by its stakeholders, the alliance approach decentralizes the corporation and alternatively visualizes each stakeholder as the center for the purpose of framing problems and generating solutions.
- Second, the alliance approach sees the corporation as a part of a system of interrelated and interdependent parts. Hence, each problem situation presents a system formed of the corporation, owners, managers, employees, suppliers, customers, local communities, and governments. Problems emerge from value conflicts within and between the constituent parts of the system. They are solved through the cooperation of the different constituencies of the alliance.
- While this approach does not lend itself to algorithms or rules, it does promise solutions by highlighting and facilitating moral imagination both in the framing of problems (problems are posed in terms of framings from multiple perspectives) and in terms of the generation of solutions (multiple problem-framings help us to visualize new solution horizons).
- See Werhane, 2007 and 2008.

## 3.3.4 What you will do ...

**Module Activities**

1. Examine the CSR challenges presented above. Compare the two responses to each challenge.
2. Learn about three models of corporate social responsibility.
3. Develop a fully articulated social contract between business and society. Use this contract to understand the basic CSRs of business corporations.
4. Prepare a Social Impact Analysis on the fictional firm, Burger Man.
5. Prepare for and participate in a board meeting for Burger Man to examine ethically its practices and develop for it a viable and sustainable program of corporate social responsibility. This requires that you give a short presentation on the interests of a particular Burger Man stakeholder
6. Develop a full blown CSR program for Burger Man that carries out the responsibilities of this company to its stakeholders.

## 3.3.5 Burger Man Stakeholders

The author became aware of the Burger Man exercise when participating in an Ag-Sat broadcast course in Agricultural Ethics in 1992. The exercise was created by the leader of the course, Dr. Paul Thompson.

**Burger Man Profile**

Burger Man is a franchise that began by selling the fast food staples of hamburgers, french fries, and milk shakes. As the company has matured and faced other competitors in this market niche, it has, of course, developed a more sophisticated set of products and services. But it has also been challenged on various issues related to corporate social responsibility. Groups representing the rights and interests of animals have criticized the agribusiness methods used by its suppliers. Recently, public interest groups have blamed Burger Man and its competitors for encouraging unhealthy dietary habits among its customers and the public in general. Shareholders, of course, are concerned that the company continue to be profitable and provide them with a good return on investment. Governmental regulatory agencies such as the EPA (Environmental Protection Agency) and OSHA (Occupational Safety and Health Administration) wish to hold Burger Man accountable for conforming to its regulations. In short there are several stakeholder groups surrounding this corporation, each vying for its particular interest. In this exercise, you will play two roles. First you will be assigned a role as one of Burger Man's stakeholders and make a presentation of your group's interest in mock shareholder meeting that will be held in class. Then you will switch to the role of Burger Man management. Here your assignment will be to articulate the different stakeholder interests and integrate them into a coherent CSR plan for your company.

**Burger Man Customers**

- Burger Man customers are the consumers who go to its restaurant and enjoy its food services. In preparing your board meeting presentation you need to explore Burger Man's social responsibilities to its customers.
- Are these reducible to providing them an enjoyable product at a reasonable price? Or does BM's social responsibilities go beyond this?
- Burger Man has extensive interactions with its suppliers that include meat packing corporations and agri-business concerns. How should Burger Man choose its suppliers? How carefully should it monitor their activities. To what extent is Burger Man responsible for the untoward activities of these groups?
- How responsible is Burger Man for shaping the dietary habits of its customers? Does it bear responsibility for the health problems that its public develops from bad dietary practices?

**Burger Man Shareholders**

- Burger Man shareholders are investors who have purchased shares of Burger Man's publicly traded stock.
- What are their stakes?
- What are their responsibilities? For example, how closely should shareholders monitor the actions of their agents, i.e., Burger Man's managers? Are shareholders responsible for holding Burger Man to certain standards of corporate social responsibility? What are these standards and how do they stand in relation to the different models of social responsibility?
- Prepare your presentation around these issues. Address shareholder interests (stakes) and responsibilities.

**Burger Man Managers**

- Burger Man managers are the agents of the shareholders/owners responsible for overseeing the day-to-day operations of the corporation.
- What are the manager's stakes? What role do they play in the different models of social responsibility? (Classical, stakeholder, and alliance views?)
- Agency theory argues that the primary corporate governance problem is overseeing and controlling the actions of managers. How closely should shareholders and their board of directors oversee corporate managers? Are managers self-interested agents or stewards of the corporation?
- What are managerial responsibilities vis a vis corporate social responsibility? Should they uncover illegal actions? Should they implement an audit process that assess the corporation's success in carrying out its social responsibilities? Should these responsibilities go beyond the legal minimum?

- Should managers go beyond the legal minimum in monitoring and carrying out corporate social responsibilities?
- Are corporate managers responsible only to shareholders or do their responsibilities extend to other stakeholders? If the latter, how do they balance conflicting stakes?
- Structure your presentation around outlining managerial stakes and roles. Choose a model of corporate social responsibility and argue for its appropriateness to Burger Man.

## Government Regulatory Agencies: OSHA and EPA

- OSHA is in charge of regulating workplace safety. EPA is in charge of setting, monitoring, and enforcing standards concerning the environment. (For example, they establish acceptable air emission and water discharge standards.)
- What are the stakes of government regulatory agencies? What is their role in the context of the Burger Man corporation?
- Write your position paper outlining your group's stakes and roles in the context of establishing Burger Man's corporate social responsibility procedures. What would you recommend? How should you back up or enforce these recommendations?

## Animal Rights Activists

- Burger Man serves hamburgers, chicken sandwiches, and dairy products. These involve animals. As animal rights activists, you are concerned with steering Burger Man and its suppliers toward morally acceptable treatment of animals.
- What are your group's stakes in this board meeting? What kind of role should you play?
- State your policy on animal treatment? Is it a position of animal welfare based on utilitarian considerations? (Peter Singer provides such a position.) Is it a deontological position based on the assertion of animal rights that impose correlative duties on humans? (Tom Regan takes this position.) Or should you base your arguments on anthropocentric issues such as human health?
- Write a position paper that responds to these questions for presentation in the Burger Man board meeting.

## Town X Committee for Economic Development

- Your town, Town X, has three Burger Man franchises. Representatives from the town council are participating in the board meeting in order to ensure that Burger Man's policies on corporate social responsibility enhance the town's economic welfare and development.
- What are your stakes? What are your roles and responsibilities?
- What kind of services and products do you provide for Burger Man? What benefits do your community draw from Burger Man? How can Burger Man activities and policies promote or demote your town's interests and stakes?
- Develop a position paper for the board meeting that addresses these issues? Pay special attention to the goods and risks that your town exchanges with Burger Man.

Insert paragraph text here.

## Exercises in CSR

- Participate in the Burger Man Stakeholder Meeting
- Take your assigned stakeholder group and prepare a short presentation(five minutes maximum) on your stakeholder's interests, rights, needs, and vulnerabilities.
- Listen to the stakeholder presentations from the other groups. Try to avoid a competitive stance. Instead, look for commonalities and shared interests. You may want to form coalitions with one or more of the other groups.

- Switch from the stakeholder role to that of Burger Man management. You are responsible for developing a comprehensive corporate social responsibility program for Burger Man. You job is to integrate the concerns expressed by the stakeholders in their presentation and form your plan around this integration.
- Try to resolve conflicts. If you cannot and are forced to prioritize, then you still must find a way of recognizing and responding to each legitimate stakeholder stake. You may want to refer to the "Ethics of Team Work" module (m13760) to look for time-tested methods for dealing with difficult to reconcile stake. These include setting quotas, negotiating interests, expanding the pie, nonspecific compensation, logrolling, cost-cutting and bridging. You should be able to establish beyond a shadow of a doubt that you have made every attempt to recognize and integrate every legitimate stakeholder stake.

### 3.3.6 What did you learn?

This module and two others (A Short History of the Corporation and Corporate Governance) are designed to help you understand the corporate context of business. In this section, you should reflect on three questions: (1) What have you learned about the social responsibilities of corporations? (2) What still perplexes you about the social responsibilities of corporations. (3) Do you find one model of CSR better than the others? (4) Can these models of CSR be combined in any way?

### 3.3.7 Appendix

**Rubric for Partial Exam on CSR**

This is an unsupported media type. To view, please see
http://cnx.org/content/m17318/latest/PE_Rubric_CLSR_F08.docx

**Figure 3.4:** This file contains the rubric to be used on the partial exam for Corporate Leadership and Social Responsibility, ADMI 3405, Fall 2008"

**Corporate Social Responsibility Frameworks: Seminal Papers**

1. Friedman, M. (1970) "The Social Responsibility of Business Is to Increase Its Profits," in **New York Times Magazine**, September 13, 1970.
2. Evan, W.M. and Freeman, E. (1988) Ä Stakeholder Theory of the Modern Corporation: Kantian Capitalism" in Beauchamp and Bowie 1988.
3. Friedman 1970 and Evan and Freeman 1988 can be found in: Beauchamp, T.L. and Bowie, N.E., editors. (1988) **Ethical Theory and Business, 3rd Edition.** New Jersey: Prentice Hall: 87-91 and 97-106.
4. See Werhane 2007 and 2008 below

**References**

1. Collins, J.C., Porras, J. I. (1994) **Built To Last: Successful Habits of Visionary Companies**. New York: Harper Collins Publishers.
2. Stone, C. D. (1975) Where the Law Ends: The Social Control of Corporate Behavior. Prospectr Heights, IL: Waveland Press, INC: 1-30.
3. Des Jardins, J.R. (1993) Environmental Ethics: An Introduction to Environmental Philosophy. Belmont, CA: Wadsworth Publishing Company: 37.

4. Clarke, T. (2004) "Introduction: Theories of Governance–Reconceptualizing Corporate Governance Theory After the Enron Experience," in Theories of Corporate Governance: The Philosophical Foundations of Corporate Governance, ed. Thomas Clarke. New York: Routledge: 1-30.

5. Donaldson, T. (1993) **The Ethics of International Business**. New York: Oxford University Press.

6. French, P.A. (1984) Collective and Corporate Responsibility. New York: Columbia University Press.

7. French, P.A. (1997) "Corporate Moral Agency" in Werhane, P.H., and Freeman, R.E. Blackwell Encyclopedic Dictionary of Business Ethics. Oxford, UK: Blackwell: 148-151.

8. May, L. (1987) The Morality of Groups: Collective Responsibility, Group-Based Harm, and Corporate Rights. Notre Dame, IN: University of Notre Dame Press.

9. Werhane, P. H. (2008) "Mental Models: Moral Imagination and System Thinking in the Age of Globalization," in Journal of Business Ethics, 78: 463–474.

10. Werhane, P. (2007) "Corporate Social Responsibility/Corporate Moral Responsibility: Is There a Difference and the Difference It Makes," in eds., May, S., Cheney, G., and Roper, J., The Debate over Corporate Social Responsibility. Oxford, UK: Oxford University Press: 459-474.

11. Fisse, B. and French, P.A., eds. (1985) Corrigible Corporations and Unruly Law. San Antonio, TX: Trinity University Press.

12. Nader, R. and Green, M.J., eds. (1973) Corporate Power in America. New York: Grossman.

13. Nader,, R. Green, M. and Seligman, J. (1976) Taming the Giant Corporation. New York: Norton.

14. Davis, M. (1998) Thinking Like an Engineer: Studies in the Ethics of a Profession. Oxford, UK: Oxford University Press: 119-156. Jackall, R. (1988) Moral Mazes: The World of Corporate Managers. Oxford, UK: Oxford University Press.

15. Carol, A. B., "Social Responsibility," in Werhane, P., and Freeman, R. E., eds. (1997, 1998) Blackwell Encyclopedic Dictionary of Business Ethics. Oxford, UK: Blackwell Publishers, INC: 593-595.

16. Dyrud, M.A. (2007) "Ethics, Gaming, and Industrial Training," in IEEE Technology and Society Magazine. Winter 2007: 36-44.

17. Ritz, Dean. (2007) "Can Corporate Personhood Be Socially Responsible?" in eds. May, S., Cheney, G., and Roper, J., Corporate Governance. Oxford, UK: Oxford University Press: 194-195.

### 3.3.8 EAC ToolKit Project

**3.3.8.1 This module is a WORK-IN-PROGRESS; the author(s) may update the content as needed. Others are welcome to use this module or create a new derived module. You can COLLABORATE to improve this module by providing suggestions and/or feedback on your experiences with this module.**

Please see the Creative Commons License[6] regarding permission to reuse this material.

**3.3.8.2 Funded by the National Science Foundation: "Collaborative Development of Ethics Across the Curriculum Resources and Sharing of Best Practices," NSF-SES-0551779**

# 3.4 Theory Building Activities: "Responsibility and Incident at Morales"[7]

## 3.4.1 Module Introduction

### 3.4.1.1 Getting Started...

Manuel, plant manager at the Phaust chemical plant in Morales, Mexico, has just died. While he was babysitting the process of manufacturing Phaust's new paint remover (monitoring on site temperature and

---

[6]http://creativecommons.org/licenses/by/2.0/

[7]This content is available online at <http://cnx.org/content/m15627/1.4/>.

pressure conditions) an explosion occurred that killed him instantly. The Mexican government has formed an independent commission to investigate this industrial accident.

This commission (headed by your instructor) has ordered key participants to testify on their role in the accident in a public hearing. Your job is to present before this commission from a stakeholder point of view. You will be divided into groups to role play the following stakeholder perspectives:

- Fred, the chief engineer involved in designing the plant,
- plant workers,
- officials from Mexican government regulatory agencies,
- Phaust management,
- representatives from the parent French company,
- officials presiding over an engineering professional society.

You will be assigned roles and given class time to prepare presentations for the commission. Then the class will enact the public hearing by having each group give a presentation from the perspective of its assigned role. Following these presentations, groups will answer questions from the investigating commission. Finally, you will work through debriefing activities to help solidify your practical understanding of the module's chief concepts. Background materials designed to help you with your presentations include sketches of moral responsibility, links to the "Incident at Morales" Case, tasks to help structure your role-playing, and activities to debrief on this exercise. This module is designed to help you learn about moral responsibility by using responsibility frameworks to make day-to-day decisions in a realistic, dynamic, business context.

### 3.4.1.1.1 Before You Come to Class...

1. Visit the link to the National Institute for Engineering Ethics. Look at the study guide and download the script for the video, "Incident at Morales." You want to have some idea of what happens in the video before you watch it.
2. Read the module. Pay special attention to the section on "What you need to know." Here you will read summaries of three senses of moral responsibility: blame responsibility, sharing responsibility, and responsibility as a virtue. Your goal here is not to understand everything you read but to have a general sense of the nature of moral responsibility, the structure of the responsibility frameworks you will be using in this module, and the difference between moral and legal responsibility. Having this background will get you ready to learn about moral responsibility by actually practicing it.
3. Come to class ready to watch the video and start preparing for your part in the public hearing. It is essential that you attend all four of these classes. Missing out on a class will create a significant gap in your knowledge about and understanding of moral responsibility.

## 3.4.2 What you need to know...

"Responsibility" is used in several distinct ways that fall under two broad categories, the reactive and the proactive. Reactive uses of responsibility refer back to the past and respond to what has already occurred. (Who can be praised or blamed for what has occurred?) Proactive uses emerge through the effort to extend control over what happens in the future. An important part of extending control, knowledge, and power over the future is learning from the past, especially from past mistakes. But proactive responsibility also moves beyond prevention to bringing about the exemplary. How do occupational and professional specialists uncover and exploit opportunities to realize value in their work? Proactive responsibility (responsibility as a virtue) explores the skills, sensitivities, motives, and attitudes that come together to bring about excellence.

### 3.4.2.1 Different meanings of Responsibility

**Reactive Senses**

1. **Causal Responsibility** refers to prior events (called causes) which produce or prevent subsequent events (called effects). Cheap, inacurate sensors (cause) required that Manual be present on the scene (effect) to monitor the high temperatures and pressures required to correctly prepare Phaust's paint stripper.
2. **Role Responsibility** delineates the obligations individuals create when they commit to a social or professional role. When Fred became an engineer he committed to holding paramount the health, safety and welfare of the public. (See NSPE code of ethics)
3. **Capacity Responsibility** sets forth those conditions under which someone can be praised or blamed for their actions. Praise and blame associate an agent with an action. Excuses are based on means for separating or disassociating an agent from their actions. Capacity responsibility helps us determine whether there are any legitimate excuses available for those who would disassociate themselves from untoward, harm-causing actions.
4. **Blame Responsibility** determines when we can legitimately praise or blame individuals for their actions.

### Proactive Senses

1. **Sharing Responsibility** extends the sphere of responsibility to include those to whom one stands in internal relations or relations of solidarity. Shared responsibility includes answering for the actions of others within one's group. It also includes coming to the moral aid of those within one's group who have gone morally astray; this involves bringing to their attention morally risky actions and standing with them when they are pressured for trying to uphold group values. While sharing responsibility entails answering for what members of one's group have done, it does not extend to taking the blame for the untoward actions of colleagues. Sharing responsibility does not commit what H.D. Lewis calls the "barbarism of collective responsibility" which consists of blaming and punishing innocent persons for the guilty actions of those with whom they are associated.
2. **Preventive Responsibility**: By using knowledge of the past, one can avoid errors or repeat successes in the future. Peter French calls this the "Principle of Responsive Adjustment." (One adjusts future actions in response to what one has learned from the past.) According to French, responsive adjustment is a moral imperative. If one fails to responsively adjust to avoid the repetition of past untoward results, this loops back into the past and causes a revaluation of the initial unintentional action. The benefit of the doubt is withdrawn and the individual who fails to responsively adjust is now held responsible for the original past action. This is because the failure to adjust inserts the initial action into a larger context of negligence, bad intentions, recklessness, and carelessness. Failure to responsively adjust triggers a retroactive attribution of blame.
3. **Responsibility as a Virtue**: Here one develops skills, acquires professional knowledge, cultivitates sensitivies and emotions, and develops habits of execution that consistently bring about value realization and excellence. One way of getting at responsibility as an excellence it to reinterpret the conditions of imputability of blame responsibility. An agent escapes blame by restricting the scope of role responsibility, claiming ignorance, and citing lack of power and control. In responsibility as a virtue, one goes beyond blame by extending the range of role responsibilities, seeking situation-relevant knowledge, and working to skillfully extending power and control.

### 3.4.2.2 Blame Responsibility

**To hold Fred responsible for the accident at Morales, we need to...**

1. Specify his role responsibilities and determine whether he carried them out
2. Identify situation-based factors that limited his ability to execute his role responsibilities (These are factors that **compel** our actions or contribute to our **ignorance** of crucial features of the situation.)
3. Determine if there is any moral fault present in the situation. For example, did Fred act on the basis of **wrongful intention** (Did he intend to harm Manuel by sabotaging the plant?), fail to exercise **due care**, exhibit **negligence or recklessness**?

4. If Fred (a) failed to carry out any of his role responsibilities, (b) this failure contributed to the accident, and (c) Fred can offer no morally legitimate excuse to get himself off the hook, then Fred is blameworthy.

Fred, and other Incident at Morales stakeholders, can escape or minimize blame by establishing morally legitimate excuses. The following table associates common excuses with the formal conditions of imputability of blame responsibility. (Conditions of imputability are those conditions that allow us to associate an action with an agent for purposes of moral evaluation.)

**Excuse Table**

| Excuse Source (Capacity Responsibility) | Excuse Statement |
|---|---|
| Conflicts within a **role responsibility** and between different role responsibilities | I cannot, at the same time, carry out all my conflicting role responsibilities |
| **Hostile Organizational Environment** which routinely subordinates ethical to financial considerations. | The environment in which I work makes it impossible to act responsibly. My supervisor routinely overrules my professional judgment, and I can do nothing about it. |
| Overly determining situational constraints: financial and time | I lack the time and money to carry out my responsibility. |
| Overly determining situational constraints: technical and manufacturing | Carrying out my responsibility goes beyond technical or manufacturing limits. |
| Overly determining situational constraints: personal, social, legal, and political. | Personal, social, legal or political obstacles prevent me from carrying out my responsibilities. |
| Knowledge Limitations | Crucial facts about the situation were kept from me or could not be uncovered given even a reasonable effort. |

**Table 3.6**

### 3.4.2.3 Proactive Responsibility

**Preventive Responsibility: Responsive Adjustment**

- Responsibility to adjust future actions in response to what has been learned from the past
- **Scenario One**: Past actions that have led to untoward results. Failure here to adjust future actions to avoid repetition of untoward results leads to reassessing the original action and retrospectively blaming the agent.
- **Scenario Two**: Past actions have unintentionally and accidentally led to positive, value-realizing results. Here the agent responsively adjusts by being prepared to take advantage of being lucky. The agent adjusts future actions to repeat past successes. In this way, the agent captures past actions (past luck) and inserts them into the scope of praise.
- **Nota Bene**: The principle of responsible adjustment sets the foundation for responsibility in the sense of prevention of the untoward.

**Responsibility as a Virtue or Excellence**

1. Virtues are excellences of the character which are revealed by our actions, perceptions, beliefs, and attitudes. Along these lines, responsibility as a virtue requires that we reformulate responsibility from its reactive, minimalist sense (where it derives much of its content from legal responsibility) to responsibility as an excellence of character.

2. Aristotle situates virtues as means between extremes of excess and defect. Can you think of examples of too much responsibility? (Does Fred try to take on too much responsibility in certain situations?) Can you think of anyone who exhibits too little responsibility. (Does Fred take on too little responsibility or shift responsibility to others?) For Aristotle, we can have too much or too little of a good thing. From the "too much" we derive vices of excess. from the"too little" we derive the vices of defect.

3. Virtues are more than just modes of reasoning and thinking. They also consist of emotions that clue us into aspects of the situation before us that are morally salient and, therefore, worthy of our notice and response. Two emotions important for responsibility are care and compassion. Care clues us into aspects of our situation that could harm those who depend on our actions and vigilance. Do Wally and Fred pay sufficient attention to the early batch leakages in the Morales plant? If not, does this stem from a lack of care ("Let operations handle it") and a lack of compassion ("Manuel can take care of himself")? Care and compassion help to sensitize us to what is morally salient in the situation at hand. They also motivate us to act responsibility on the basis of this sensitivity.

4. Responsibility as a virtue manifests itself in a willingness to pick up where others have left off. After the Bhopal disaster, a worker was asked why, when he saw a cut-off valve open, he didn't immediately close it as safety procedures required. His response was that shutting off the value was not a part of his job but, instead, the job of those working the next shift. This restriction of responsibility to what is one's job creates responsibility gaps through which accidents and other harms rise to the surface. The worker's lack of action may not constitute moral fault but it surely signifies lack of responsibility as a virtue because it indicates a deficiency of care and compassion. Those who practice responsibility as a virtue or excellence move quickly to fill responsibility gaps left by others even if these tasks are not a part of their own role responsibilities strictly defined. Escaping blame requires narrowing the range of one's role responsibilities while practicing responsibility as a virtue often requires effectively expanding it.

5. Finally, responsibility as an excellence requires extending the range of knowledge and control that one exercises in a situation. Preventing accidents requires collecting knowledge about a system even after it has left the design and manufacturing stages and entered its operational life. Responsibility requires that we search out and correct conditions that could, under the right circumstances, produce harmful accidents. Moreover, responsibility is a function of power and control. Extending these and directing them toward good results are clear signs of responsibility as a virtue.

## Reponsibility as Virtue

- The Incident at Morales provides us with a look into a fictionalized disaster. But, if it is examined more carefully, it also shows opportunities for the exercise of responsibility as a virtue. The following table will help you to identify these "responsibility opportunities" and allow you to imagine counbterfactuals where had individuals acted otherwise the "incident" could have been avoided and moral value could have been realized.
- Think of virtuous or even heroic interventions that could have prevented the accident. These represents, from the standpoint of the film, lost opportunities for realizing responsibility and other virtues.

### Responsibility as a Virtue: Recovering Lost Opportunities

| Characteristic | Relevance to Incident at Morales |
|---|---|
| Change goal from avoiding blame to pursuing professional excellence. | Could this have led participants to look for more creative responses to EPA environmental regulations? |
| | *continued on next page* |

| Develop a flexible conception of your role responsibilities and move quickly to extend it to fill responsibility gaps left by others. | Could this have structured differently the relation between those responsible for plant design/construction and those responsible for its operation? |
| --- | --- |
| Extend the scope and depth of your situational knowledge, especially regarding accumulating information on the operational history of newly implemented technologies. | Would this have led to further follow-up on the early signs of leakage of the couplings? |
| Extend control and power. This includes finding ways of more effectively communicating and advocating ethical and professional standards in the context of group-based decision-making. | Could Fred have handled more proactively the last minute change in the chemical formulation of the paint remover? |

**Table 3.7**

### Section Conclusion

Integrate the retroactive and proactive senses of responsibility into your group's presentation for the public hearing. Don't just work on the reactive approach, i.e., try to avoid blame and cast it on the other stakeholder groups. Think proactively on how to prevent future problems, respond to this accident, and turn the events into positive opportunities to realize value.

### Questions to Get Started

- Is Fred (blame) responsible for the accident and even Manuel's death? (Use the conditions of imputability and the excuse table to get started on this question.)
- Did Wally and Chuck evade their responsibility by delegating key problems and decisions to those, like plant manager Manuel, in charge of operations? (Start the answer to this question by determining the different role responsibilities of the stakeholders in this situation.)
- What kind of responsibility does the parent French company bear for shifting funds away from Phaust's new plant to finance further acquisitions and mergers? (Looking at the modules on corporate social responsibility and corporate governance will help you to frame this in terms of corporate responsibility.)
- Do engineering professional societies share responsibility with Fred? (The CIAPR and NSPE codes of ethics will help here. Try benchmarking corporate codes of ethics to see if they provide anything relevant.
- Look at the positive, proactive moral responsibilities of professional societies. What can they do to provide moral support for engineers facing problems similar to those Fred faces? Think less in terms of blame and more in terms of prevention and value realization.

## 3.4.3 What you are going to do...

**In this module, you will...**

1. apply and integrate the concept of moral repsonsibility (blame responsibility, sharing responsibility, responsibility as a virtue) to situations that arise in the video, "Incident at Morales."
2. learn the basic facts, character profiles, and decision-situations portrayed in the video, "Incident at Morales." You will see the video in class and examine the script and Study Guide at the NIEE website.
3. work in groups to develop and play a stakeholder role in a fictional public hearing. Your group's specific tasks are outlined below in one of the group profiles provided. In general, you will prepare a statement advancing your group's interests and points of view. The responsibility frameworks will help you anticipate questions, prepare responses, and defend your role against those in other roles who may try to shift the blame your way. But most important, this module provides tools to help you go beyond the reactive, blame standpoint.

4. participate in a mock public hearing by playing out your group's assigned role.

5. work with the other groups to debrief on this activity. The public hearing will generate a lot of information, ideas, and positions. Debriefing will help you to structure and summarize this material. The objective here is to learn by doing. But to truly learn from what you have done, you need to reflect carefully.

### 3.4.3.1 Stakeholder Roles

#### Mexican Government Regulatory Agencies

- Look at OSHA regulations on safety. Do any of these apply to the incident at morales. Pay particular attendion to responsibilities for providing safe working conditions and to mandated procedures for accident prevention. How as a government agency can you encourage companies to take active and positive measures to increase workplace safety and prevent accidents?

- Look at EPA or JCA for ideas on environmental issues. What are Phaust's responsibilities regarding local environmental conditions? (Should the Mexican government require lining waste water ponds?)

- As an official representing Mexican government regulatory agencies, how do you balance the safety and environmental needs of Mexican citizens and workers with the need to attract foreign companies and investors to Mexico to promote economic development. Should safety and environmental values ever be traded off to promote economic development?

#### Workers at Morales Plant

- Manuel, your plant manager, has just died. You and your co-workers are concerned about the safety of this new plant. Can you think of any other issues that may be of concern here?

- Develop a statement that summarizes your interests, concerns, and rights. Are these being addressed by those at Phaust and the parent company in France?

- The Mexican Commission established to investigate this "incident" will ask you questions to help determine what cause it and who is to blame. What do you think some of these questions will be? How should you respond to them? Who do you think is to blame for the incident and what should be done in response?

#### Designing Engineer: Fred

- Examine Fred's actions and participation from the standpoint of the three responsibilty frameworks mentioned above.

- Develop a two minute position paper summarizing Fred's interests, concerns, and rights.

- Anticipate questions that the Commission might raise about Fred's position and develop proactive and effective responses..

- Be sure to use the three responsibility frameworks. Is Fred to blame for what happened? In what way? What can professional societies do to provide moral support to members in difficult situations? How can interested parties provide moral support? Finally, what opportunities arose in the video practicing moral responsibility as a virtue? (Think about what an exemplary engineer would have done differently.)

#### Phaust Management: Wally and Chuck

- Chuck and Walley made several decisions reponding to the parent company's budget cuts that placed Fred under tight constraints. Identify these decisions, determine whether there were viable alternatives, and decide whether to justify, excuse,or explain your decisions.

- Develop a two minute position paper that you will present to the commission.

- Anticipate Commission questions into your responsibility and develop effective responses to possible attempts by other groups to shift the blame your way.

**Corporate Governance: French Parent Company**

- You represent the French owners who have recently required Phaust Chemical. You have recently shifted funds from Phaust operations to finance further mergers and acquisitions for your company.
- What are your supervisory responsibilities in relation to Phaust?
- Develop a preliminary two minute presentation summarizing your position and interests.
- Anticipate likely commission questions along with possible attempts by other groups to shift the blame your way.

**Engineering Professional Society**

- You represent the professional engineering society to which Fred belongs.
- Develop a two minute presentation that outlines your group's interests and position.
- Anticipate possible Commission questions, develop responses, and anticipate attempts by other groups to shift the blame your way.
- Respond to whether your professional society should extend moral support to engineers in difficult positions like Fred's. Should they clarify code provisions? Provide legal support and counseling? Make available a professional/ethical support hotline?

**Investigative Commission**

This role will be played by your instructor and other "guests" to the classroom. Try to anticipate the commissions questions. These will be based on the conditions of blame responsibility, the principle of responsive adjustment, and responsibility as a virtue.

### 3.4.3.2 Module Time Line

- Module Preparation Activities: Read module and visit niee.org to get general orientation to "Incident at Morales"
- **Class One**: Watch Video. Receive group role. Begin preparing your group role.
- **Class Two**: Work within your group on preparing your group's statement, anticipating questions, and developing responses.
- **Class Three**: Participate in the Public Hearing. The group representing the Mexican Commission will convene the public hearing, listen to the group's statements, ask questions, and prepare a brief presentation on the Commission's findings
- **Class four**: Class will debrief on the previous class's public hearing. This will begin with the Commission's findings

## 3.4.4 What have you learned?

**Listen to the findings of the Mexican Government Commision. Write a short essay responding to the following questions. Be prepared to read parts of your essay to your professor and to your classmates.**

1. Do you agree with the Commissions findings? Why or why not? Be sure to frame your arguments in terms of the responsibility frameworks provided above.
2. Were there any opportunities to offer Fred moral support by those who shared responsibility with him? What were these opportunities. How, in general, can professional societies support their members when they find themselves in ethically difficult situations?
3. What opportunities arise for exercising resonsibility as an excellence? Which were taken advantage of? Which were lost?
4. Finally, quickly list themes and issues that were left out of the public hearing that should have been included?

## References

1. F. H. Bradley (1962) Ethical Studies, Essay I. Oxford, UK: Oxford University Press.
2. Herbert Fingarette. (1967) On Responsibility. New York: Basic Books, INC: 3-16.
3. Larry May (1992) Sharing Responsibility. Chicago: University of Chicago Press.
4. Larry May (1996) The Socially Responsive Self: Social Theory and Professional Ethics. Chicago: University of Chicago Press: 28-46.
5. Michael Pritchard (2006) Professional Integrity: Thinking Ethically. Lawrence,KS: University of Kansas Press.
6. Lawrence Blum (1994) Moral Perception and Particularity. Cambridge, UK: Cambridge University Press: 30-61
7. Aristotle. Nichomachean Ethics, Book 3, Chapters 1-3.
8. Edmund L. Pincoffs (1986) Quandaries and Virtues: Against Reductivism in Ethics. Lawrence, KS: University of Kansas Press.
9. W.H. Walsh (1970) "Pride, Shame and Responsibility," The Philosophical Quarterly, Vol 20, no 78, January 1970: 1-13.
10. Albert Flores and Deborah G. Johnson (1983) "Collective Responsibility and Professional Roles" in Ethics April 1983: 537-545.

# 3.5 Ethical Issues in Risk Management for Business[8]

NOTE: These links will help you to explore different topics related to this module's contents.

```
     - Epidemological studies are "natural" experiments.  But allowing
naturally occurring harms to continue without abatement and withholding
information from risk bearers creates serious ethical problems.
Read the Tuskegee case as presented at the Western Michigan University
Ethics Center to learn about a nororious case in which
patient rights were egregiously violated for the sake of "continuing
the experiment."


- Risk has meaning only in relation to the socio-technical system
in which it operates.  Click on the link above to find out more
about STS analysis and how it can be used to anticipate problems.


- Informed consent is a fundament right in the responsible
management of risk.  Click on the link to the Belmont Report to
find out more about this right and its historical importance.


- The Online Ethics Center's definition of informed consent
includes the conditions necessary for fulfilling this right.
```

---

[8]This content is available online at <http://cnx.org/content/m19085/1.1/>.

**Word Version of this Template**

This is an unsupported media type. To view, please see http://cnx.org/content/m19085/latest/ EAC TK STD TEMPLATE.doc

**Figure 3.5:** This is an example of an embedded link. (Go to "Files" tab to delete this file and replace it with your own files.)

### 3.5.1 Introduction

**Tilting at Windmills in Puerto Rico**
The company, Windmar, has purchased land adjacent to the Bosque Seco de Guanica in Puerto Rico. Their plan is to build a small windmill farm to generate electricity that can be sold to the public utility, the Autoridad de Energia Electrica. Windmill technology is considered desirable because wind is an abundant, clean, and renewable resource. But local opposition has stalled this effort. Concerned citizens object, first of all, to being excluded from the public hearings that were held to assess Windmar's windmill project. Opponents also claim that windmill technology can kill birds on the endangered species list and damage the fragile ecosystems protected in the Boseque Seco de Guanica, an important nature preserve in Puerto Rico. They also suspect that the windmill project has the ulterior motive of attracting industrial development into southern Puerto Rico. What risks accompany windmill technology, and how can they be dealt with ethically?

**The real price of cell phones**
Recently, a series of microwave antennas have been built in Puerto Rico in the Atalaya hills between the western cities of Mayaguez and Moca. Different kinds of antennas serve different purposes; some provide citizens with cell phone service while others make it possible to track hurricanes and other weather developments. The problem is the impact on the people who live in the surrounding areas. Many antennas have been built within five hundred yards of private residences with some as close as one hundred yards. Local residents were not consulted when the decision was made to build them. They claim that they have suffered a disproportionate number of health problems caused by the EMFs (electro-magnetic fields) generated by the antennas. Construction and repair activities occur at all hours, day and night, disrupting sleep and other normal activities. How should the cell phone companies, government agencies, and other stakeholders respond to these health and safety concerns? How should the possible risks to health and safety associated with antennas be assessed and communicated?

**No Copper Mines in Puerto Rico**
Starting in the mid-1950's, several international mining companies have attempted to receive permission from the Puerto Rican government to construct mines for gold and copper. Orebodies located in the mountainous central region of the island, have attracted several proposals for mining projects ranging from large to small scale. Concerns about **water pollution** (produced by tailings or mining waste products), **air pollution** (accompanying the proposed copper smelting plants), and **disruption of the agrarian lifestyle** still alive in central Puerto Rico became focused into considerable political and environmental opposition. Several mining proposals were defeated as citizens' interest groups formed and intensively lobbied the government not to permit mining. One mining site, located in the Cala Abajo region, has been reclassified as a nature preserve to block further attempts at mining. Mining could benefit the areas around the proposed mining sites by generating much needed jobs and tax revenue. But these benefits come accompanied by increased

risks to the environment as well as public safety and health. How should these risks be assessed? Under what conditions, if any, could they be deemed acceptable? What processes should be set into place by the government to ensure adequate public participation in determining whether these risks are acceptable? How should risk information be communicated to a public which is isolated and still largely illiterate?

## "No" to the Coal Plant

In the early to mid-1990's, a consortium of U.S. and Spanish power generation companies proposed an electricity-generating plant for the Mayaguez area that employed co-generation technology fueled by coal. Not only would this privately owned plant sell the electricity it produced to the Autoridad de Energia de Electrica; it would also sell the steam by-product to the two local tuna canning plants that had been operating in the area since the 1960s. But local opposition arose to derail the project. Coal is a non-renewable resource that produces noxious by-products that contribute to acid rain and global warming. Geologists pointed out that the plant would be located dangerously close to an active earthquake fault. Environmental groups raised concerns about water pollution, especially further deterioration of the already endangered coral reef in the Mayaguez Bay due to the discharge of the heated water employed to cool the components of the proposed plant. In televised public hearings, company engineers testified on design modifications to keep endangered species such as manatee from being sucked into the plant through water intake pipes. On the other side of the debate, the Puerto Rico energy utility, the Autoridad de Energia Electrica, predicted energy shortages beginning around the year 2000. (These warnings have been vindicated by the frequent brown-outs and black-outs that residents currently suffer through.) They also argued that the western part of the island needed its own energy-generating facilities to hold onto crucial industries like the textile and tuna canning plants located in the area. Finally, they turned to the use of coal to generate electricity as an effective substitute for petroleum which is used to generate most of the electricity used by Puerto Ricans. Since the rejection of the project, the textile industry has all but disappeared and one of the two tuna canning plants has relocated to Taiwan. Can government play the role of "honest broker" between private industry and a suspicious public? Should public utilities contract with private industry to meet energy and other infrastructure needs? What are the environmental risks of co-generating technology? How can these be responsibly communicated to the public? How should all stakeholders weigh environmental, safety, and health risks against infrastructure expansion and economic development?

## Ethical Issues in Risk Management for Business

Each of these cases raises risk issues that cannot be settled by process alone but require substantive debate focusing on the fragile ethical values embedded in the surrounding socio-technical system. The stakeholders have at times worked together but more often engage in conflict over seemingly incompatible yet essential interests. Private industry has designed these projects to respond to real, market-based needs. For example, Puerto Rico desparately needs clean, renewable and sustainable sources of energy to protect its fragile environment and reduce its dependency on foreign oil. Yet other stakeholders, especially a public with complex and vital interests, have banded together to oppose these and other initiatives. Local residents demand a right to a livable environment, raise health and safety concerns, and assert civil rights based on distributive justice, free and informed consent, and due process. Past experiences with ambitious but poorly designed and executed business and government projects have consumed social capital and undermined public trust. Continuing development under these conditions has proven difficult. The Puerto Rican government has consistently been in the middle attempting to mediate between these contending parties. Can government play the role of "honest broker" and help lead conflicting stakeholders to political and social consensus? Can government lead the substantive ethical debate into applications of distributive justice, informed consent, and sustainable environmental value? Or should it step out of the way and let the public and private industry fight it out on their own? What role do free (or semi-controlled) markets have to play in mediating this conflict? This module will help you explore these problems through the prism of risk. You will study the different aspects of risk and learn about their ethical and social implications. The final objective is to help you manage risk ethically through responsible assessment, perception and communication.

## 3.5.2 What you need to know ...

Working responsibly with risk requires careful integration of substantive ethical issues, distinguishing different senses of risk, and mastering the skills required in morally responsible risk communication. In other words, it is more than just implementing a mechanical process that imposes unwanted consensus on disparate groups and individuals. (See Sandel for an argument that past ethical controversies such as slavery had to be settled by means of substantive debates rather than procedural maneuvers.) Ethics is important to risk because scientific risk assessment is value-laden. Values permeate decisions such as choice of method as well as decisions on how to distribute the burden implied by the uncertainty involved in risk assessment and management. This section will introduce you to basic moral concepts involved in risk and offer information on how risk is assessed, managed, perceived, and communicated.

**Responsible Risk Management: Associated Basic Moral Concepts**

1. **Right**: A capacity of action that others are obliged to recognize and respect. A key right in the context of risk is free and informed consent. (See below)
2. **Duty**: The obligation to recognize and respect the essential capacities of actions of others. Duties are correlative to rights. For example, the duty to avoid paternalism in the management and communication of risk is correlative to the right of free and informed consent.
3. **Virtue**: Responsible risk management can also be formulated as a virtue. Virtues are traits that extend "deep down" into an individual's character. They include an orientation toward excellence in decision and execution, perceptual sensitivities that help to uncover moral relevance, and emotions/attitudes that help motivate decisions and actions oriented toward achieving excellence. For example, a responsible risk communicator has curiosity that drives understanding and appreciating risk, a concern for the well being of the risk bearer, and a strong desire to communicate risk information truthfully and clearly.
4. **Justice**: Justice can be generally defined as giving each his or her due. Distributive justice, in the context of risk, prescribes a fair distribution of the benefits and harms associated with taking a certain risk. Ideal pattern approaches argue that distribution should conform to a pattern such as **equality** (equal shares to everyone), **need** (greatest share to those with the greatest needs), and **merit** (greatest share to those who demonstrate superior merit). **Ideal pattern approaches** require continual redistribution by government through measures such as a progressive income tax. **Historical process approaches** prefer maintaining current patterns of distribution provided the historical process leading to them has been free of force or fraud. Justice in the context of risk lies in determining how the benefits and harms associated with risk are distributed, and how the uncertainty that permeates the risk assessment and management process is distributed among those involved.
5. **Responsibility**: Herbert Fingarette defines responsibility (in the context of criminal insanity) as (moral) response to (moral) relevance. Different senses of responsibility include causal, legal (vs. moral), role, capacity, and blame. Responsibility can be reactive when it focuses on the past and the assigning of praise and blame; or it can be proactive when it turns to preventing harm (minimizing risk) and realizing value.
6. **Trust**: The expectation of moral behavior on the part of others. Trust is built out of the social capital accumulated through successful interactions with others. It is consumed or undermined by those who choose to free ride on social cooperation, i.e., compete while others are cooperating. The prisoner's dilemma (see link above) provides a simplified model to show the fragility of trust (m17367).

**Key Terms in Risk Practices**

1. **Safety**: "A thing is safe if, were its risks fully known, those risks would be judged acceptable in light of settled value principles." (IEE 108)
2. **Risk**: "A risk is the potential that something unwanted and harmful may occur." (IEE 108)
3. **NIMBY**: This acronym stands for "Not in my backyard." Citizens often find the risks associated with a project or product acceptable only if these are located somewhere else, i.e., in another person's

backyard. NIMBY has made it next to impossible for the U.S. DOE (Department of Energy) to find an acceptable permanent storage facility for nuclear waste.

4. **Free and Informed Consent**: The right to decide if a risk is acceptable based on access to pertinent information and absence of compulsion. The **Belmont Report** defines informed consent in the following way: "[that] subjects, to the degree that they are capable, be given the opportunity to choose what shall or shall not happen to them. This opportunity is provided when adequate standards for informed consent are satisfied." The Online Ethics Center spells out conditions necessary for fulfilling informed consent: (a) **disclosure** (of information to the patient/subject); (b)**comprehension** (by the patient/subject of the information being disclosed); (c) **voluntariness** (of the patient/subject in making his/her choice); (d) **competence** (of the patient/subject to make a decision); and (e) **consent** (by the patient/subject).

5. **Paternalism**: Often experts are tempted to act as overly concerned parents and take over the decision-making perogatives of the public because they (the experts) "know better." Paternalism, while well motivated, is based on the misconception that the public doesn't understand risk because it often reaches different conclusions on the acceptability of a given risk than the expert. But the public often appreciates risk from a broader, richer standpoint, especially if the expert has properly and clearly communicated it. As will be seen below, the public perception of risk is rational because it is predictable.

## Dimensions of Risk

- **Risk Assessment**: The process of determining the degree of risk associated with a certain product or process using scientific methods such as epidemological study or animal bioassay. While using scientific procedures to gain a measure of exactness, risk assessment still brings with it a remainder of uncertainty that cannot be eliminated. A risk assessment issues into two uncertainties, the uncertainty as to whether the harm will occur and the uncertainty as to who (out of the many exposed) will be harmed. Ethics enters into the picture as stakeholders negotiate how to deal with and distribute this uncertainty. Responsible risk practice requires integrating the conflicting values and interests of the involved stakeholders in assessing, communicating, perceiving, and managing risk. It also requires a basis of trust that is difficult to build up given the diverse players that make up the risk taking and bearing situation.

- **Risk Management**: The political/social/ethical process of determining if a risk of a certain degree is acceptable given the settled value principles generally held in the community of the risk bearers. Responsible risk management requires (a) assessing harm through the responsible exercise of scientific method and (b) communicating the assessed risk to those likely to bear it. Responsible risk management (i) honors rights such as free and informed consent and due process, (ii) avoids conflicts of interests in determining and communicating risk, (iii) conscientiously works toward a just distribution of risks and benefits, and (iv) avoids paternalism.

- **Risk Perception**: How people perceive risk differs from the strict, scientifically determined degree of risk. For example, risk perception factors in voluntariness, control, expected benefits, lack of knowledge, and dread of adverse consequences in working toward a judgment on the acceptability of a given risk by the community of risk bearers. Because the public perceives risk over this broad background of scientific, social, political, and ethical factors, it frequently arrives at conclusions at odds with judgments reached using strictly scientific methods. Those taking a paternalistic attitude toward the public take this difference as evidence of the irrationality of the public and the need for the experts to taken things into their own hands. However, the public attitude toward risk is intelligible and rational when this broader, risk perception perspective is taken into account.

- **Risk Communication**: This dimension focuses on how to communicate risk information to risk bearers in order to facilitate distributive justice, free and informed consent, and due process. Responsible risk communication requires translating scientifically determined information into a non-technical vocabulary. Analogies and comparisons help as does the use of concrete language and commonly understood images. But improper use of comparisons and analogies confuses the public and undermines trust.

- **Public**: "those persons whose lack of information, technical knowledge, or time for deliberation renders them more or less vulnerable to the powers an engineer wields on behalf of his client or employer" Davis

## Assessing Risk

- **Epidemiological Studies**: We are constantly exposed to different risks that have become inherent in our socio-technical circumstances. These ongoing, unintentional experiments are exploited through epidemiological studies which are designed to measure the correlation between exposure to risk factors and the occurrence of harm. For example, are those living close to EMFs (electro-magnetic fields generated by technologies like electrical power lines) susceptible to certain harms like leukemia? An epidemiological study would compare incidents of this disease occurring in a population exposed to EMFs with incidents of this disease occurring in a population, unexposed to EMSs. If there were a significant risk ratio (usually set at three times the incidents of the harm in the unexposed, control group) then this provides evidence that exposure to EMFs somehow causes leukemia. (Further study would be required to confirm this hypothesis and uncover the causal mechanism by which exposure produces the harm.) Epidemiological studies are difficult to carry out and are always accompanied by uncertainty due to the limitations of the methods employed. Typically, the harm may take years to become manifest after exposure. Finding a population stable enough to determine the effects of long term exposure is difficult because individuals frequently move from place to place. Such natural experiments also bring with them a great deal of "noise"; factors other than EMFs could be causing leukemia or EMFs could be interacting with other elements in the environment to cause the harm. Finally, there is the Tuskegee factor. In the notorious Tuskegee experiment, doctors refused to treat African Americans for syphilis in order to study the long term progression of the disease. Exposing a population to a risk factor without informing them of the potential harm in order to gain scientific information violates the right of free and informed consent and the duty not to harm.

- **Animal Bioassays**: Risk information can often be obtained by exposing animals to the risk factor and checking for emerging harms. While useful, animal bioassays are subject to several problems. Experimenting on animals raises many of the same ethical concerns as experimenting on humans. Utilitarians argue that animals merit moral consideration because they are sentient and can suffer. Animal experiments are thus subject to the three Rs: reduce, refine, and avoid replication. (See Bernard Rollins) Second, these experiments create two kinds of uncertainty. (a) Projections from animal to human physiology can lead researchers astray because of the differences between the two; for example, animals are more sensitive to certain harms than humans. (b) Projecting the results from intensive short term animal exposure into the long term can also introduce errors and uncertainty. Thus, as with epidemiological studies, there are uncertainties inherent in animal bioassays.

- Risk assessment, while useful, is burdened with uncertainty due to the limits of what we know, what we can know, and what we are able to learn within the ethical parameters of human and animal experimentation. Crucial ethical issues arise as we decide how to distribute this uncertainty. Do we place its burden on the risk taker by continuing with a project until it is proven unsafe and harmful? Or do we suspend the activity until it is proven safe and harm-free. The first gives priority to advancing risky activities. The second gives priority to public safety and health, even to the point of suspending the new activities under question.

## Risk Perception

- The framework from which the public perceives risk is broader and richer than that of risk assessment. The following five factors influence how the public judges the acceptability of a risk assessed at a given magnitude.

- **Voluntariness**: A risk that is voluntarily taken is more acceptable than a risk of the same magnitude that taken involuntarily. Thus, driving one's car to a public hearing on the risks of a proposed nuclear power plant may be riskier than living next to the plant. But driving to the public hearings is done voluntarily while living next to the plant is suffered involuntarily. According to studies, a voluntary risk is as much as 1000 times more acceptable than an involuntary risk of the same magnitude.

- **Control**: Closely related to voluntariness is control. A risk under one's control (or under the control of someone trusted) is more acceptable than a risk of the same magnitude that is not under control. Charles Perrow, in **Normal Accidents** argues against nuclear energy technology because its design allows for components that are tightly coupled and interact with nonlinear patterns of causality. These two characteristics make it possible for small events to start chain reactions that issue into large scale disasters. Because these small events cannot be isolated (they are "tightly coupled") and because they interact unpredictably (they display nonlinear causality), they escape control and lead to unacceptable risks.

- **Perceived/Expected Benefits**: A risk of a given magnitude is more acceptable if it comes accompanied with substantial expected benefits. One takes the risk of driving to the hearings on the proposed nuclear plant because the benefits of getting crucial information on this project outweigh the risks of having a car accident. Riding a motorcycle is a risky venture. But the benefits received from this activity in the form of enjoyment make the risk more acceptable than a risk of the same magnitude accompanied with less benefits.

- **Unknown Factors**: A risk that is not understood is less acceptable than one that is well understood. Riding a bicycle is a risky venture but, because its risks are well known, it is more acceptable than other activities accompanied by risks of similar magnitudes. This factor is highly pertinent to EMFs (electro-magnetic fields). While EMFs are associated with certain illnesses like leukemia, their effects are not well known and are not understood by the public. This unknown element makes living near EMF producing technologies less acceptable.

- **Dread Factors**: A risk may be known and its causal relation to certain illnesses well understood. Nevertheless it may be less acceptable because the condition it causes is one that is highly dreaded. EMFs, because they have been associated with leukemia in children, are much less acceptable because of this "dread factor." The causes of radiation sickness are well known as are the stages of the illness. But because this kind of illness is highly dreaded, accompanying risks are less acceptable than other risks of the same magnitude with less of the dread factor. Again, compare crashing on a bicycle with coming down with cancer to get an idea of how dread permeates the perception of risk.

- **Against Paternalism**: Consider the possibility that predictability is one component of rationality. Then test this hypothesis in the cases presented at the beginning of this module. Can the risks posed by each project be examined in terms voluntariness, susceptibility to control, expected benefits, unknown factors, and dread factors? If so, then the public perception of this risk is rational because it can be predicted and understood. Thus, even though members of the public might find other risks of the same–or even greater–magnitude more acceptable, these perceptual factors would render the public's judgment intelligible and predictable. If all of this is so (and you will be testing this hypothesis in the exercises below) then paternalism on the part of the expert would not be justified. Furthermore, these insights into how risk is perceived by the public should provide you with valuable insight into how to communicate risk to the public.

## Responsible Risk Communication

- **Telling the Truth**: Certainly, responsible risk communication should start with the commitment to tell the truth. But the virtue of truthfulness is more complicated than it might seem at a first glance. For example, were an expert to tell nonexperts the whole truth this might confuse them, especially if the account is loaded with complex technical explanations and jargon. Truthfulness might require some simplification (holding some things back or putting them in different terms), **judicious** comparisons, and the use of concrete images. Thus, the virtue of truthfulness requires (a)understanding the audience and (b) outlining their perceptions, concerns, feelings, and needs. With this in mind, here are some factors that are useful in communicating risk responsibly and truthfully.

- **Know the audience**: What is their level of understanding, their needs, and their perceptions. For example, do they perceive the risk as voluntary, under control, accompanied with substantial benefits, accompanied by effects that are well known, and of a low dread factor? The risk perception framework described above will help you to communicate risk in a helpful and responsible manner.

- **Take measures to avoid deceiving the audience**: The gap between the expert (those in the know) and the public is sometimes quite large. This creates the temptation to fill that gap with less then truthful content. Avoiding deception requires more than just refraining from telling outright lies. It also requires taking measures to avoid subtle manipulation and unintentional deception.

- **Guard against unintentional deception**: (a) Be careful when using rhetorical devises. (b) Use risk comparisons and analogies to provide the public with benchmarks, not to persuade them that because they accept risk X they should accept risk Y. (c) Be sure to point out the limits of comparisons and analogies. (Driving to the public hearing is a risk of a greater magnitude than living next to a nuclear plant but this does not include key factors such as voluntariness, control, and expected benefits. (d) Avoid conflicts of interest. In exercise one below, you will be looking at an example of risk communication taken from the movie **Silkwood**. Think about whether this communication is reponsible and honest. Do the interests of the risk communicators coincide with those of the audience? Do the interests of the communicators bias the content of the communication in any way? (For example, does the upcoming vote to keep the union play a role in this risk communication act?)

### 3.5.3 What you will do ...

In this section, you will practice managing and communicating risk information. In managing risk information, you will practice how to empower, inform, and involve the risk-bearing public. In communicating risk, you will practice different ways of helping the public to deliberate on the acceptability of certain risks.

**Exercise One**

- Listen to the doctors communicating the risks associated to exposure to plutonium while working in the Kerr-McGee plant in the movie, Silkwood. How effective is this communicative act? (Explain your assertion.) How truthful is this communicative act? (Is truth about risk value-free scientific information or do values play a crucial role in our deliberations on risk? What kind of values are at stake here?)

- Listen to Charlie Bloom's presentation to the Milagro citizens' meeting on the economic and social risks associated with the Devine Recreational Center. Describe in detail the audience's reaction. Analyze both the content and style of Bloom's short speech. Does he facilitate or impede the process and substance of deliberation over risk? Rewrite Bloom's speech and deliver it before the class as if they were citizens of Milagro.

- Paul Slovic pictures a part of the risk perception process in terms of unknown and dread factors. In general, the higher the dread and unknown factors, the less acceptable the risk. Other factors that enter into the public perception of risk are voluntariness, control, expected benefits, and the fairness of the distribution of risks and benefits. Given this depicting of the public's perception of risk, how do you expect the Kerr McGee employees to react to the risk information being presented by the doctors? How will the citizens of Milagro react to the risk information they are receiving on the ethical, social, and economic impacts of the Devine Recreational Project?.

**Exercise Two: Risk Perception**

- Choose one of the cases presented above in the Introduction to this module.
- Describe those who fall into the public stakeholder group in this case. (See the above definition of "public")
- Identify the key risks posed in your case..
- Describe how the public is likely to perceive this risk in terms of the following: voluntariness, perceived benefits, control, unknown factors and dread factors.
- Given this perception of the risk, is the public likely to find it acceptable?

**Exercise Three: Risk Communication**

- You are a representative from one of the private business involved in the above case
- Your job is to communicate to the public (whose risk perception you studied in exercise two) the risk assessment data you have collected on the project in question
- Develop a strategy of communication that is based on (a) legitimate risk comparisons and analogies, (b) that is non-paternalistic, (c) that responds to the manner in which the public is likely to perceive the risk(s) in question, and (d) is open to compromise based on legitimate public interests and concerns.

**Exercise Four (optional)**

- Carry out exercises two and three using either the **Milagro Beanfield War** town meeting or the union meeting from **Silkwood**.
- Pretend you are Charlie Bloom and are charged with outlining the various risks that accompany the Devine Recreational Facility. The rest of the class, your audience, will play the role of the different stakeholders. These could include the (1) townspeople (owners of local businesses such as Ruby Archuleta's car body shop and the general store owner, Nick Real), (2) farmers (such as Joe Mondragon), (3) local and state law enforcement officers (such as Bernabe Montoya and Kyril Montona), (4) Ladd Devine Recreation Center employees (such as Horsethief Shorty who leads the construction crew), (5) local government officials (such as mayor Sammy Cantu) and state government officials (including the governor), and Ladd Devine himself.
- Give a short presentation. Then respond to questions and commentaries from your classmates who are working with the different roles outlined above.
- Take a vote on whether to go ahead with the Ladd Devine project.

## 3.5.4 What did you learn?

**Business and Risk**

You are a Corporate Ethics Compliance Officer developing an ethics program for your organization. How should your program respond to the ethics of risk issues discussed in this module? How should your corporation go about identifying and communicating risk factors to employees? How should your corporation go about identifying and communicating risk factors to other stakeholders such as customers, local community, and government agencies?

## 3.5.5 Appendix

**Bibliography**

1. Covello, V.T., Sandman, P.M. and Slovic, P. (1991) "Guidelines for Communicating Information About Chemical Risks Effectively and Responsibly," in **Acceptable Evidence**: 66-92.
2. Cranor, C.F. (1993) **Regulating Toxic Substances: A Philosophy of Science and the Law**. Oxford University Press: London.
3. Fingarette, H. (1971) **Criminal Insanity**. University of California Press, Berkeley, CA: 171.
4. Mayo, D.G., Hollander, R.D., Editors. (1991) **Acceptable Evidence: Science and Values in Risk Management**. Oxford University Press: London.
5. Mayo, D.G. (1991) "Sociological Versus Metascientific Views of Risk Assessment," in **Acceptable Evidence**. Oxford University Press: London: 249-280.
6. Slovic, P. (1991) "Beyond Numbers: A Broader Perspective on Risk Perception and Risk Communication," in **Acceptable Evidence**: 48-65.
7. Perrow, C. (1984) **Normal Accidents: Living with high-risk technologies**. Basic Books, NY,NY.
8. Reason, J. (1990/1999) **Human Error** Cambridge University Press: London.
9. Sagoff, M. (1985) **Risk-Benefit Analysis in Decisions Concerning Public Safety and Health**. Kendall/Hunt: Dubuque, Iowa.

10. Sagoff, M. **The Economy of the Earth: Philosophy, Law, and the Environment**. Cambridge University Press: London.

11. Sandel, M.J. (1982/1998) **Liberalism and the Limits of Justice, 2nd Ed**. Cambridge University Press, London.

12. Shrader-Frechette. (1991) "Reductionist Approaches to Risk," in **Acceptable Risk**. 218-248.

13. Thompson, P.B., (1999) "The Ethics of Truth-Telling and the Problem of Risk." **Science and Engineering Ethics** 5(4): 489-510.

14. "Glossary" Online Ethics Center for Engineering 1/31/2006 6:57:46 PM National Academy of Engineering Accessed: Saturday, December 27, 2008 www.onlineethics.org/CMS/glossary.aspx

This optional section contains additional or supplementary information related to this module. It could include: assessment, background such as supporting ethical theories and frameworks, technical information, discipline specific information, and references or links.

### 3.5.6 EAC ToolKit Project

**3.5.6.1 This module is a WORK-IN-PROGRESS; the author(s) may update the content as needed. Others are welcome to use this module or create a new derived module. You can COLLABORATE to improve this module by providing suggestions and/or feedback on your experiences with this module.**

Please see the Creative Commons License[9] regarding permission to reuse this material.

**3.5.6.2 Funded by the National Science Foundation: "Collaborative Development of Ethics Across the Curriculum Resources and Sharing of Best Practices," NSF-SES-0551779**

---

[9]http://creativecommons.org/licenses/by/2.0/

# Chapter 4

# CG (Corporate Governance)

## 4.1 Different Approaches to Corporate Governance[1]

-The first link refers to a news story on Dunn's resignation from the Hewlett-Packard board. It is taken from PBS's Online NewsHour in a report delivered by Margaret Warner on September 22, 200

-The second link provides background information on the Hughes Aircraft case profiled just below.

NOTE:

**Arthur Andersen**

Once a highly respected company, Arthur Andersen no longer exists having gone bankrupt in the wake of the Enron disaster. Arthur Andersen provided Enron with consulting and accounting services. The consulting division was more successful but the accounting division, with its long tradition of outstanding ethical service, was the corporation's backbone. Arthur Andersen signed off on Enron's use of mark-to-market accounting which allowed Enron to project optimistic earnings from their deals and then report these as actual profits years before they would materialize (if at all). They also signed off on Enron's deceptive use of special purpose entities (SPE) to hide debt by shifting it from one fictional company to another. With Arthur Andersen's blessing, Enron created the illusion of a profitable company to keep stock value high. When investors finally saw through the illusion, stock prices plummeted. To hide their complicity, Arthur Andersen shredded incriminating documents. For federal prosecutors this was the last straw. The Justice Department indicted the once proud accounting firm convinced that this and previous ethical lapses (Sunbeam and Waste Management) showed a pattern of unabated wrongdoing. Arthur Andersen was conficted of obstructing justice on June 15, 2002 and closed its doors shortly after.

**AA Timeline (Taken from Smartest Guys in the Room)**

- 1913–Founded by Arthur Andersen: "think straight, talk straight"
- Stood up to Railroad company in early years. When asked to change accounting standards, Andersen said, "There is not enough money in the city of Chicago [to make AA give into client demands]"
- 1947-1963–Leonard Spacek became president of AA succeeding Arthur Andersen.
- Spacek helped motivate the formation of the Financial Accounting Standards Board. AA also served as conscience of accounting profession criticizing the profession and the SEC (Securities and Exchange Commission) for "failing to square its so-called principles with its professional responsibility to the public."
- 1963-1989–Slow erosion of standards and development of competition between accounting and consulting divisions. (Consulting division was developed to take advantage of a profitable direction in the financial induistry.)

---

[1]This content is available online at <http://cnx.org/content/m17367/1.1/>.

- 1989–Consultants achieve relative autonomy as "separate business unit." (McLean: 144)
- 1997–Consultants break from firm.
- 1988-1991–Arthur Andersen receives 54 million in fees from Enron
- 2000–Enron pays AA 52 million. The lion share of this was for consulting fees.
- June 15, 2002–AA found guilty of obstruction of justice. "Today's verdict is wrong....The reality here is that this verdict represents only a technical confiction." (McLean: 406)

**Hughes Aircraft**

Howard Hughes founded this company at the beginning of the twentieth century. Hughes became a regular supplier of military hardware to the U.S. military. In the 1980's this included parts for surface to air misiles and fighter aircraft. One division specialized in computer chips designed to convert analogue information to digital for use in guidance systems and decision support systems. For example, these chips interacted with radar to help pilots of fighter aircraft avoid enemy missiles and also served as an essential component for missile guidance systems, the so-called smart bombs. Hughes had won the competitive bids for these highly profitable military projects but they had also committed themselves to tight delivery schedules with inflexible deadlines. And on top of this, the U.S. Airforce demanded that these computer chips and the systems that integrated them be rigorously tested to show that they could withstand the severe environmental stresses of battle. Hughes soon fell behind on the delivery of these computer chips causing a chain reaction of other delays both within the company and between the company and other links in the military supply chain. The environmental tests carried out by quality control under the supervision of Frank Saia had worked hard to complete the time-consuming tests and still remain on schedule with deliveries; hot parts (parts in high demand) were pulled to the front of the testing line to keep things running but soon even this wasn't enough to prevent delays and customer complaints. Giving way to these pressures, some Hughes supervisors pushed employees to pass chips without testing and even to pass chips that had failed tests. Margaret Gooderal and Ruth Ibarra resigned from the company and blew the whistle on these and other ethical failings that had become rampant in Hughes. So the corporate social responsibility question becomes how to change this culture of dishonesty and restore corporate integrity to this once innovative and leading company. (Background information on Hughes can be found at computingcases.org.)

**Patricia Dunn v. Tom Perkins on Corporate Governance**

When Patricia Dunn became a "non-executive" chairman of Hewlett-Packard's board on February 7, 2005, she brought with her an outstanding reputation in corporate governance. Her top priorities were to oversee the election of a new CEO after the firing of Carly Fiorina whose management of the recent acquisition of Compaq had lost her the HP board's support. Dunn also was determined to stop leaks to the press from high-level HP officials. She viewed the latter task as a fundament component of the post-Enron corporate governance approach she felt was needed as Hewlett-Packard moved into the 21st century. But her formal take on CG was at odds with powerful board member and successful venture capitalist, Tom Perkins. In his opinion, too strict an approach to CG stood in the way of HP culture and took focus away from competing with Dell and IBM as well as staying on the cutting edge in the development of new technology. As the leaks continued, Dunn's investigation into their source (most likely a discontented HP board member) became more active and rigorous. And the disagreements between her and board member Perkins deepened; their incompatible views on CG (and other disagreements) led to Perkins's resignation from the HP board. Things became critical when Perkins received a letter from A.T. and T. informing him that an account had been established in his name (but without his knowledge or consent) using the last 4 digits of his social security number and his private phone number. During the HP-led investigation into the press leaks, a private investigation firm used an illegal technique known as "pretexting" to obtain confidential information about HP board members and news reporters including private phone and social security numbers. Perkins reported this to the SEC, and Patricia Dunn, as chairman and de facto head of the leak investigation, was indicted on four criminal charges including identity theft.

Dunn focused on incompatible views of corporate governance as one of the causes of the rift that had developed between her and Perkins's: **"Tom's model of governance may be appropriate in the world of venture capital, but it is outmoded and inappropriate in the world of public company governance."** (Stewart, 165) She also made clear her strong views on board members leaking confidential information shared during board meetings to the press: **"The most fundamental duties of a director–the duties of deliberation and candor–rely entirely upon the absolute trust that each director must have in one another's confidentiality. This is true for trivial as well as inmportant matters, because even trivial information that finds its way from the boardroom to the press corrodes trust among directors. It is even more critical when discussions can affect stock prices....Leaking "good" information is as unacceptable as leaking "bad" information–no one can foretell how such information may advantage or disadvantage one investor relative to another."** (Stewart, 156)

**Questions**

How can successful corporate governance programs be integrated into companies with free-wheeling, innovative cultures without dampening creative and imaginative initiatives? How does one make sense of the fundamental irony of this case, that a conscientious pursuit of corporate governance (attacking violations of board confidentiality) can turn into violation of corporate governance (violation of the privacy and persons of innocent board members)?

---

**Word Version of this Template**

---

This is an unsupported media type. To view, please see http://cnx.org/content/m17367/latest/ EAC TK STD TEMPLATE.doc

---

**Figure 4.1:** This is an example of an embedded link. (Go to "Files" tab to delete this file and replace it with your own files.)

---

## 4.1.1 Introduction

James B. Stewart, in a **New Yorker** article about Patricia Dunn and Hewlett-Packard, describes corporate governance as "a term that technically refers to all aspects of running a corporation but in recent years has come to emphasize issues of fairness, transparency, and accountability." This module looks at corporate governance from the macro perspective, (1) examining the management strategies adopted by a firm to ensure compliance and pursue excellence and (2) from the standpoint of government as it seeks to minimize unethical corporate behavior and to maximize the corporation's contribution to social welfare.

## 4.1.2 What you need to know ...

### 4.1.2.1 Prisoner's Dilemma: Cooperation or Competition?

Scholarly debates on corporate governance have turned on the advocacy of different approaches, many of which can be modeled mathematically. Two approaches are based on the concepts of agency and stewardship. (See Davis et. al. in Clarke 2004) To enter into this debate, you will reenact the "Prisoner's Dilemma." Imagine that two patriotic spies, A and B, have just been captured by the enemy. Both are placed in separate interrogation cells and are being pressured to confess and provide details about their spying activities. A and B would like to coordinate their actions but the enemy has kept them apart to prevent this. Their objective is to pit A against B another in order to get the desired information. To do this, they have set forth the following systems of motivations, i.e., punishments and rewards.

**Options for the Prisoners**

- **If both A and B confess**. A and B are put in jail for five years each. The net loss in this scenario is 10. This is the least desirable alternative from the collective standpoint.
- **If one confesses and the other does not**. The confessor is released immediately while the non-confessor gets seven years in prison. This maximizes the confessor's self interest but severaly punishes the patriotic, non-confessor. Net loss is 7.
- **If both do not confess**. After six months of half-hearted interrogation (most of this time is for processing the prisoners' release), both are set free for lack of evidence. While not maximizing self interest (this lies in confessing while the other remains silent) this does maximizes overall welfare by producing a net loss of only 1.

**Prisoner Dillema Options Summarized**

| Prisoner A / Prisoner B | Confess | Not Confess |
|---|---|---|
| **Confess** | Both go to jail for 5 years (Net loss is 10) | A goes to jail for 7 years.  B is released. (Net loss is 7) |
| **Not Confess** | B goes to jail for 7 years.  A is released (Net loss is 7) | Both held for six months, then released. (Net los is 1.0) |

**Table 4.1**

### Assumptions in the Prisoner Dilemma

- Cooperation produces the best collective option and the second best individual option. This, in turn, assumes that cooperation produces more social welfare than competition.
- Free riding (competing) on the cooperation of others produces the most individual gains (for the free rider) but the second worst collective results. Society suffers loses from the harm done to the trusting, non-confessor and from the overall loss of trust caused by unpunished free-riding.
- Unlimited, pure competition (both prisoners confess) produces the worst collective results and the second worst individual results.
- Multiple iterations of the prisoner's dilemma eventually lead to cooperative behavior. But what causes this? (1) The trust that emerges as the prisoners, through repeated iterations, come to rely on one another? Or (2) the fear of "tit-for-tat" responses, i.e, that free riding on the part of one player will be punished by free riding on the part of the other in future iterations?
- Does the Prisoner's Dilemma assume that each player is a rational, self-interest maximizer? Are the players necessarily selfish in that they will seek to maximize self interest even at the expense of the other players unless rewards and punishments are imposed onto the playing situation from the outside?

The Prisoner's Dilemma is designed to model the reality of corporate governance where the directors/owners of a corporation delegate responsibility for the corporation's operations to managers who are charged with pursuing, not their own interests, but those of their directors. The problem of corporate governance is how this cooperative arrangement is institutionalized. Can managers be left alone and trusted to pursue the best interests of the corporation? This is implied in stewardship theory. Or is it necessary to design a system of controls to keep the managers from diverting the operations of the corporation toward their exclusive, self-interests? This is the approach taken in agency theory. Modeling this in terms of repeated iterations of the prisoner's dilemma, does cooperation emerge as the most reliable strategy in the long run? Or does it need to be manufactured by introducing a system of incentives such as fear of tit-for-tat strategies? The Prisoner's Dilemma models the central problems of corporate governance by asking whether cooperation naturally emerges between managers and directors or whether it needs to be manufactured through a system of punishments and rewards.

### 4.1.2.2 A Short Footnote on Human Nature

- One important means for classifying different approaches to corporate governance is to reflect on the associated account of human nature. This is a very complex issue but, fortunately, political philosophy provides us with some useful insights.

- Thomas Hobbes in the **Leviathan** presents a comprehensive psychological analysis of human nature based on seventeenth century physics. The focal point of this analysis is the human individual's unlimited pursuit of desire. Without external checks (primarily the threat of punishment imposed by a powerful sovereign) the **State of Nature** (where human individuals pursue self interest without external checks) is identical to a **State of War**. This war of all against all is **"solitary, poore, nasty, brutish, and short."**

- Hobbes's view has been characterized by C.B. Macphearson as "possessive individualism" which portrays the self as the possessor of its own attributes including the property acquired through its actions. This leads to a view called atomic individualism which is based on the claim that the self has its characteristics and determinate structure prior to and independently of any social interaction.

- Jean-Jacques Rousseau offers a brilliantly original criticism of Hobbes' conception of human nature in his Second Discourse, the **Discourse on the Origin of Inequality**. According to him, Hobbes's characterization of human nature in the State of Nature is actually a description of the human corrupted by society and the acquisition of property. **"The first person who, having enclosed a plot of land, took it into his head to say this is mine and found people simple enough to believe him, was the true founder of civil society. What crimes, wars, murders, what miseries and horrors would the human race have been spared, had someone pulled up the stakes or filled in the ditch and cried out to his fellow men: "Do not listen to this imposter.""** Rousseau argues that before the notion of property, the human's desire to preserve self was balanced by the social feeling of pity brought forth by the suffering of others. Only the unchecked pursuit of property (seen in terms of exclusive possession) would bring the motive of self-interest into conflict with natural pity.

- In opposition to Hobbes's atomic and individualistic self, a group of political philosophers, beginning with Aristotle, see the self as primarily social. Aristotle characterizes the human as a political animal (a being who naturally constructs a social organism called the "polus"). Sandel describes a "thick self" constructed out of familial, social and political content; this content is integrated into the core of the self. Werhane's description of this "social animal" is worth quoting in full: **"In that socialization process, we develop a number of interests, roles, memberships, commitments, and values such that each individual is an historical, cultural, and social product, a pluralistic bundle of overlapping spheres of foci, a thick self or selves....[T]here is no self as precritical, transcendental subject, totally ideal spectator or dispossessed subject.**

- Thus a series of views of human nature emerge that are instrumental in forming different approaches to corporate governance. Hobbes's atomistic individualism will favor the compliance approach mandated by agency theory as directors set up external checks to self-serving managers. Rousseau's more nuanced view would require structures to hold the pursuit of self-interest in check while strengthening the equally natural impulses toward socializability and cooperation. The social conception of the self would treat the corporation as an environment where managers, as stewards, recruit employees who will quickly commit to the central corporate values and then develop supporting structures and procedures to help their colleagues find meaningful work while fulfilling social, corporate objectives.

### 4.1.2.3 Approaches to Corporate Governance

**Summary Table**

| (1,1) | Description(1,2) | Theory of Human Nature(1,3) | Owner Role(1,4) | Manager Role(1,5) | Corporate Ethics Focus(1,6) |
|---|---|---|---|---|---|
| **Agency Theory**(2,1) | Managers act as agents of the corporation fulfilling the goals established by the owners / directors(2,2) | Managers are rational, but self-interested beings who must be controlled from the outside(2,3) | Owners are principals, that is, they originate the action and bear primary moral responsibility.(2,4) | Managers are agents, that is, responsible for acting in the interest of the principals who hire them. Faithful agency implies avoiding conflicts of interests and maintaining confidences.(2,5) | Compliance focus uses (1) rule-based codes, (2) systems of monitoring, and (3) punishments and rewards to motivate compliance from outside.(2,6) |
| **Stockholder Approach**(3,1) | Corporation is property of stockholders who dispose of it as they see fit.(3,2) | Stockholders pursue self interest. They are rational (instrumental), economic self-interest maximizers.(3,3) | Owners invest in corporation and seek a return (profit) on their investment.(3,4) | Managers are responsible for ensuring that owners get maximum return on investment.(3,5) | Stockholders direct compliance toward manager control and external conformity to laws.(3,6) |
| **Stakeholder Approach**(4,1) | Owners drop out of center focus. Corporation is run for the sake of its stakeholders.(4,2) | Groups have special interests but recognize the need to integrate these. Humans possess capacity for procedural reasoning.(4,3) | Owners drop to one of a group of equal stakeholders. Still advocate their financial interests but not to exclusion of other stakeholders.(4,4) | Managers are meta-stakeholders. They treat stakeholders and stakes equally and integrate these to the fullest extent possible.(4,5) | (4,6) |
| | | | | *continued on next page* | |

*continued on next page*

| Stewardship Model(5,1) | Managers act as stewards for absentee owners; oversee the operations of corporation and exercise care over them. Emotion (care) plays an equal role with instrumental rationality.(5,2) | Desire and self interest are balanced out by social motives such as Rousseau's pity and Aristotle's virtues.(5,3) | Owners still set cardinal objectives but they also are responsible for providing managers with a meaningful work environment.(5,4) | Managers are stewards exercising care over the property of the owners in their absence. Stewardship is based on internally generated and self-imposed motives toward care.(5,5) | Value-based: (1) identify and formulate common standards of excellence, (2) develop training programs to foster pursuit of these excellences, and (3) develop support structures to help reduce value "gaps."(5,6) |

**Table 4.2**

## Agency Theory

1. In agency theory, the owners/directors set the central objectives of the corporation. Managers, in turn, are responsible for executing these objectives in the corporation's day-to-day operations. Corporate governance consists of designing structures and procedures to control management, i.e., to keep their actions in line with director-established objectives.

2. Managers cannot be trusted to remain faithful agents, i.e., to stay faithful to the interests and goals of the owners/directors. This presupposes a particular view of human nature. Humans are rational, egoists. They have desires and use reason to devise means to realize them. Since one desire can be checked only by another desire, this egoism is potentially without limit. Agency theory assumes that managers will divert corporate resources to pursue their own selfish ends unless checked by some system of external controls. Thus, another key element of corporate governance under agency theory is to find the most efficient systems of controls to keep manager egoism in check.

3. The owners/directors play the role of principal in agency theory. The principal originates the action and bears primary moral and legal responsibility for it. Most of the time the principal of an action is also its executor. But there are times when the principal lacks the knowledge and skill necessary for executing the objectives he or she originates. In this case, the principal contracts with an agent. The principal authorizes the agent to act on his or her behalf. This requires that the agent remain faithful to the goals and interests of the principal. See Hobbes's **Leviathan**, Chapter 16 for an important historical account of the agent-principal relation.

4. Managers are agents. Their primary responsibility is to serve as faithful executors of the goals and interests of the principals. This requires, first, that, managers are responsible for exercising their professional judgment in a competent way. Managers are also responsible for remaining faithful to the interests of their principals. To do this they must avoid conflicts of interests and maintain confidentialities (i.e., keep secrets). Agent can also range from being free (unguided by principals) to bound (tightly monitored and controlled by principals).

5. How does ethics enter into corporate governance under agency theory? Primary emphasis is placed on compliance, i.e., enforced conformity to rules that constitute minimum thresholds of acceptable behavior. Compliance approaches develop (1) rule based codes, (2) systems of monitoring to detect violations, and (3) punishments and rewards to deter non-compliance and reward compliance. Trevino and Weaver provide an empirical analysis to the goals achieved through compliance ethics: "[4] the perception that better decisions are made because of the ethics program [5] ethical advice seeking, [6]

decreased unethical behavior in the organization...[7] ethical awareness." (Weaver and Trevino, 1999: 333.)

## Stockholder Theory

1. The stockholder approach is quite similar to that set forth in agency theory. The difference is that it views the corporation as the property of its owners (stockholders) who may dispose of it as they see fit. Most of the time this involves using it to receive maximum return on investment.

2. Stockholders are oriented toward self-interest, so stockholder theory, along with agency theory, takes an egoistic/Hobbesian view of human nature. Humans are rational, self-interest maximizers. Owners should expect this from the corporation's managers and employees. They should integrate procedures and controls that channel the corporation and its members in the direction of their (owners) self-interest.

3. The owners invest in the corporation and seek a return (profit) on this investment. But this narrow role has been expanded into overseeing the operations of the corporations and its managers to ensure that the corporation is in compliance with ethical and legal standards set by the government. Just as the master, under tort law, was responsible for injury brought about by the negligence of a servant, so also are directors responsible for harm brought about by their property, the corporation.

4. Managers are role-responsible for ensuring that investors get maximum return on their investment. This includes exercising good business judgment and avoiding conflicts of interests and violations of confidences.

5. Like corporations operating within agency theory, stockholder corporations focus on compliance strategies to monitor managers and make sure they remain faithful agents. However, directors under the stockholder approach also take seriously oversight responsibility which include ensuring corporate compliance with laws such as Sarbanes-Oxley and the Federal Sentencing Guidelines.

## Stakeholder Theory

1. Owners drop out of the center of attention in this approach to become one of several, equal stakeholders. A stakeholder is any group or individual that has a vital interest, right, good, or value in play or at risk. (A gambler's stake is the money on the table in play as the roulette wheel turns. Depending on the outcome of the situation, the gambler either keeps or loses the stake.) Examples of corporate stakeholders include stockholders, employees, customers, suppliers, local community, and government. The corporation on this view exists for the sake of its stakeholders, not stockholders.

2. The stakeholder view can be closely tied to egoism if it is assumed that the different stakeholder groups exist to maximize their selfish interests. But the stakeholder approach to corporate governance goes beyond the egoistic account of human nature. The corporation (and its managers) become responsible for mediating between these different, often conflicting, stakeholder interests, always keeping in mind that all stakeholders deserve equal respect. If stakeholders have any solidarity with one another, it is because the interest set of each includes the interests of the others. (This is how Feinberg defines solidarity.) The ability to envision the interests of each stakeholder and to work toward integrating these must be built on a view of human nature that is as altruistic as egoistic. While not embracing the social view of human nature outlined above, the stakeholder view assumes that stakeholders are capable and willing to negotiate and bargain with one another. It begins, in other words, with enlightened and long term self interest.

3. The first feature of the owner role is the reduction in centrality mentioned just above. They advocate their interests in the same arena as the other stakeholders, but they also must work to make their interests compatible with the other stakeholders. This requires integrating interests when possible and drawing integrity-preserving compromises when necessary. (See Benjamin 1990).

4. Managers play an important meta-role here. They are faithful agents but of all stakeholders, not just stockholders. Thus, they becomes referees or (to switch metaphors) brokers between stakeholders. They oversee the generation of expansive corporate values capable of absorbing and integrating narrower stakeholder interests.

5. Stakeholder approaches combine compliance and value-based approaches. In compliance, corporate officers define a moral and legal minimum; this consists of the minimum set of rules necessary for stakeholder coexistence. Beyond this, value-based approaches seek to create common, broader objectives, aspirations that can unite the different stakeholders in the pursuit of excellence. Stakeholder approaches need both; the compliance approach gets things started and the values-based approach sets them on the path to excellence.

## Stewardship Theory

- Managers and employees can be trusted to act as stewards or guardians of the corporation. This means that while they do not own the corporation's resources, they will safeguard these for the owners. A steward is a caretaker who looks after the owner's property and interests when the owner is absent
- This approach definitely makes use of the social approach to human nature. Humans, naturally and spontaneously, realize their innermost natures by forming social unions. The corporation, under this view, is such an organization. While taking on the characteristics of a social contract with the other approaches, especially agency theory, the corporation under the stewardship view is more of a cooperative, collaborative enterprise. Humans can act and find meaning in interests and concerns well beyond the confines of the ego. In fact, to organize the corporation around egoistic assumptions does harm to those capable of action on altruistic motives. The emphasis here is on building trust and social capital to strengthen the social potentialities of human nature.
- Owners still establish the cardinal objectives for the sake of which the corporation exists. But they are also responsible for providing managers with an environment suitable developing human potentialities of forming societies to collaborate in meaningful work.
- Managers act as stewards or caretakers; they act as if they were owners in terms of the care and concern expressed for work rather than merely executors of the interests of others. In other words, the alienation implied in agency theory (acting not out of self but for another), disappears as the managers and employees of the corporation reabsorb the agent function.
- Stewardship approaches are primarily value-based. They (1) identify and formulate common aspirations or values as standards of excellence, (2) develop training programs conducive to the pursuit of excellence, and (3) respond to values "gaps" by providing moral support.

## 4.1.2.4 External Controls: Fining, Stock Dilution, Changing Internal Governance, Court Ordered Adverse Publicity, and Community Service

### Classifications of Corporate Punishments

|  | Description | Example | Target of Punishment | Deterrence Trap Avoided? | Non-financial Values Addressed? | Responsive Adjustment | Interference with Corporate Black Box |
|---|---|---|---|---|---|---|---|
| continued on next page | | | | | | | |

| Monetary Exaction | Fines | Pentagon Procurement Scandals | Harms innocent | Fails to Escape | Few or None Targeted | None | No interference |
|---|---|---|---|---|---|---|---|
| **Stock Dilution** | Dilute Stock and award to victim | | Stockholders (Not necessarily guilty) | Escapes by attacking future earnings | Few or None | Limited | No interference |
| **Probation** | Court orders internal changes (special board appointments) | SEC Voluntary Disclosure Program | Corporation and its Members | Escapes since it mandates organizational changes | Focuses on management and subgroup values | Passive adjustment since imposed from outside | Substantial entry into and interference with corporate black box |
| **Court Ordered Adverse Publicity** | Court orders corporation to publicize crime | English Bread Acts (Hester Prynne shame in **Scarlet Letter**) | Targets corporate image | Escapes (although adverse publicity indirectly attacks financial values) | Loss of prestige / Corporate shame / Loss of Face/Honor | Active adjustment triggered by shame | No direct interference (corporation motived to restore itself) |
| **Community Service Orders** | Corporation performs services mandated by court | Allied chemical (James River Pollution) | Representative groups/individuals from corporation | Escapes (and targets non-financial values) | Adds value to community | Passive or no adjustment: sometimes public does recognize that cs is punishment | None |

**Table 4.3**

## Requirements of Sarbanes-Oxley (From Dyrud: 37)

- Provide increased protection for whistle-blowers
- Adhere to an established code of ethics or explain reasons for non-compliance
- Engage in "full, fair, timely and understandable disclosure"
- Maintain "honest and ethical" behavior.
- Report ethics violations promptly
- Comply with "applicable governmental laws, rules, and regulations"
- Dyrud cites: ELT, **Ethics and Code of Conduct**, n.d.; http://www.elt-inc.com/solution/ethics _and_code_of_conduct_training_obligations.html

## Ammended Federal Sentencing Guidelines (Dyrud 37)

- Establishing standards and procedures to prevent and detect criminal conduct

- Promoting responsibility at all levels of the program, together with adequate program resources and authority for its managers
- Exercising due diligence in hiring and assigning personnel to positions with substantial authority
- Communicating standards and procedures, including a specific requirement for training at all levels
- Monitoring, auditing, and non-internal guidance/reporting systems
- Promiting and enforcing of compliance and ethical conduct
- Taking reasonable steps to respond appropriately and prevent further misconduct in detecting a violation

## 4.1.3 What you will do ...

### Module Activities

- Study the Prisoner's Dilemma to help you formulate the central challenges of corporate governance.
- Study four different approaches to corporate governance, (1) agency theory, (2) the stockholder approach, (3) the stakeholder approach, and (4) stewardship theory.
- Examine corporate governance from the macro level by (1) looking at the structural changes a company can make to comply with legal and ethical standards and (2) examining the balances that government must make to control corporate behavior and yet preserve economic freedom.
- Design a corporate governance program for an actual company that you and your group choose. It should be a company to which you have open access. You will also be required to take steps to gain the consent of this company for your study.
- Reflect on how to integrate this module's macro description of corporate governance with the micro perspective presented in the module on moral ecologies and corporate governance.

### Corporate Governance Plans

- A corporate code of ethics that responds to the specific ethical problems uncovered by your profile of the corporation you are studying.
- A corporate ethics training program designed to acquaint employees, owners, and managers with the company's value aspirations and compliance objectives.
- A Corporate Ethics Audit designed to identify and minimize ethical risks.
- A comprehensive ethics compliance program that responds to the requirements set forth in Sarbanes and Oxley as well as the Federal Sentencing Guidelines.
- A program in corporate excellence designed to articulate and realize the core values that define your company's identity and integrity.

## 4.1.4 What did you learn?

This material will be added later. Students will be given an opportunity to assess different stages of this module as well as the module as a whole.

## 4.1.5 Appendix

### Bibliography

1. Benjamin, M. (1990) **Splitting the difference: Compromise and Integrity in Ethics and Politics**. Lawrence, KS: University of Kansas Press.
2. Carol, A. B., "Social Responsibility," in Werhane, P., and Freeman, R. E., eds. (1997, 1998) **Blackwell Encyclopedic Dictionary of Business Ethics**. Oxford, UK: Blackwell Publishers, INC: 593-595.

3. Clarke, T. (2004) "Introduction: Theories of Governance–Reconceptualizing Corporate Governance Theory After the Enron Experience," in **Theories of Corporate Governance: The Philosophical Foundations of Corporate Governance**, ed. Thomas Clarke. New York: Routledge: 1-30.

4. Davis, J.H., Schoorman, D., and Donaldson, L. "Toward a Stewardship Theory of Management,"in **Theories of Corporate Governance: The Philosophical Foundations of Corporate Governance**, ed. Thomas Clarke. (2004) New York: Routledge: 1-30.

5. Dyrud, M.A. (2007) "Ethics, Gaming, and Industrial Training," in **IEEE Technology and Society Magazine**. Winter 2007: 36-44.

6. Feinberg, J. (1970) "Collective Responsibility" in **Doing and Deserving: Essays in the Theory of Responsibility**. Princeton, NJ: Princeton University Press: 234.

7. Fisse, B. and French, P.A., eds. (1985) **Corrigible Corporations and Unruly Law**. San Antonio, TX: Trinity University Press.

8. French, P.A. (1984) **Collective and Corporate Responsibility**. New York: Columbia University Press..

9. Hobbes, T. (1651, 1968) **Leviathan**. Middlesex, England: Penguin Books: 186.

10. Macpherson, C.B. (1962) **The Political Theory of Possessive Individualism: Hobbes to Locke**. London, UK: Oxford University Press: 3.

11. May, L. (1987) **The Morality of Groups: Collective Responsibility, Group-Based Harm, and Corporate Rights**. Notre Dame, IN: University of Notre Dame Press.

12. McLean, B., and Elkind, P. (2003) **The Smartest Guys in the Room: The Amazing Rise and Scandalous Fall of Enron**. New York: Portfolio: 141-149.

13. Paine, L.S. (1994) "Managing for Organizational Integrity," in **Harvard Business Review**, March/April 1994.

14. Rousseau, J.J. (1987) **Jean-Jacques Rousseau: The Basic Political Writings** Translated by Donald A. Cress. Indianapolis, IN: Hackett Publishing Company: 60.

15. Stewart, J.B. (2007) "The Kona Files: How an obsession with leaks brought scandal to Hewlett-Packard," in **The New Yorker**, February 19 and 26, 2007: 152-167.

16. Stone, C. D. (1975) **Where the Law Ends: The Social Control of Corporate Behavior**. Prospectr Heights, IL: Waveland Press, INC: 1-30.

17. Swartz, M., Watkins, S. (2003) **Power Failure: The Inside Story of the collapse of Enron**. New York: Doubleday: 356.

18. Weaver, G.R. and Trevino, L.K. (1999) "Integrated and decoupled social performance: Management commitments, external pressures, and corporate ethics practices." **The academy of Management Journal**, 42: 539-552.

19. Werhane, P.H. (1999) **Moral Imagination and Management Decision Making**. Oxford, UK: Oxford University Press: 39.

20. Werhane, P. H. (2008) "Mental Models: Moral Imagination and System Thinking in the Age of Globalization," in **Journal of Business Ethics**, 78: 463–474.

21. Werhane, P. (2007) "Corporate Social Responsibility/Corporate Moral Responsibility: Is There a Difference and the Difference It Makes," in eds., May, S., Cheney, G., and Roper, J., **The Debate over Corporate Social Responsibility**. Oxford, UK: Oxford University Press: 459-474.

## 4.1.6 EAC ToolKit Project

**4.1.6.1 This module is a WORK-IN-PROGRESS; the author(s) may update the content as needed. Others are welcome to use this module or create a new derived module. You can COLLABORATE to improve this module by providing suggestions and/or feedback on your experiences with this module.**

Please see the Creative Commons License[2] regarding permission to reuse this material.

---

[2]http://creativecommons.org/licenses/by/2.0/

**4.1.6.2 Funded by the National Science Foundation: "Collaborative Development of Ethics Across the Curriculum Resources and Sharing of Best Practices," NSF-SES-0551779**

# 4.2 Developing a Statement of Values[3]

## 4.2.1 Module Introduction

Codes of ethics evoke opposite reactions from people who teach, do research in, or are practitioners of occupational and professional ethics. Some hold that teaching codes of ethics is essential to preparing students for their future careers. Corporations, for example, have come to view codes as the cornerstone of a successful compliance program. Professional societies, such as the **Puerto Rico State Society of Professional Engineers and Land Surveyors**, also make the drafting, revising, and disseminating professional codes of ethics a central part of practicing professional engineering ethics. But many strongly oppose codes because they promote the wrong sorts of attitudes in those who would be influenced by them. As you will see below, philosophical ethicists raise objections to codes because they undermine moral autonomy, lead to uncritical acceptance of authority, and replace moral motives with fear of punishment. These polar stances are grounded in the very different perspectives from which different groups approach codes. But they are also grounded in the fact that codes take many different forms and serve distinct functions. For example, consider the introductory considerations presented in the following:

**Codes: Introductory Considerations**

- Managers and administrators have used them to maintain positions of control and authority.
- Professional societies use codes to communicate and enforce minimum standards of acceptable behavior.
- Codes can be used to support those who would be ethical in the face of difficulties. For example, codes that uphold public welfare can be used as "clear mandates of public policy" in a legal defense created to support those who suffer organizational retaliation for refusing to carry out illegal or immoral directives.
- This leads to an important fact about codes of ethics: they serve several different functions such as educating, fostering dialogue, disciplining unethical behavior, encouraging and supporting ethical behavior, articulating values and aspirations, and even presenting a group in a favorable way to the general public.
- This module has been designed to get you to recognize these different functions at play in codes of ethics.

**Difficulties With Codes**

- The following objections lead many to omit teaching codes in practical and professional ethics classes.
- Codes can **undermine moral autonomy** by habituating us to act from motives like deference to external authority and fear of punishment.
- Codes take on more than they can handle when they purport to provide us guidance for complex situations. The ineliminable gap between **rules** (which are general and abstract) and **action-situations** (which are particular and concrete) leads to serious **application problems**.
- Codes **fail to provide guidance** in complex situations that present new and unexpected challenges. Arguing that codes should provide action-recipies for all situations neglects the fact that effective moral action requires more than just blind obedience to rules.
- Codes of ethics can **encourage a legalistic attitude** that turns us away from the pursuit of moral excellence toward just getting by or staying out of trouble. Compliance codes are most effective when they establish minimum standards of acceptable behavior. They break down when they turn to more elevated standards that reflect aspirations rather than minimum thresholds. Thus, compliance codes habituate individuals to the idea that morality can be reduced to carrying out minimal standards of moral decency.

---

[3]This content is available online at <http://cnx.org/content/m14319/1.6/>.

This module is designed to steer you through these complex issues by having you draft a **Statement of Values** for students at your university. As you work through your Statement of Values, you will learn that codes have strengths and weaknesses, serve different functions, and embody values. To get you started in this process, you will study a defective code, the Pirate Credo. A quick glance is all that is needed to see that codes are "all too human" and need to be approached critically. In a second activity you will identify the values embedded in professional, corporate, and academic codes. Working with these values, you will develop a list upon which your group will build its own Statement of Values in a third activity. Finally, you will construct value profiles that include a general description, sample provisions, value-based challenges, and value principles. These will all contribute to motivating those in your community to commit to and work in concert to realize these values.

## 4.2.2 A Failure and a Success Story

### A Cautionary Tale

The faculty of the Arts and Sciences College of University X decided to form a committee to write a code of ethics. This committee met several times during the course of an academic semester to prepare the first draft. When they finished, they circulated copies throughout the college. Then they held a series of pubic hearings where interested members of the College could criticize the code draft. These were lightly attended and those attending had only a few suggestions for minor changes. However, when the code was placed before the faculty for approval, considerable opposition emerged. For example, a provision discouraging faculty from gossiping was characeized by opponents as an attempt by a hostile College administration, working through the committee, to eliminate faculty free speech. Several opponents expressed opposition to the very idea of a code of ethics. "Does the administration think that our faculty is so corrupt," they aked, "that the only hope for improvement is to impose upon them a set of rules to be mindlessly followed and ruthlessly enforced?" At the end of this debate, the faculty overwhelmingly rejected the code.

### Reflections on "A Cautionary Tale"

- Why do you think this university faculty failed to adopt, or even consider, the draft code?
- What leads different members of a group to view the same code provisions in different, and even opposed, ways? What considerations guide individuals as they interpret codes of ethics?
- Can codes of ethics be used by those in positions of power to strengthen that power and extend control?.

### A Success Story

- Three years later at the same university, another faculty group set out to construct a code of ethics in order to respond to accreditation requirements. They began with the idea of constructing a stakeholder code.
- First, they identified the stakeholders of the college's activities, that is, groups or individuals who had a vital interest in that community's actions, decisions and policies.
- Second, they identified the goods held by each of these stakeholders which could be vitally impacted by the actions of the college. For example, education represented the key good held by students that could be vitally impacted by the activities and decisions of the College.
- Working from each stakeholder relation and the good that characterized that relation, members of the college began crafting code provisions. Some set forth faculty duties such as keeping regular office hours, grading fairly, and keeping up to date in teaching and research. Others emphasized student duties such as working responsibly and effectively in work teams, adhering to standards of academic honesty, and attending classes regularly.

Because stakeholder codes embody a community's values, the individuals in charge of drafting the code decided that a more direct approach would be to identify the embodied values and refine them into a Statement of Values. This formal statement could later be developed in different directions including a more detailed compliance code.

Turning their efforts toward preparing a Statement of Value Process, the Business Administration community went through the following steps:

1. They discussed a flawed document, the Pirate Credo. This brought about three positive results: participants came to see how codes embody values, that codes serve different functions, and that codes clarify relations between the insiders and outsiders of a community.

2. Participants examined "bona fide" codes of ethics such as academic codes, codes of honor, corporate codes, and professional codes. Since codes embody values, they developed lists of the values these codes embodied.

3. The sample provisions crafted in the earlier stakeholder code effort were presented so that participants could identify the values these embodied. Previous efforts in developing a stakeholder code could be benchmarked against the codes studied in the previous step. Convergences and divergences were noted and used to further characterize the college's community in terms of its similarities and differences with other communities.

4. In this step, faculty members were asked to reduce the values list to a manageable number of five to seven. This led to the most contentious part of the process. Participants disagreed on the conception of value, the meaning of particular values like justice, and on whether rights could be treated as values.

5. To resolve this disagreement, discussion leaders proposed using ballots to allow participants to vote on values. This process was more than a simple up or down vote. Participants also ranked the values under consideration.

6. After the top five values were identified, efforts were made, in describing each of the remaining values, to find places to include at least components of the values left out. For example, while confidentiality was not included in the final value list, it was reintegrated as a component of the more general value of respect. Thus, the final values list could be made more comprehensive and more acceptable to the faculty community by reintegrating some values as parts of other, more general values. Another way of picking up values left behind in the voting process was to combine values that shared significant content. Values that did not make it into the final list were still noted with the provision that they could be integrated into subsequent drafts of the Statement of Values.

7. A committee was formed to take each value through a value template. After describing the value, they formulated a principle summarizing the ethical obligations it entailed, crafted sample provisions applying the value, and posed different challenges the value presented to help guide a process of continuous improvement.

8. The committee presented its results to the faculty who approved this first draft Statement of Values

9. The faculty then developed a schedule whereby the Statement of Values would be revisited, expanded, revised, and improved.

### 4.2.3 Textbox 1: Responding to the Federal Sentencing Guidelines

Recent efforts to develop ethics codes in the academic context for both students and faculty may, in part, stem from the success of ethics compliance programs developed in business and industry in response to the Federal Sentencing Guidelines. Organizational codes of ethics have been integrated alongside other compliance structure and activities to prevent criminal behavior, to detect criminal behavior, and to ensure prompt and effective organizational response once such behavior has been detected.

**The following section contains short exerpts from the Federal Sentencing Guidelines. For more details consult the materials referenced in note 5 below.**

- "The hallmark of an effective program to prevent and detect violations of law is that the organization exercised due diligence in seeking to prevent and detect criminal conduct by its employees and other agents. Due giligence requires at a minimum that the organization must have taken the following types of steps:

- The organization must have established compliance standards and procedures to be followed by ite employees and other agents that are reasonably capable of reducing the prospect of criminal conduct.

- Specific individual(s) within high levelpersonnel of the organization must have been assigned overall responsibility to oversee compliance with such standards and procedures.
- The organization must have used due care not to delegate substantial discretionary authority to individuals whom the organization knew, or should have known through the exercise of due diligence, had a propensity to engage in illegal activities.
- The organization must have taken steps to communicate effectively its standards and procedures to all employees and other agents, e.g., by requiring participation in training programs or by disseminating publications that explain in a practical manner what is required.
- The organization must have taken reasonable steps to achieve compliance with its standards, e.g., by utilizing monitoring and auditing systems reasonably designed to detect criminal conduct by its empoyees and other agents and by having in place and publicizing a reporting system whereby employees and other agents could report criminal conduct by others within the organization without fear of retribution.

**Recommendations by the Federal Sentencing Guidelines for an Effective Compliance Program**

- Appointing individuals to serve as ethics or compliance officers
- Developing corporate credos and codes of ethics that effectively communicate an organization's ethical standards and expectations to employees.
- Designing ethics training programs for all employees
- Designing and implementing monitoring and auditing systems
- Designing and implementing an effective system of punishments and sanctions. These must be accompanied by investigative procedures that respect employee due process rights.

## 4.2.4 Textbox 2: Compliance Oriented Codes and Programs Versus Values Oriented Codes and Programs

**Compliance Strategy**

1. The initial and still probably the most prevalent method for responding to the Federal Sentencing Guidelines is the compliance strategy. This strategy is based on three interrelated components:
2. **Rules**: Compliance strategies are centered around strict codes of ethics composed of rules that set forth minimum thresholds of acceptable behavior. The use of rules to structure employee action does run into problems due to the gap between rule and application, the appearance of novel situations, and the impression that it gives to employees that obedience is based on conformity to authority.
3. **Monitoring**: The second component consists of monitoring activities designed to ensure that employees are conforming to rules and to identify instances of non-compliance. Monitoring is certainly effective but it requires that the organiztion expend time, money, and energy. Monitoring also places stress upon employees in that they are aware of constantly being watched. Those under observation tend either to rebel or to automatically adopt behaviors they believe those doing the monitoring want. This considerably dampens creativity, legitimate criticism, and innovation.
4. **Disciplining Misconduct**: The last key component to a compliance strategy is punishment. Punishment can be effective especially when establishing and enforcing conduct that remains above the criminal level. But reliance on punishment for control tends to impose solidarity on an organization rather than elicit it. Employees conform because they fear sanction. Organizations based on this fear are never really free to pursue excellence.

**Values Orientation**

1. **Development of Shared Values**: Using a process similar to the one described above, a company develops a Statement of Shared Values. These provide guidelines that replace the hard and fast rules of

a compliance code. Statements in values-oriented codes play a different logical function that statements in compliance codes. "Principles of Professional/Organizational Conduct" in compliance codes specify circumstances of compliance: time, agent, place, purpose, manner, etc. These circumstances provide sufficient content to set forth principles of professional conduct as rules that can be violated. This, in turn, allows them to be backed by punishment for violation. "Ideals of the Profession/Organization state a community's shared aspirations. They set forth levels of behavior well beyond the minimum. And they chart out directions for continuous improvement.

2. **Support for Employees**: Since Statements of Values set forth excellences or aspirations, the role of the organization changes from monitoring and then punishing misbehavior to finding ways of opening avenues for employees to realize key values in their day to day activity. In other words, the role of the organization changes from the punitive to the supportive.

3. **Ethical Aspirations**: In summary, values orientations set forth higher standards for behavior. Going well beyond the moral or legal minimum, these values, clarified in an organization's statement of values, serve as aspirations. A values orientation requires that an organization find ways to reinterpret basic values as excellences. Hence, it is most compatible with a virtue orientation and virtue ethical theory.

## 4.2.5 Exercise 1: Evaluating the Pirate Credo

**Read the Pirate Credo. Then answer the following questions individually**

- What is good about the Pirate Credo?
- What is bad about the Pirate Credo?
- What is the purpose served by the Pirate Credo? For the Pirate Community? For non-members?

## 4.2.6 Exercise 2: Evaluating Bona Fide Codes of Ethics

**Form small work teams of four to five individuals. Carry out the following fours steps and report your results to the rest of the group.**

1. **Review** a few sample codes per team.
2. **List** the values you identify in the codes. Express each value as a word or in as few words as possible.
3. **Identify** any recurring values.
4. **Record** and post the list of values.

## 4.2.7 Exercise 3: Do a Statement of Values for Students at Your University

**In this third exercise, work with your group to develop a refined list of five to seven values. You can refine your list by integrating or synthesizing values, grouping specific values under more general ones, and integrating values into others as parts. Do your best to make your list comprehensive and representative.**

1. **Brainstorm**: list the values for your group. Keep in mind that values are multi-dimensional. For example, in the academic context, the values will break down into dimensions corresponding to stakeholder: faculty, students, administration, and other academic stakeholders.
2. **Refine**: reduce your list to a manageable size (5-7). Do this by rewording, synthesizing, combining, and eliminating.
3. **Post**: share your list with the entire group.
4. **Revise**: make any last minute changes.
5. **Combine**: a moderator will organize the lists into a ballot
6. **Vote**: Each person ranks the top five values

## 4.2.8 Exercise 4–Conveying Our Values: Crafting a Values-Based Code

Each value in your Statement of Values needs to be accompanied by a Value Profile. Give a description of the value in everyday, non-technical terms. Think concretely. For example, those who exemplify your value behave in a certain fashion, exhibit certain commitments, pursue certain projects, and show certain attitudes and emotions. Try to think of general guidelines to keep in mind when working to realize your value. Finally, values challenge us because portray our aspirations. Think of specific ways values challenge us. For example, students may set for themselves the challenge of working responsibly in teams. They can further spell out what kinds of actions and attitudes this might require. Faculty members might set for themselves the challenge of grading more fairly. This could require actions like developing rubrics and refining exams to make them clearer. The purpose of this fourth exercise is to provide content to your statement of values and begin its implementation in your community. The following steps ennumerated below will help.

1. **Value**: Responsibility
2. **Description**: a responsible person is a person who...
3. **Principle**: The faculty, students, and staff of the college of business Administration will...
4. **Commitments**: Keep office hours, do your fair share in work teams, divide work into clear and coordinated tasks, tec.

## 4.2.9 Exercise 5: Creating Awareness of the UPRM College of Business Administration Statement of Values

This exercise provides you an opportunity to study and discuss the UPRM College of Business Administration Statement of Values (available via the PREREQUISITE LINKS). Your task consists of the following tasks:

- Read the entire UPRM CBA Statement of Values (individually)
- Discuss the particular section/value assigned to your group and briefly describe what commitments or challenges does this value present for the students, faculty and/or staff of the CBA
- List the most important commitments or challenges as precise and concise principles

## 4.2.10 Exercise 6: Assessing the UPRM College of Business Administration Statement of Values

This exercise offers four scenarios in academic integrity. Your job is to discuss each scenario in terms of the values listed in the UPRM College of Business Administration Statement of Values (available via the PREREQUISITE LINKS).

**Marta Acevedo, a business administration student, has a report due tomorrow. She has been overwhelmed for the last few weeks with assignments from other classes and doesn't really have time to complete this exercise. She discovers that her roommate took this same class the previous semester and has a complete report on disk. She considers using her roommate's report. Should she? What would you do if you were her?**

- Is Marta threatening any of the values listed in the ADEM SOV? Which ones?
- What can be done prevent this kind of problem from arising in the first place? Should Marta have planned her course load better when registering? Can teachers coordinate to prevent overloading students with the same deadlines? Whose fault is this? The students? The teachers? The system?
- Can this problem be posed as a conflict between ADEM values and other values held by students and teachers? If so, what are values that are in conflict? How can these conflicts be addressed?
- Do you think the ADEM SOV adequately addresses this problem? If not, how can it be improved?

You are head of your department. A recent study has revealed that plagiarism, which is a university-wide problem, is especially bad in your department. Imagine your relief when a member of your faculty brings you his latest software project, a super-effective and comprehensive anti-plagiarism software program. This program does everything. It detects subtle changes in style in student papers. Its new search engine quickly connects to existing online paper data bases, greatly expanding the ability of a professor to detect the sources from which their students have copied. Furthermore, it allows professors to upload papers and projects from past semesters and provides fast and flexible indexing to help them identify recycled student work. Professors can zero in on students using recycled papers, and the former students who have become their suppliers. Following the recent lead of Ohio State University, you can now revoke the degrees of past students who participate in this version of academic dishonesty. In short, this new and exciting software package allows you to monitor the work of present and past students to a degree thought impossible even in the recent past. "Plagiarism," your colleague tells you, "will now become a thing of the past."

- Does this anti-plagiarism program threaten any of the values in the ADEM SOV? If so, which values?
- Is the department chairperson treating students disrespectfully by adopting and implementing the anti-plagiarism software? Can faculty treat students disrespectfully as "justifiable" retaliation for student cheating and plagiaring? Do two wrongs make a right?
- What is the cause of plagiarism? Do students do it out of ignorance of standards and practices of documentation and achnowledgment? Do they do it because they procrastinate until they do not have time to do the assignment properly? Do students resort to plagiarism because they have too many conflicting obligations such as family, job, large course loads, etc.?

You teach an advanced course in Engineering Economics that has both graduate and undergraduate students. At the end of the semester the students turn in a group project that comprises 40% of their grade. One of the groups complains to you that only 4 out of the 5 members have done any work. The fifth student, the one who allegedly has done no work, is an undergraduate. The others are graduate students. You talk with the undergraduate who claimed that she tried to involve herself in the group activities but was excluded because she was an undergraduate. What should you do?

- ADEM faculty have identified students not working together effectively in groups as a major concern. Do you find this a problem? What do you think are the causes of students not participating effectively in work groups?
- Assume that the teacher in this case is committed to implementing the ADEM SOV. Which values are at play in this case? Design an action for the teacher that realizes these values?
- Assume you are a member of this student work group. What can groups do to ensure that every member is able to participate fully? What do group members do to exclude individuals from participating?

You are studying frantically for your exam in a computer engineering course. It will be very difficult. But your roommate, who is also taking the course and has the exam tomorrow, seems unconcerned. When you ask why, he tells you that he has a copy of the exam. Apparently, a group of students in the class found out how to hack into the professor's computer and download the exam. (They installed a Trojan horse called Sub-Seven into the professor's computer which allows unauthorized access; then they searched through the professor's files, found the exam and downloaded it.) Your roommate has the exam in his hand and asks you if you would like to look at it. What should you do?

- A group of students in a computer ethics class created a survey that asked students if they would avail themselves of exams obtained through means such as that described in the scenario above. Sixty percent of the respondents said that they would. Compare this to the value commitments expressed in the ADEM SOV? Is there a gap between aspiration and behavior? What can be done to reduce this gap?

- Suppose you took the exam. Would this have any long term effects on your character? Would acting dishonestly this time make it easier to do so in the future?
- Suppose you wish to uphold standards of academic integrity in this case and not take the exam. Should you turn your roommate in to the teacher? Would keeping this exam theft a secret undermine any of the UPRM ADEM values? If so, which ones?

You have now discussed some or all of the above cases in terms of the ADEM Statement of Values. What do you think are the strengths of this document? What are its weaknesses? Do you recommend any changes? What are these?

**Sources for Cases**

- Case 1 has been developed by William Frey, Chuck Huff, and José Cruz for their book, Good Computing: A Virtue Approach to Computer Ethics. This book is currently in draft stage and is under contract with Jones and Bartlett Publishing Company.
- Cases 2 and 3 were developed by UPRM faculty teams from the College of Engineering during workshops held for the ABET 2001 Steering Committee and the Department of Industrial Engineering. These workshops took place April 6, 2001 and May 14, 2001.
- Case 4 has been modified from "The Plagiarism Detector" written by Moshe Kam. It can be found at the beginning of the ethics chapter in Practical Engineering Design, edited by Maja Bystrom and Bruce Eisenstein. Moshe Kam. "The Plagiarism Detector", in Practical Engineering Design, edited by Maja Bystrom and Bruce Eisenstein. Boca Raton, FLA: CFC Press, 2005: 27-28.

## 4.2.11 Assessment Tools

### Ethics Across the Curriculum Matrix

This is an unsupported media type. To view, please see
http://cnx.org/content/m14319/latest/EACMatrix_Template_ADEM_Feb_17.doc

**Figure 4.2:** This table will help you document your class discussion of the ADEM Statement of Values.

### Muddy Point Exercise

This is an unsupported media type. To view, please see http://cnx.org/content/m14319/latest/MP.doc

**Figure 4.3:** Clicking on this media file will open a word format for the Muddiest Point Exercise. Students are invited to discuss the strongest and weakest facets of the ADEM Statement of Values.

**Module Assessment Form**

This is an unsupported media type. To view, please see http://cnx.org/content/m14319/latest/MAP.doc

**Figure 4.4:** Clicking on this media file will open a general module assessment form taken from Michael Davis' IIT EAC workshop. This form will help you assess the SOV activity as well as other EAC modules.

### 4.2.12 Bibliography

1. Lynn Sharp Paine (1994) "Managing for Organizational Integrity," in Harvard business review, March-April: 106-117
2. Gary R. Weaver and Linda Klebe Trevino (1999) "Compliance and Values Oriented Ethics Programs: Influences on Employees' Attitudes and Behavior," in Business Ethics Ethics Quarterly 9(2): 315-335
3. Stuart C. Gilman (2003) "Government Ethics: If Only Angels Were to Govern," in Professioinal Ethics, edited by Neil R. Luebke in Ph Kappa Phi Forum, Spring 2003: 29-33.
4. Stephen H. Unger (1994) Controlling Technology: Ethics and the Responsible Engineer, 2nd Edition. New York: John Wiley and Sons: 106-135.
5. "Federal Sentencing Guidelines–Sentencing of Organizations," in Ethical Theory and Business, 5th Edition, edited by Tom L Beauchamp and Norman E. Bowie, New Jersey: Prentice Hall: 182-187. This article was reprinted with permission from The United States Law Week, Vol. 50 pp. 4226-29 (March 26, 1991) (Bureau of National Afairs, Inc.

## 4.3 Pirate Code for Engineering Ethics[4]

### 4.3.1 Statements of Value/Codes of Ethics

- William J. Frey
- Center for Ethics in the Professions
- University of Puerto Rico at Mayaguez

### 4.3.2 Module Introduction

In this module, you will learn about professional and occupational codes of ethics by looking at a bad code, writing your own code, and then critically examine a professional code of ethics, the engineering code for the Colegio de Ingenieros y Agrimensores de Puerto Rico. Three exercises will take you through the process of examining the Pirate Creed, writing your own code, and examining the Colegio's code. Text boxes will provide helpful background information on purposes served by professional codes, philosophical objections, and a framework for working your way through a stakeholder-based code like that of the CIAPR or the National Society of Professional Engineers. This module provides a Spanish translation of the Pirate Creed prepared by Dr. Dana Livingston Collins of the Department of Humanities in the University of Puerto Rico at Mayagüez.

---

[4]This content is available online at <http://cnx.org/content/m13849/1.10/>.

Concluding this module are two word documents uploaded as media files. One provides the exercises that are presented in this module in XML format. The other provides the background information that has been presented in this module as Textboxes.

### 4.3.3 Module Activities

1. You will analyze the Pirate Creed in terms of (a) its different functions, (b) the community values it embodies, and (c) how it stands toward nonmembers of the pirate community as well as members.
2. You will write a code of ethics for an occupational or professional area such as business or engineering.
3. You will debrief the rest of the class on your group's code, clarify its functions and values, and defend it if necessary.
4. This module will conclude with a look at the code of ethics of the Puerto Rico State Society of Professional Engineers and Land surveyors or **Colegio de Ingenieros y Agrimensores de Puerto Rico**.

### 4.3.4 Pirates Creed of Ethics (translated into Spanish by Dana Collins)

1. El capitán tendrá comando total durante una batalla y tendrá la autoridad para dirigir el barco. El que no sigua al capitán podrá ser castigado se la tripulación no vota en contra del castigo.
2. Si el barco naufraga, la tripulación permanecerá unidos hasta el capitán consigue otra nave. Si la nave es propiedad común de la tripulación, la primera nave capturada pertenecerá al capitán con una (1) parte de botín.
3. El cirujano del barco recibirá doscientas (200) coronas para el mantenimiento de su equipo médico y recibirá una (1) parte del botín.
4. Los otros oficiales recibirán una (1) parte cada uno, y si se distinguen, la tripulación determinará cuanto recibirán como recompensa.
5. El botín de una nave capturada será distribuido en partes iguales.
6. El primero que señale la aparición de un barco que sea capturado recibirá cien (100) coronas.
7. El que pierda un ojo, una mano, o una pierna mientras está en servicio, recibirá hasta seis esclavos o seiscientas (600) coronas.
8. Los suministros y raciones serán compartidos por igual.
9. La penalidad por traer una mujer disfrazada a bordo es la muerte.
10. Si un hermano roba de otro, perderá su nariz u orejas. Se peca de nuevo, se le darán un mosquete, municiones, plomo y una botella de agua y será abandonado en una isla.
11. Si hay duda en una disputa entre hermanos, una corte de honor determinará el veredicto. Si un hermano es encontrado culpable, la primera vez será perdonado, pero al ofender de nuevo, será atado a un cañón y recibirá un latigazo de cada miembro de la tripulación. El mismo castigo será dado a todos, incluyendo oficiales, quienes se emborrachen al punto de perder sus sentidos mientras estén en el barco.
12. El que se duerma mientras está trabajando como centinela, recibirán latigazos por todos los miembros de la tripulación. Se repite el crimen, su cabeza será rajada.
13. A todos quienes conspiren para desertar, o lo que hayan desertado y sean capturados, sus cabezas serán rajadas.
14. Pelas entre varios hermanos mientras estén a bordo será resueltos en tierra con pistolas y espadas. El que saque primera sangre será el vencedor. No pueden golpear a otro mientras estén a bordo de la nave.

### 4.3.5 Exercise 1: Pirate Creed

- What is good about the Pirate Creed of Ethics?

- what is bad about the Pirate Creed of Ethics?
- What is the purpose of the Creed for the Pirate Community?
- What values are embedded in the Pirate Creed
- How does the Pirate Creed deal with nonmembers?

## 4.3.6 Exercise 2: Writing a Code of Ethics for Engineers

- **Step One:** Identify the purpose behind your engineering code of ethics. For example, is it to punish wrongful behavior, provide a set of guidelines, educate the community, support ethical behavior, or create an ethics dialogue?
- **Step Two:** Identify the contributions that engineering makes to society.
- **Step Three:** Identify the stakeholders of the engineering profession. A stakeholder is any group or individual with a vital or essential interest tied to what engineers do. along with these stakeholders, identify their stakes, that is, the goods, rights, interests or values that are maintained, promoted, or diminished by what engineers do?
- **Step Four:** Enumerate the obligations or duties that engineers have toward each of these stakeholders. In other words, what can engineers do to maintain, promote, or diminish the stakes of each stakeholder?
- **Step Five:** Identify the conflicting obligations that arise from the fact that engineers have different stakeholders who hold conflicting stakes? Do any of these stakeholders or stakes have obvious priority over the others?
- **Step Six:** Step back and reflect on what you have written. For example, look for different kinds of provisions. Does your code use **ideals of the profession** which set forth the profession's central or cardinal objectives? Does your code contain **principles of professional conduct** which set forth minimal levels of behavior and prerscribe sanctions and punishments for compliance failures? In the CIAPR (**Colegio de Ingenieros y Agrimensores de Puerto Rico**) code of ethics, the fundamental principles and basic canons set forth the ideals of the profession. The principles of professional conduct fall in the section on practical norms.
- **Step Seven:** The Final Audit. Submit your code to an overall audit to see if anything has been left out. Have you included all the stakeholders and their stakes? Have you left out any ethical considerations such as rights and duties? Compare your code to the law. Are your code's provisions legal? Do they overlap with existing law? Do they imply criticisms of existing laws? If they imply punishments or sanctions, what measures does your code prescribe to administer justly and properly these sanctions? Finally, be sure to guard against the equal but opposite sins of over-specificity and too much generality. Overly specific codes try to provide a rule for every possible situation. Because this is impossible, these codes tend toward rigidity, inflexibility, and irrelevance. Codes that are too general fail because they can be interpreted to rationalize any kind of claim and, thus, mask immoral actions and intentions.

## 4.3.7 Exercise 3: Studying the code of Ethics of the Colegio de Ingenieros y Agrimensores de Puerto Rico

- Identify the provisions that touch upon the relation of the engineer to the public. What goods are at stake in this relation? What can engineers do to preserve or promote these goods?
- Identify provisions that touch upon the relation of the engineer to the client. What goods are at stake in this relation? What can engineers do to preserve or promote these goods?
- Identify provisions that touch upon the relation of the engineer to the CIAPR (professional engineering society) What goods are at stake in this relation? what can engineers do to preserve or promote these goods?.
- Finally, identify provisions that touch upon the relation of the engineer to other engineers (peer relations). What goods are at stake in this relation? What can engineers do to preserve or promote these goods?

### 4.3.8 Textbox 1: Code of Ethics of Colegio de Ingenieros y Agrimensores de Puerto Rico (Puerto Rico State society of Professional Eng

- The CIAPR code of ethics has three parts:
- Part One: Three Fundamental Principles which express cardinal objectives for engineering practice in Puerto Rico
- Part Two: Ten Canons which set forth general rules for ethical engineering practice
- Part Three: Each canon is repeated followed by several practical norms. by setting forth detailed rules, practical norms specify and interpret the basic canons. They also set forth specific and concrete rules for professional and ethical conduct
- The CIAPR code of ethics is a stakeholder code. This means it identifies engineering stakeholders, the goods they depend upon, and the duties engineers have in protecting or promoting these goods.

**Key Engineer Relations**

- The relation between engineer and **public** is founded on the goods of health, safety and welfare.
- The relation between engineer and **client** is founded on the good of faithful agency (trust).
- The relation between the individual engineer and the **profession** is founded on the engineer working to maintain the good reputation and integrity of the profession.
- The **peer** relation between practicing engineers is founded on the good of collegiality.

**Engineer and Public**

- Duties arising in this relation are tied to maintaining or promoting the goods of health, safety, and welfare. They include minimizing harm, avoiding paternalism (making decisions for others who have the right and ability to make these for themselves), free and informed consent (the right of those taking a risk to consent to that risk).
- FP1: Deberán considerar su principal función como profesionales la de servir a la humanidad. Su relación como professional y cliente, y como professional y patrono, deberá estar sujeta a su función fundamental de promover el bienestar de la humanidad y la de proteger el interés público.
- Canon 1: Velar por sobre toda otra consideración por la seguridad, el ambiente, la salud y el bienestar de la comunidad en la ejecución de sus responsabilidades profesionales.
- Practical Norm 1d: Cuando tengan conocimiento o suficiente razón para creer que otro ingeniero o agrimensor viola las disposiciones de este Código, o que una persona o firma pone en peligro la seguridad, el ambiente, la salud o el bienestar de la comunidad, presentarán tal información por escrito a las autoridades concernidas y cooperarán con dichas autoridades proveyendo aquella información o asistencia que les sea requerida.

**Engineer to Client**

- Duties stemming from this relation arise out of faithful agency, that is, the responsibility of an engineer to remain true to the client's interests. Positively this includes exercising due care for the client by carrying out the client's interests through the exercise of sound, competent engineering professional judgment. Negatively this entails avoiding conflicts of interest and revealing the client's confidential information.
- **Faithful Agency**: Canon 4—Actuar en asuntos profesionales para cada patrono o cliente como agentes fieles o fiduciarios, y evitar conflictos de intereses o la mera apariencia de éstos, manteniendo siempre la independencia de criterio como base del profesionalismo.
- **Conflict of Interest**: 4a—Evitarán todo conflicto de intereses conocido o potencial con sus patronos o clientes e informarán con prontitud a sus patronos o clientes sobre cualquier relación de negocios, intereses o circunstancias que pudieran influenciar su juicio o la calidad de sus servicios.
- **Confidentiality**: 4i—Tratarán toda información, que les llegue en el curso de sus encomiendas profesionales, como confidencial y no usarán tal información como medio para lograr beneficio personal si

tal acción es adversa a los intereses de sus clientes, de sus patronos, de las comisiones o juntas a las que pudiera pertenecer o del público.

### Engineer to Profession

- This includes working to promote the profession's **autonomy and independence** as well as maintaining its **good reputation**. Moreover it requires that engineers participate in their professional society, work to advance engineering, be objective and impartial in their work, and associate only with persons of **good reputation**.
- **Canon 3**: Emitir declaraciones públicas únicamente en una forma veraz y objetiva.
- **Practical Norm 3a**: Serán objetivos y veraces en informes profesionales, declaraciones o testimonios. Incluirán toda la información relevante y pertinente en tales informes, declaraciones o testimonios.

### Engineer to Engineer

- This relation is based on the good of **Collegiality**. It requires that engineers work to maintain friendly and collaborative relations with other engineers by avoiding disloyal competition and comparative advertising and by always giving peers due credit for their contributions to engineering projects and designs.
- **Practical Norm 4l**: Antes de realizar trabajos para otros, en los cuales puedan hacer mejoras, planos, diseños, inventos, u otros registros, que puedan justificar la obtención de derechos de autor o patentes, llegarán a un acuerdo en relación con los derechos de las respectivas partes. (Give due credit to colleagues for their work).
- **Canon 5**: Edificar su reputación profesional en el mérito de sus servicios y no competir deslealmente con otros. (**Avoid disloyal competition**)
- **Practical Norm 6b**: Anunciarán sus servicios profesionales sin auto-alabanza y sin lenguaje engañoso y de una manera en que no se menoscabe la dignidad de sus profesiones. (**Non-comparative advertising**)
- **Practical Norm 5h**: No tratarán de suplantar, ni suplantarán otro ingeniero o agrimensor, después de que una gestión profesional le haya sido ofrecida o confiada a éste, ni tampoco competirá injustamente con él. (**Avoid disloyal competition**)

## 4.3.9 Professional Codes as Social Contracts

- What some have said about defining ethics could also be applied to defining a profession: it's a bit like "nailing jello to a tree." Nevertheless, we can make to reasonable claims about professions: tye can be treated as social contracts, and they have someting to do with specialized knowledge. If these two claims hold, then a third claim can be made, namely, that professions have an ineliminable ethical dimension.
- A legitimate contract between two parties requires a **quid pro quo** (a mutually beneficial exchange) and **free consent** (consent that includes full information and excludes force or deception). The social contract between engineering and society can be pictured int he following way:

### Profession as Social Contract

| Society grants to Profession | Profession grants to Society |
| --- | --- |
| Autonomy | Self-Regulation |
| Prestige | Primacy of public health, safety, and welfare |
| Monopoly | Developing and enforcing ethical and professional standards |

**Table 4.4**

**Society grants autonomy, prestige, and monopoly control to the profession of engineering.**

1. Autonomy includes freedom from regulation and control from the outside through cumbersome laws, regulations, and statutes.
2. Prestige includes high social status and generous pay.
3. Monopoly status implies that the profession of engineering itself determines who can practice engineering and how it should be practiced.
4. The profession promises to use its autonomy responsibly by regulating itself. it does this by developing and enforcing professional and ethical standards. By granting prestige to the profession, society has removed the need for the profession to collectively bargain for its self-interest.
5. Not having to worry about its collective self-interest, the profession is now free to hold paramount the health, safety, and welfare of the public.
6. This contract explains why professions develop codes of ethics. Codes document to the public the profession's commitment to carry out its side of the social contract, namely, to hold paramount public welfare. They can do this because society will honor its side of the contract, namely, to remove from the profession the need to fight for its self-interest

**This social contract is more symbolic and explanatory than real.**

- Codes allow the profession to document to society that it has developed proper standards and intends to enforce them. They express the profession's trust in society to keep its side of the bargain by granting autonomy, prestige, and monopoly. Of course this contract has never been explicitly enacted at a point in historical time. But the notion of a social contract with a mutually beneficial exchange (a quid pro quo) provides a useful device for modeling the relation that has actually evolved between society and its professions.

**Professions and Responsibility**

- Professions have been created to exercise stewardship over knowledge and skill domains.
- Exercising stewardship over X generally means watching over, preserving, protecting, and even improving X. Stewardship is a forward-looking kind of responsibility similar to the responsibility that a parent exercises toward his or her children. The steward is a trusted servant or agent of the landowner who acts in the owner's place while the later is absent or incapacitated.
- "Stewardship," thus, refers to the profession's responsibility to safeguard its specific domain of knowledge and skill. This domain is essential to society in some way (it provides society with a basic, common good) and society delegates responsibility for this domain to its members who are specially suited to exercise it.
- So, generally speaking, professions can be characterized in terms of epistemological and ethical responsibilities.
- The epistemological responsibility refers to stewardship over the knowledge and skills that characterizes the profession. The profession preserves, transmit, and advances this domain of knowledge and skill. (Epistemology = study of knowledge.)
- The ethical dimension refers to the responsibility of the profession to safeguard knowledge and skill for the good of society. Society trusts the profession to do this for the sake of the comnmon good. Society also trusts the profession to regulate its own activities by developing and enforcing ethical and professional standards.

## 4.3.10 Objections to and Mischievous Side Effects of Codes of Ethics

**These objections are taken from John Ladd, "The Quest for a Code of Professional Ethics: An Intellectual and Moral Confusion." This article can be found in Deborah G. Johnson, editor, (1991) Ethical Issues in Engineering, New Jersey: Prentice Hall: 130-136. The author of this module has taken some liberties in this presentation.**

- **Codes "confuse ethics with law-making"** (Ladd, 130). Ethics is deliberative and argumentative while law-making focuses on activities such as making and enforcing rules and policies.
- **A code of ethics is an oxymoron.** Ethics requires autonomy of the individual while a code assumes the legitimacy of an external authority imposing rule and order on that individual.
- **Obedience to moral law for autonomous individuals is motivated by respect for the moral law. On the other hand, obedience to civil law is motivated by fear of punishment.** Thus, Ladd informs us that when one attaches "discipinary procedures, methods of adjudication and sanctions, formal and informal, to the principles that one calls 'ethical' one automatically converts them into legal rules or some other kind of authoritative rules of conduct...."(Ladd 131) Accompanying code provisions with punishments replaces obedience based on respect for the (moral) law with conformity based on fear of punishment.
- **Codes lead to the dangerous tendency to reduce the ethical to the legal.** Ethical principles can be used to judge or evaluate a disciplinary or legal code. But the reverse is not true; existing laws cannot trump ethical principles in debates over ethical issues and ethical decisions. As Ladd puts it, "That is not to say that ethics has no relevance for projects involving the creation, certification and enforcement of rules of conduct for members of certain groups....[I]ts [ethics's] role in connection with these projects is to appraise, criticize and perhaps even defend (or condemn) the projects themselves, the rules, regulations and procedures they prescribe, and the social and political goals and institutions they represent." (Ladd 130)
- **Codes have been used to justify immoral actions.** Professional codes have been misued by individuals to justify actions that go against common morality. For example, lawyers may use the fact that the law is an adversarial system to justify lying. Ladd responds in the following way to this dodge: "{T}here is no special ethics belonging to professionals. Professionals are not, simply because they are professionals, exempt from the common obligations, duties and responsibilities that are binding on ordinary people. They do not have a special moral status that allows them to do things that no one else can." (Ladd 131)

**Mischievous Side-Effects of Codes (from John Ladd)**

- **Codes make professionals complacent.** (Ladd 135) First, they reduce the ethical to the minimally acceptable. Second, they cover up wrongful actions or policies by calling them–within the context of the code–"ethical". For example, the NSPE code of ethics used to prohibit competitive bidding. Enshrining it in their code of ethics gave it the appearance of being ethical when in fact it was motivated primarily by self interest. This provision was removed when it was declared unconstitutional by the U.S. Supreme Court for violating the Anti-Trust law.
- Because codes focus on micro-ethical problems, **"they tend to divert attention from macro-ethical problems of a profession."** (Ladd 135) For example, in Puerto Rico, the actions of the Disciplinary Tribunal of the Colegio de Ingenieros y Agrimensores de Puerto Rico tend to focus on individual engineers who violate code provisions concerned with individual acts of corruption; these include conflicts of interest, failing to serve as faithful agents or trustees, and participating in corrupt actions such as taking or giving bribes. On the other hand, the CIAPR does not place equal attention on macro-ethical problems such as "the social responsibilities of professionals as a group" (Ladd 132), the role of the profession and its members in society (Ladd 135), and the "role professions play in determining the use of technology, its development and expansion, and the distribution of the costs." (Ladd 135)

### 4.3.11 Exercise: Questions for Reflection

1. Which of Ladd's criticisms apply to the Pirate Creed?
2. How does your group's code of ethics stand in relation to Ladd's criticisms?
3. Do Ladd's objections apply t the ABET, NSPE, or CIAPR codes?

---

**WORD FILE**

---

This is an unsupported media type. To view, please see
http://cnx.org/content/m13849/latest/Code_EX_Bx_1.doc

---

**Figure 4.5:** Module Exercises.

---

## 4.4 Corporate Ethics Compliance Officer Report[5]

NOTE: This module has been designed to bring together the following modules responding to the AACSB four ethics themes, corporate leadership, ethical decision-making, corporate social responsibility, and corporate governance. The links in this module tie it directly to EAC Toolkit modules that will help in preparation of the CECO report. The include the following:

```
- Type or paste the content directly into the appropriate section

- Socio-Technical Systems in Professional Decision Making (m14025)

- Developing a Statement of Values (m14319)

- Pirate Code for Engineering Ethics (m13849)

- Moral Ecologies in Corporate Governance (m17353)

- Three Views of Corporate Social Responsibility (m17318)

- Different Approaches to Corporate Governance (m17367)
```

```
These modules have links of their own that will prove invaluable for this activity.  An example
is the Leeds School of Business at the University of Colorado; this link connects to a search
engine for finding codes of ethics and corporate social responsibility programs.
```

```
The media file below provides a generic poster presentation template geared toward this assignment.
```

---

[5]This content is available online at <http://cnx.org/content/m18646/1.1/>.

**Template for CECO Poster Presentation**

This is an unsupported media type. To view, please see http://cnx.org/content/m18646/latest/Corporate Governance Presentation.pptx

**Figure 4.6:** This media file provides a template of the poster presentation required for ADME 3405, the course "Corporate Leadership and Social Responsibility." The different sections can be filled in by preparing PowerPoint slides, pressing control + Print Screen when in presentation viewing mode, and copy-pasting into appropriate part of poster template slide.

## 4.4.1 Introduction

You are the CECO of your company. Being familiar with the requirements of Sarbanes-Oxley and the Federal Sentencing Guidelines, you have been charged with developing a comprehensive ethics program that includes (1) a socio-technical system study, (2) a corporate code of ethics, (3) an ethics training program for new and ongoing employees, (4) an ethics hotline or some other reporting mechanism, (5) a CSR (corporate social responsibility) challenge, and (6) recruitment and leadership strategies for implementing ethics. Your report will begin with an executive summary and end with a concluding section that discusses implementation issues and needs.

## 4.4.2 What you need to know ...

**Sections of CECO Corporate Ethics Report**

1. Executive Summary (1 page)
2. Socio-Technical System Table plus written explanation. (3-5 pages)
3. Corporate Code of Ethics that provides core values, a description of each value, and how you plan to disseminate and implement your code. (3-5)
4. CSR (Corporate Social Responsibility) Challenge
5. Description of Ethics Training Program including activities and required resources (3-5 pages)
6. Recruitment and Leadership Strategies for Implementing Ethics into your organization (3-5 pages)
7. A Conclusion that includes a summary of the report, a time frame for implementing your ethics program, and an inventory of program needs and resources (1 page)

## 4.4.3 What you will do ...

**Executive Summary**

The executive summary should be no more than one page. Expect to write this several times because it needs to be the clearest and best written section. Written for your CEO, it should provide a quick two minute summary of your ethics plan. Write it in active voice, use ordinary language, and make references throughout the summary to the sections of the report that provide more in-depth analysis of the issue at hand. In this section you will tell your reader what you are going to say in the report.

**Socio-Technical System**

- This section will provide both a table and written description to help your reader understand the socio-technical system in which your company works and which provides the ethical and social challenges to which your program will respond.
- For information on how to compose a STS table and the different frames covered refer to module m14025, Socio-Technical Systems in Professional Decision-Making. The table for Burger Man provides frames that will be most relevant to this module but there are also other STS tables adopted for use in power engineering and engineering practice in Puerto Rico.
- Your written analysis should summarize and explore in more detail the STS issues that you are addressing in your corporate ethics plan. These would include compliance issues as well as fields in which your corporation's aspirations could be realized.

## Corporate Code of Ethics

- Your job here is to write a code of ethics for your corporation emphasizing the key value aspirations and CSR challenges that your are targeting in your ethics program. Your code should include...
- The values that form your corporation's highest and central commitments.
- A description or profile of each value. See the Developing a Statement of Values module for more on this.
- How your values apply to both the corporation's stakeholders and to its key CSR challenges.
- You should be clear about the function your code is playing both within your ethics plan and within the corporate organization. Six key functions are (1) to educate, (2) to foster an ethical dialogue, (3) to discipline employees, (4) to support employees in their efforts to realize the corporation's core commitments/values, (5) to communicate these commitments/values to employees and other stakeholders, and (6) to serve as a public testament of the key ethical and value commitments that define the integrity of your organization.

## Ethics Training Program

- This section details how you educate employees on the key components of your ethics program including the core ethical and value commitments. It should also provide means for getting employee buy-in for the ethics program as well as components that help employees with special ethical challenges. It should include the following:
- How you plan to educate employees on the company's code of ethics.
- How the company's core ethical values and principles should be integrated in the company's key operations including setting policy, strategic planning and decision-making.
- How your ethics program addresses your company's moral ecology. (Is it finance-, customer-, or quality driven? How do employees develop successful moral careers and modes of ethical advocacy within each of these companies? How does your ethics training program support this process?)

## CSR Challenges

- Several companies have special challenges in CSR. For example, Coca Cola when operating in India finds itself sharing scarce water resources with local, subsistence farmers. What are their responsibilities in this context? Relate your CSR challenge to the STS description in the second section.
- Develop a response to this CSR challenge. How does this realize your company's key moral values?
- Contextualize your company's CSR response within a general CSR perspective: shareholder, stakeholder, alliance.

## Recruitment and Leadership Strategies for Implementing Ethics

- In this section you will describe how you will realize your core objectives in recruiting new employees and in developing a leadership style.

- Consider, for example, how you will integrate values into the different components of your corporation's recruiting mechanism. Justice in the job description. Communicating to new employees their job and moral responsibilities. Recruiting employees who will be able to develop successful moral careers in the moral ecology of your company.
- Recognizing and responding to ethical risks such as maintaining privacy and property.

**Conclusion**

In the executive summary, you have told your reader what you are going to say in this report. The main body of the report contains what you need to say. This final section tells the reader what you have said by recapitulating and summarizing the report's high points. Include a time frame for implementing your ethics program as well as a description of the program's needs.

## 4.4.4 What did you learn?

**Check List**

- Each group will turn in this checklist, fully filled out and signed. Checking signifies that your group has completed and turned in the item checked. Failure to submit this form will cost your group 20 points
- _ _ _ _ _Executive Summary
- _ _ _ _ _Socio-Technical System Table and Written Explanation
- _ _ _ _ _Code of Ethics
- _ _ _ _ _Ethics Training Program
- _ _ _ _ _Corporate Social Responsibility Challenge and Response
- _ _ _ _ _Recruitment and Leadership Strategies for Implementing Ethics
- _ _ _ _ _Conclusion

**Group Self Evaluation Requirements**

- Group Self-Evaluation Form including...
- _ _ _ _ a list of the goals your group set for itself
- _ _ _ _ a carefully prepared, justified, and documented assessment of your group's success in reaching these goals
- _ _ _ _ a careful assessment of what you did and did not learn in this activity
- _ _ _ _ a discussion of obstacles you encountered and the measures your group took to overcome these
- _ _ _ _ a discussion of member participation and contribution including the member contriution forms
- _ _ _ _ a general discussion of what worked and what did not work for you and your group in this activity
- _ _ _ _ _Each member will turn in a filled out a Team Member Evaluation Form. This form can be accessed through the media file listed above. It is suggested that you do this anonomously by turning in your Team Member Evaluation Form in a sealed envelop with the rest of these materials. You are to evaluate yourself along with your teammates on the criteria mentioned in the form. Use the scale suggested in the form.Your first item here

**Team Member Evaluation Form**

---

This is an unsupported media type. To view, please see http://cnx.org/content/m18646/latest/TEAM MEMBER RATING SHEET.docx

---

**Figure 4.7:** This Team Member Evaluation Form must be filled out by each team member. Evaluate yourself and each member in terms of the criteria. It is preferable if you do this anonymously.

**Group Pledge**

- I certify that these materials have been prepared by those who have signed below, and no one else. I certify that the above items have been checked and that those items with check marks indicate materials that we have turned in. I also certify that we have not plagiarized any material but have given due acknowledgment to all sources used. All who sign below and whose names are included on the title page of this report have participated fully in the preparation of this project and are equally and fully responsible for its results.
- Member signature here _____
- Member signature here _____
- Member signature here _____
- Member signature here _____
- Member signature here _____
- Member signature here _____

## 4.4.5 Appendix

## 4.4.6 EAC ToolKit Project

**4.4.6.1 This module is a WORK-IN-PROGRESS; the author(s) may update the content as needed. Others are welcome to use this module or create a new derived module. You can COLLABORATE to improve this module by providing suggestions and/or feedback on your experiences with this module.**

Please see the Creative Commons License[6] regarding permission to reuse this material.

**4.4.6.2 Funded by the National Science Foundation: "Collaborative Development of Ethics Across the Curriculum Resources and Sharing of Best Practices," NSF-SES-0551779**

# 4.5 Being an Ethical Job Candidate[7]

## 4.5.1 Module Introduction

Chances are that you are either actively involved in an effort to find work or soon will be. Based on stories that come from the job-hunting experiences of UPRM students in Practical and Professional ethics classes, this module presents the employment guidelines put out by the IEEE, challenges these guidelines with realistic cases and scenarios, and provides you with decision-making tools to tackle these ethical complexities. This

---

[6]http://creativecommons.org/licenses/by/2.0/
[7]This content is available online at <http://cnx.org/content/m14468/1.7/>.

module was developed for and recently presented in Mechanical Engineering Capstone Design courses. It forms a part of the EAC Toolkit funded by the National Science Foundation, SES 0551779.

The details of the IEEE Professional Employment Guidelines for Engineers and Scientists have been reprinted by Stephen Unger in his book, Controlling Technology: Ethics and the Responsible Engineer, 2nd Ed. NY, NY: John Wiley and Sons, Inc.: 315-329. We condense these guidelines to a few concepts. Each concept will be presented and followed by one or more cases designed to test the concept in its application.

## 4.5.2 Sincere Interest

- Job candidates are obliged to apply only for those positions in which they are sincerely and seriously interested.
- "Sincere interest" has several meanings but two stand out here. First, they should not agree to an interview after having accepted a job offer from another company. Second, they should be qualified according to the requirements listed in the job application.
- The following scenarios test this concept in different ways. "Bring Your Friends" raises the issue of whether not being seriously interested in a job is ok if the interviewer knows this and initiates the interview for other reasons. "Working for Mega Weapons" asks whether moral or conscience-based conflicts cancel out "sincere interest."

### 1. Bring Your Friends:
Maria, a talented student in mechanical engineering has accepted an offer to work for a prestigious firm. Then she receives a call for an interview with firm X. She tells them that she has already accepted an offer from Y, but the caller says that doesn't matter. "We want to interview you anyway so that we can document affirmative action compliance. In fact, if you have any friends who are similarly situated [i.e., women who come from minority groups] please give us their names. We will fly all of you to our central headquarters for interviews at our expense. It will be a good vacation.

**What would you do if you were in Maria's place?**

- Accept the interview offer but not try to recruit any of your friends.
- Accept the interview offer and try to recruit some of your friends to go along.
- Refuse to accept the interview on moral grounds.
- Refuse to accept the interview because it would interfere with the class in Practical and Professional Ethics that you are currently taking.
- Report this company to the appropriate governmental agency since they are clearly distinguishing against candidates from so-called minority groups
- Your solution....

### 2. Working for Mega Weapons
Jorge is an unemployed computing professional. He is also a pacifist. Antonio, a friend, has a job prospect. Mega Weapons is looking for someone with Jorge's expertise. Yes, he will be spending time developing the guidance systems for "smart bombs." But the accurate, smart bombs will be less likely to go astray and kill innocent civilians. Jorge, however, remains unimpressed by this. "They're still bombs," he says, "and their primary purpose is to kill human beings. Besides, I would compromise myself by even accepting an interview. What if they ask me about my views on war? I would have to tell them the truth and then they would dismiss me as a candidate." Jorge tells his wife about the job prospect. While she supports his pacifism, she tells him that she can't continue indefinitely as a waitress; her job is preventing her from completing her college degree and keeps her away from the children. She asks Jorge if there is any way he can reconcile this job with his pacifism. What should Jorge do?

**What should Jorge do is he receives a request to interview with Mega Weapons?**

- Jorge should not go to the interview because he is not "sincerely interested" in this position. His pacifism cancels out any possibility of "sincere interest".

- Jorge should accept this interview request because his obligations to his family outweigh matters of personal morality and personal conscience such as his pacifism.
- Jorge should accept this interview and a job offer, if one follows, precisely because of his pacifism. If he refuses then Mega Weapons will find a war monger who will do all kinds of harm. By taking the job and using his skills to minimize harm in weapons development Jorge is doing his best to realize the pacifist agenda.
- Jorge should set aside his pacifism and use his engineering skills to carry out politically sanctioned weapons projects just as a doctor should set aside personal likes or dislikes of a patient and exercise his or her skills dispassionately and professionally.
- Your solution...

### 4.5.3 Full and Honest Disclosure

- The job candidate is required to provide full information relative to the job description as advertised. This would include elements such as:
- Educational Experience
- Prior work experience
- Other job relevant skills and knowledge
- Do religion, sexual preference, marital status, political viewpoints, and recreational practices constitute job relevant matters? In other words, are these matters private to the job candidate or are there occasions when the prospective employer has a right to access this information?
- Distinguish between information to which an interviewer has a right and the means the interviewer has the right to use to uncover this information. Do interviewers have the right to require that job candidates (1) take polygraph examinations, (2) undergo drug tests, (3) take psychological profiling exams, (4) be subjected to "staged crises" to find out how a candidate would handle such an event? These may constitute information areas to which the prospective employer has a right, but does the interviewer also have a right to use these means to obtain this information?

**The following scenario examines whether full disclosure requires that one make known one's personal moral convictions.**

**3. Are You a Bleeding-Heart Pacifist?**
Jorge is a pacifist. He is also an unemployed computing professional. Against his better judgment, his wife and friend, Antonio, have talked him into interviewing with Mega Weapons for a new opening working on the guidance systems of non-nuclear missiles. During the interview, the employer remarks that Mega Weapons has had trouble in the past with employees who have moral qualms about working on weapons projects. He then turns to Jorge and asks, "You're not one of those bleeding-heart pacifists are you?" How should Jorge answer this question?

- Jorge should not reveal his pacifism. It is obvious that this would prejudice Mega Weapons against hiring him. He must try to get the job at all costs.
- Jorge should take the time to explain his pacifism, and how he sees himself fitting into different military projects. For example, he could emphasize his concern and expertise in making weapons guidance systems as accurate as possible to minimize "collatoral" damage during use. He could use this interview to negotiate guidelines for projects that he would find compatible with his convictions.
- Jorge should immediately exit the interview. It is obvious that Mega Weapons would exhibit no sympathy or support for his pacifism.
- Your solution.

## 4.5.4 Moral Conflicts and Full and Honest Disclosure

### Consider this Analogy

You are a physician on call for Saturday night in a remote country hospital. You receive an emergency call to come immediately and perform, life-saving surgery on a patient in critical condition. The surgery is routine for someone of your skills but the situation for the patient is critical. You can save his life if you act quickly. You speed to the hospital, scrub, suit up and walk into the operating room. There lying unconscious on the operating table is your worst enemy. This is a person whose entire life has been devoted to making you miserable. You have no doubt that if you save his life he will continue to inflict even more suffering on you. You hesitate. You could botch the operation and probably get away with it. But no one else can perform the surgery. You successfully execute the operation and save the patient's life. After all, as a physician you have the obligation to set aside personal issues and feelings and do your duty as a professional to the best of your abilities.

The general consensus is that the doctor is morally, professionally, and even legally obligated to perform the operation. Professionalism, most argue, requires that we set aside personal issues and personal morality and do our duties as professionals. Samuel Florman argues that engineers as professionals have the same duty by analogy. If society asks an engineer to carry out a task that is socially sanctioned and politically validated, then the engineer has the duty to set aside whatever moral or conscience-based objections he or she may have and carry out the engineering activity. So even those who are pacifists and object to weapons projects may have, under the right conditions, the obligation or duty to set aside personal morality and work on the project. Do you think Florman's analogy holds? Put yourself into the position of Jorge? Does he have the obligation to set aside his pacifism as a merely personal belief and carry out his orders as an engineer?

### Here is the central part of Florman's argument from analogy quoted from his article, "Moral Blueprints" (Harper's, October 1978, pp. 0-33):

If each person is entitled to medical care and legal representation, is it not equally important that each legitimate business entity, government agency, and citizens' group should have access to expert engineering advice? If so, then it follows that engineers (within the limits of conscience) will sometimes labor on behalf of causes in which they do not believe. Such a tolerant view also makes it easier for engineers to make a living.

### What do you think Florman means by "within the limits of conscience"?

Nathaniel Borenstein a widely respected expert on intelligent systems found himself under just this kind of situation. A committed pacifist, he assiduously avoided getting involved in military projects, even when asked repeatedly by representives of the military. But something said to him by one of these military representatives led him to reassess his position. Borenstein was asked to develop a training simulation to teach individuals how to work with the nuclear missile launching system. When he found that it involved "embedded training" he became very concerned. To appreciate the full extent of his concern and the reasons that persuaded him to get involved in **this** project, it is best to turn to his own words:

### Borenstein on Embedded Training

Embedded training, in particular, struck me as a very poor idea. Training by computer simulation has been around for a long time. Embedded training takes this one step further: it does the simulation and training on the actual command and control computer. To exaggerate slightly, whether or not anyone actually dies when you press the "launch missiles" button depends on whether or not there is a little line at the top of the screen that says "SIMULATION."

### Borenstein continues

Such a system seems almost designed to promote an accidental nuclear war, and this thought was what persuaded me to attend the workshop in the first place. One can all too easily imagine human error–"I could have **sworn** it was in the 'simulation' mode–as well as frightening technical possibilities. Perhaps, due to some minor programming bug, the word "SIMULATION" might fail to disappear when it was supposed to. Someone approaching the computer would get the wrong idea of what it was safe to type.

**These quotes are taken from: Nathaniel S. Borenstein, "My life as a NATO collaborator" in the Bulletin of the Atomic Scientists, April 1989: 13-20.**

**A Thought Exercise**

- Think of Borenstein's concerns and eventual actions in light of Florman's analogy.
- Does Borenstein have the obligation to set aside his pacifism to work on correcting this training problem?
- Does Florman's analogy provide the justification for this? Or is Borenstein acting on the basis of a very different set of arguments?
- Assume that you are a committed pacifist. Was Borenstein right to set aside his beliefs to work on this project? Did he really set aside his beliefs?

## 4.5.5 Honoring Confidentiality Agreements and Waiving Employment Rights

- More and more, prospective job candidates are being required to sign "non-disclosure agreements" as a part of their employment contract. These agreements commit engineers and professionals, not only to non-disclosure of company secrets, but to not seeking employment with competitors for three to five years after leaving the company.
- Non-disclosure agreements are designed to balance an employer's concern for protecting confidential information with an employee's right to job mobility based on freedom of association. But a new and vital concern to engineers and professionals on the point of employment is just what they are commiting themselves to when they agree to such contractual provisions.
- The prospective employee's responsibility to honor confidentiality agreements is grounded in the employer's obligation to full disclosure of the terms of employment. Balancing these is difficult in the interviewing and hiring processes as the following cases demonstrate.
- New employees are also being asked to sign agreements waiving their right to sue the company should they be fired. In lieu of the right to sue for wrongful dismissal, companies ask that employees agree to binding arbitration carried out by an outside arbitrator. Binding arbitration is...binding, that is, it obligates both of the disputing parties to a decision decided upon by an outsider. And the company reserves the right to name the arbitrator. Companies have done this to protect themselves against the erosion of the doctrine of "employment at will" toward the notion of "just cause." But the scenarios below invites you to think about how much job candidates are being asked to give up when they waive their right to sue for wrongful dismissal.

### 4. We Protect Our Property

Pedro has a job offer from Z-Corp, a manufacturer of computer chips. Z-Corp has recently had problems with its competitors who have tried to hire away its employees to get information about their chip production process. In response, Z-Corp now includes a clause (non-disclosure agreement) in its employment contract that prohibits employees from working with competitors for up to five years. Should Pedro be concerned about this? What should he do?

**What should Pedro do?**

- He should refuse to sign such an agreement even if it costs him the job.
- He should sign the agreement without complaint. It's a nasty world out there, and he is lucky to have this job.
- Pedro should ask the company to be more explicit about the confidentiality concerns they are trying to protect. He should also ask whether it is necessary to restrict his future employment options to such an extent.
- Your solution....

### 5. You Can't Sue Us

Marta, a student at an Hispanic university has just accepted a job with a major U.S. corporation. The job seems ideal. However, she notices that her employment contract includes a clause to the effect that she cannot sue the corporation for wrongful dismissal should she be fired or laid off. Instead, the dispute would be resolved by an outside arbitrator. The arbitrator's decision would be binding on both parties. Moreover, the arbitrator would be chosen by the company. Marta suspects that this agreement represents a "hard line" stance that the company has taken on wrongful dismissal suits. What should she do?

**What should Marta do?**

- She should refuse to agree to waiving any of her legal rights. Not to do so would leave her vulnerable to being fired by the company for any reason whatsoever, even morally questionable reasons.
- She should ask for more time to study the employment contract before signing. Then she should examine very carefully the company's past employment issues. Maybe the company's record is questionable and this has led them to take such a stance toward wrongful dismissal suits.
- Marta should ask for more time to think about the employment offer and the contractual terms. Then she should try to find another position and only if she fails in this effort should she accept the offer as the best thing she can do.
- Your solution....

### 6. Can I use what I have already learned?

Mega Weapons, Inc. (MW) has been awarded a lucrative contract with the U.S. military to develop guided, non-nuclear missiles. This contract is based on MW's considerable success in developing highly accurate computer guidance systems. While working with MW, you have had access to the details of these guidance systems, including information owned by MW and protected by the law. Recently, you have received a job offer from Amaco Arms, Inc. (AA). This offer came about through an unsolicited recommendation by a former classmate of yours; he now works for Amaco, is familiar with your experience and expertise, and suggested to his supervisors at Amaco that they try to hire you away from Mega Weapons. You will be helping them develop guidance systems for missiles and will be doing work similar to the work you are doing with Mega Weapons. AA competes directly with ME for military weapons contracts. It is more than likely that protected information you have had access to while working with Mega Weapons would be useful for what you would be doing with Amaco.

**What would you do if you were in this position>**

- You should accept the new job. After all, your classmate has done you a favor. It's a lot more money, and you are certainly in a position to help AA.
- You should not accept this job offer since it is clear that your former classmate and AA are only interested in the proprietary and confidential information you have about MW.
- You should accept the job but only after you have done two things. First, you need to consult with MW to define precisely the boundaries of your confidentiality obligations. Then you should make these boundaries clear to AA and only if they accept these boundaries should you agree to work for them.
- Your solution....

### 7. You Can't Take It With You

You are leaving Computing Systems, Inc. to work for Compware, Inc,. a competitor. Before you leave Computing Systems, you are debriefed by the Personnel Office and a company lawyer on the proprietary information you have had access to while working with Computing Systems. They have itemized the information that you cannot divulge to or use in your work with Compware. It is your professional judgment that they are including information that is general knowledge and should not be considered confidential or proprietary. It is also information that would be useful—even essential—for what you will be doing in your new job. You feel that this confidentiality agreement is overly restrictive and would handicap you in your new job. What should you do?

**How should you respond to CSI's restrictions on what you can and cannot disclose in your new work with Compware?**

1. You should assert your rights to make use of all the information that your training has provided you. This includes especially the innovations you introduced to CSI. Because this is the result of your hard work you should be able to take it with you to your new job.

2. Even though CSI's confidentiality boundaries are, in your opinion, restrictive, you have no choice but to accept them. Make these boundaries clear to Compware and hope that they still want your services.

3. You need to consult a lawyer here. Clearly CSI is trampling on your legal rights but you will need expert help to assert them.

4. Your solution....

### 4.5.6 More on Full and Honest Disclosure: Terms of Interview

**Full Disclosure also pertains to providing full disclosure of the terms of the interview as well as full disclosure of the terms of employment should the search reach this point.**

- Full disclosure would include providing the job candidate with a detailed itinerary of the interview process. As we will see in the case below, some interviewers deliberately leave off certain items to create surprises.

- Full disclosure of the nature of the job should include a detailed description of routine activities as well as non-routine possibilities. An example of a significant non-routine task would be that occasions may arise where an employee may at some point be called upon to work on a weapons project.

- In short, the job candidate should be given, during the interview, an orientation on work responsibilities, places in which the work will be carried out, and the colleagues with whom he or she will be working.

**8. Oh, by the way...**

Pedro, who will graduate at the end of the current semester, is a student at a well known Hispanic serving university. He and two of his classmates are flown by Comp-Org for an interview at company headquarters. During a phone conversation with the company representative setting up the interview, he asks if there is anything he should do to prepare for the interview. The company representative answers, "No." Pedro receives a faxed itinerary of the interview–it looks routine. So Pedro and his classmates board the plane and arrive at their destination, the company headquarters. The company official who meets them at the airport tells them that the first item on the interview agenda is a drug test. When Pedro objects–"Why weren't we told about this before we agreed to the interview?"–he is told that if this is unacceptable to him, he can get right back on the plane because the interview is over for him.

**What should Pedro do?**

- He should get on the plane. This act on the part of the interviewer violates his right of prior disclosure of the terms of the interview.

- He should submit to the drug test. After all, he should have reasonably expected that the company would do something like this. Since whether or not he has a drug habit is highly job relevant, the company has a right to this information.

- He should file a grievance against the company for discriminating against Hispanics.

- Your solution....

**Employers should also treat information about job candidates and employees as confidential**
In the following case, examine whether information about why a former employee with your company had been fired is or is not confidential and should or should not be included in any recommendation you write for that employee.

**9. The Recommendation**

A worker under your supervision has recently been fired for incompetence and repeated violations of confidentiality. Several weeks later, the worker returns to ask you for a letter of recommendation. He says you owe it to him; you fired him and he has not been able to find any work and has a family to support.

**What should you do?**

1. Write the letter and withhold information about the employee being fired. While he may be a slacker, you should help him as a means of helping his family.

2. Write the letter but include the information about the employee being fired. If you frame it properly, maybe he will get a job and be able to support his family.
3. Refuse to write a letter. If you leave out what the prospective employer considers crucial information you may be liable for any harm this slacker causes. And you wouldn't be doing the former employee any favor in writing the letter because you would be wrong to conceal information about his being fired.
4. Your solution....

**Finally, interviewers and employers have the obligation to treat job candidates and employees with dignity. This includes respecting privacy and refraining from harassment. The following case raises interesting questions about just what constitutes harassment during an interview.**

- A recent graduate from University X, Marta has a strong and successful interview with a representative from a local, respected company. She discussed her skills, experience, and asked several perceptive questions about working conditions, job responsibilities, and benefits. The interviewer, obviously impressed, asked Marta back for a second interview with his supervisor.
- The second interview followed a different course. The interviewer, an older man, did not ask her about her skills or experience. Instead he reminisced about his days as a college student. He talked about his children–what they were studying and their career plans. He mentioned his wife in passing. Then he told Marta that the people who do well in his company are hard workers. "The strongest person," he said, "will do whatever is necessary to survive in a harsh, competitive environment." Then he looked at her hands and asked if she was single and if she still lived with her parents.
- How should Marta answer these questions?
- Do these questions invade Marta's privacy?
- Do the interviewer's questions, comments, and gestures constitute sexual harassment?

## 4.5.7 Decision Making Exercise and Ethics Tests

**Your Task**

- You will be divided into groups and assigned a scenario.
- Each scenario involves a difficulty with interpreting and applying an employee guideline concept.
- Interpret and apply the concept as best you can.
- Develop a value integrative solution that resolves the decision point of your scenario.

**Values**

- **Value**: A value "refers to a claim about what is worthwhile, what is good. A value is a single word or phrase that identifies something as being desirable for human beings." Brincat and Wike, Morality and the Professional Life: Values at Work
- **Justice**: Justice as fairness focuses on giving each individual what is his or her due. Three senses of justice are (1) the proper, fair, and proportionate use of sanctions, punishments and disciplinary measures to enforce ethical standards (retributive justice), (2) the objective, dispassionate, and impartial distribution of the benefits and burdens associated with a system of social cooperation (distributive justice), (3) an objectively determined and fairly administered compensation for harms and injustices suffered by individuals (compensatory justice), and (4) a fair and impartial formulation and administration of rules within a given group.
- **Respect**: Recognizing and working not to circumvent the autonomy in others and ourselves. (Autonomy is the capacity to make and execute decisions as well as to set forth ends and goals, integrate them into life plans, and use these to constitute active identities.) Respect involves recognizing and respecting rights such as privacy, property, free speech, due process, and free (and informed) consent. Disrespect undermines autonomy through deception, force, or manipulation.

- **Responsibility**: The ability to develop moral responses appropriate to the moral issues and problems that arise in one's day-to-day experience. Responsibility includes several senses: (1) individuals are (capacity) responsible when they can be called upon to answer for what they do; (2) individuals have (role) responsibilities when they commit to carry out tasks that arise from social and professional roles; (3) responsibility also refers to the way in which one carries out one's obligations. It can range from indifference and negligence to care and diligence. Responsibility in this sense turns into a virtue that formulates diligence and care as excellences worth striving for.

- **Honesty** – Is honesty telling the truth, the whole truth, and nothing but the truth? Or is it a virtue that involves a more delicate balance between extremes of excess and defect? Too much honesty results in harmful bluntness and tactlessness. ("Your child is a hopeless slob. You should disown him." The former may be true but there are gentler and ultimately more productive ways to communicate this information to the concerned parent.) We are all familiar with too little honesty, the dishonesty that results from lying, deceiving, manipulating, exaggerating, distorting, etc.

- **Reasonableness** - Defusing disagreement and resolving conflicts through integration. Characteristics include seeking relevant information, listening and responding thoughtfully to others, being open to new ideas, giving reasons for views held, and acknowledging mistakes and misunderstandings. Thus, reasonableness as a virtue includes much more than rationality. (From Michael Pritchard, Reasonable Children)

**In making your decision...**

1. Try to design a solution that realizes as many values as possible.
2. Wike: "Although values can compete, they don't conflict." Try to solve the value competitions in your scenario by integrating the competing values in a solution.
3. Wike: "No value necessarily overrides any other."
4. Wike: "Aim to realize all values, but where that is impossible, enact the most important values and/or the greatest number of values."

**Having Trouble? Try this...**

1. **Nolo Contendere**. Take the path of least resistance. (Just go along with what the dominant person in the situation says.)
2. **Negotiate**. Try to persuade those in the situation to accept a value-integrative solution, compromise, or trade off.
3. **Oppose**. Someone is trying to force you to so something wrong. Get some courage. Oppose the wrongdoer.
4. **Exit**. You can't win in this situation so find a way of getting out. Let someone else deal with it.
5. These options can be evaluated and ranked in terms of the values they realize (or don't realize) and how feasible they are in the given situation.

**Try these ethics tests**

1. **REVERSIBILITY**: Would I think this a good choice if I were among those affected by it?
2. **PUBLICITY**: Would I want this action published in the newspaper?
3. **HARM**: Does this action do less harm than any available alternative?
4. **FEASIBILITY**: Can this solution be implemented given time, technical, economic, legal, and political constraints?

### 4.5.8 References

1. Victoria S. Wike, "Professional Engineering Ethical Behavior: A Values-based Approach". **Proceedings of the 2001 American Society for Engineering Education Annual Conference and Exposition**, Session 2461.

2. Michael S. Pritchard (1996) **Reasonable Children: Moral Education and Moral Learning**. Lawrence, KS: University of Kansas Press: 11.
3. Stephen H. Unger (1994) **Controlling Technology: Ethics and the Responsible Engineer**. New York: John Wiley and Sons: 315-325 (Reprinted with permission of IEEE)
4. Robert C. Solomon (1999) **A Better Way to Think About Business: How Personal Integrity Leads to Corporate Success**. Oxford, UK: Oxford University Press: 71-114.
5. See Onlineethics, www.onlineethics.org, for case on which "Oh, By the Way" is based.

## 4.5.9 Conclusion

**What have you achieved?**

1. You have become aware of how ethical issues can arise in the job candidacy process.
2. You have a better of your obligations and rights in the job candicacy process.
3. You have practiced decision making by evaluating and ranking solutions to ethics cases.
4. You have worked with integrating important ethical values into solutions to ethical problems.

## 4.5.10 Presentation of Module before Mechanical Engineering Class

**Presentation: Being an Ethical Job Candidate**

This is an unsupported media type. To view, please see
http://cnx.org/content/m14468/latest/Be_Et_Job_V2.ppt

**Figure 4.8:** This figure contains a powerpoint presentation of this module used in a Mechanical Engineering Capstone Design course during Spring and Fall semesters, 2007.

**Gray Matters in Job Searches**

This is an unsupported media type. To view, please see http://cnx.org/content/m14468/latest/Gray Matters in Job Searches.doc

**Figure 4.9:** This word file presents four of the above scenarios in Gray Matters form. It provides a useful handout as well as an abbreviated version of this activity.

# Chapter 5

# Business Ethics Case Studies

## 5.1 Biomatrix Case Exercises - Student Module[1]

NOTE: Write your module for a student audience. To complete or edit the sections below erase the provided textual commentaries then add your own content using one or more of the following strategies:

```
    - Type or paste the content directly into the appropriate section

  - Link to a published CNX module or an external online resource
    using the ''Links'' tabs (see example on the right)

  - Link to a document or multimedia file within the content after
    uploading the file using the ''Files'' tab (see example below)

  - Cite content not available online
```

---

**Word Version of this Template**

---

This is an unsupported media type. To view, please see http://cnx.org/content/m15187/latest/ EAC TK STD TEMPLATE.doc

---

**Figure 5.1:** This is an example of an embedded link. (Go to "Files" tab to delete this file and replace it with your own files.)

---

### 5.1.1 Introduction

In this module you will study a real world ethical problem, the Biomatrix case, and employ frameworks based on the software development cycle to (1) specify ethical and technical problems, (2) generate solutions that

---

[1]This content is available online at <http://cnx.org/content/m15187/1.3/>.

integrate ethical value, (3) test these solutions, and (4) implement them over situation-based constraints. This module will provide you with an opportunity to practice integrating ethical considerations into real world decision-making and problem-solving in business and computing. This whole approach is based on an analogy between ethics and design (Whitbeck).

Large real world cases like Biomatrix pivot around crucial decision points. You will take on the role of one of the participants in the Biomatrix case and problem-solve in teams from three decision points. Problem-solving in the real world requires perseverance, moral creativity, moral imagination, and reasonableness; one appropriates these skills through practice in different contexts. Designing and implementing solutions requires identifying conflicting values and interests, balancing them in creative and dynamic solutions, over-coming technical limits, and responding creatively to real world constraints.

Each decision point requires that you take up the position of a participant in the case and work through decision-making frameworks from his or her perspective. You may be tempted to back out and adopt an evaluative posture from which to judge the participants. Resist this temptation. This module is specifically designed to give you practice in making real world decisions. These skills emerge when you role play from one of the standpoints within the case. You will learn that decision-making requires taking stock of one's situation from within a clearly defined standpoint and then accepting responsibility for what arises from within that standpoint.

Cases such as Biomatrix are challenging because of the large amount of information gathering and sorting they require. Moral imagination responds to this challenge by providing different framings that help to filter out irrelevant data and structure what remains. Framing plays a central role in problem specification. For example, Biomatrix could be framed as the need to develop quick and decisive responses to cyber-smear. Or it could be framed legally as employing legal tools (John Doe suits to pierce anonymity) that set a dangerous precedent against free speech. Yet again, it could be framed as a cautionary tale on the dangers of thinking that you are anonymous when you speak online. What is important at this stage is that you and your group experiment with multiple framings of the case around your decision point. This makes it possible to open up avenues of solution not possible under just one framing.

Tackling large cases in small teams also helps develop the communication and collaboration skills that are required for group work. Take time to develop strategies for dividing the work load among your team members. The trick is to distribute equally but, at the same time, to assign tasks according the different abilities of your team members. Some individuals are better at research while others excel in interviewing or writing. Also, make sure to set aside time when you finish for integrating your work with that of your teammates. Start by quickly reviewing the information available on the case. This is called "scoping the case." Then formulate specific questions to focus further research on information relevant to your problem solving efforts. This includes information pertinent to constructing a socio-technical analysis, identifying key "embedded" ethical issues, and uncovering existing best and worst practices.

A case narrative, STS (socio-technical system) description, and two ethical reflections have been published at http://computingcases.org. This module also links to websites on free speech and privacy law, advice to corporate officials on how to respond to cyber-smear, and information useful in understanding the products manufactured by Biomatrix.

## Biomatrix Abstract

Biomatrix manufactures a medical product called Synvisc, a lubricant injected into the knee to take the place of natural lubricants that disappear with age. From April 1999 to August 2000, a series of messages (some 16,000 in all) highly critical of Biomatrix were posted on a Yahoo bulletin board. These messages, sent by three individuals operating under 23 pseudonyms, make a series of defamatory claims about Biomatrix officials, employees, the company's financial status, and its key products. Biomatrix vigorously denied each of these claims. Yet the quality and quantity of this information may have had negative effects on the financial well being of the company. During the period in which the messages appeared in Yahoo, Biomatrix stock dropped from $35 per share to $21. In response, Biomatrix petitioned the court to subpoena Yahoo to reveal the identities of the persons sending the messages. Yahoo complied identifying Raymond Costanzo, Richard Costanzo, and Ephraim Morris as the authors of the messages. In a summary judgment, all three were found guilty of defamation.

# Biomatrix Time Line

| Date | Event | Actors |
|------|-------|--------|
| April 1999 through August 2000 | Posting of anti-Biomatrix messages | Richard Costanzo, Raymond Costanzo, Ephraim Morris |
| April 1999 to July 2000 | Biomatrix Shares drop from 35 to 21 | Caused by BXM Police? |
| March 2000 | Announcement of Genzyme's intention to buy Biomatrix for $245,000,000 | Biomatrix and Genzyme Top Management |
| June/July 2000 | Initiation of John Doe Lawsuit | Plaintiffs: Biomatrix, Balazs, and Denlinger |
| July 2000 | Court subpoenas Yahoo for identities of message posters (BXM Police) | Plaintiffs: Biomatrix, Balazs, and Denlinger |
| August 3, 2000 | Summary Judgment against Raymond Costanzo, Richard Costanzo, and Ephraim Morris | Plaintiffs: Biomatrix, Balazs, and Denlinger |
| November 7, 2000 | SEC approval of Genzyme plan to purchase Biomatrix | Genzyme and Biomatrix Top Management plus SEC |
| November 7, 2000 | Biomatrix stock rises from $19 to $19.94 | |
| January 3, 2001 | Yahoo alters bulletin board policies | |

**Table 5.1**

## 5.1.2 What you need to know ...

### 5.1.2.1 What you need to know about socio-technical systems

**1. STS have seven broad components: hardware, software, physical surroundings, people/groups/roles, procedures, laws, and data/data structures.**

**2. Socio-technical systems embody values**

- These include moral values like safety, privacy, property, free speech, equity and access, and security. Non-moral values can also be realized in and through Socio Technical Systems such as efficiency, cost-effectiveness, control, sustainability, reliability, and stability.
- Moral values present in Socio Technical Systems can conflict with other embedded moral values; for example, privacy often conflicts with free speech. Non-moral values can conflict with moral values; developing a safe system requires time and money. And, non-moral values can conflict; reliability undermines efficiency and cost effectiveness. This leads to three problems that come from different value conflicts within Socio Technical Systems and between these systems and the technologies that are being integrated into them.
- Mismatches often arise between the values embedded in technologies and the Socio Technical Systems into which they are being integrated. As UNIX was integrated into the University of California Academic Computing STS (see Machado case at Computing Cases), the values of openness and transparency designed into UNIX clashed with the needs of students in the Academic Computing STS at UCI for privacy.

- Technologies being integrated into Socio Technical Systems can magnify, exaggerate, or exacerbate existing value mismatches in the STS. The use of P2P software combined with the ease of digital copying has magnified existing conflicts concerning music and picture copyrights.
- Integrating technologies into STSs produces both immediate and remote consequences and impacts.

## 3. Socio-technical systems change

- These changes are bought about, in part, by the value mismatches described above. At other times, they result from competing needs and interests brought forth by different stakeholders. For example, bicycle designs, the configuration of typewriter keys, and the design and uses of cellular phones have changed as different users have adapted these technologies to their special requirements.
- These changes also exhibit what sociologists call a "trajectory", that is, a path of development. Trajectories themselves are subject to normative analysis. For example, some STSs and the technologies integrated into them display a line of development where the STS and the integrated technology are changed and redesigned to support certain social interests. The informating capacities of computing systems, for example, provide information which can be used to improve a manufacturing processes can or to monitor workers for enhancing management power. (See Shoshanna Zuboff, **The Age of the Smart Machine**
- Trajectories, thus, outline the development of STSs and technologies as these are influenced by internal and external social forces.

In this section, you will learn about this module's exercises. The required links above provide information on the frameworks used in each section. For example, the Socio-Technical System module provides background information on socio-technical analysis. The "Three Frameworks" module provides a further description of the ethics tests, their pitfalls, and the feasibility test. These exercises will provide step by step instructions on how to work through the decision points presented above.

**For more information see Huff and Jawer below.**

**Decision Point One:**

You are the publicist for the company Biomatrix, a manufacturer of biotechnology products including Synvisc, a promising treatment for osteoarthritis. The CEO, Endre Balazs, and Vice President, Janet Denlinger, come to you. It seems that they are quite upset. Biomatrix and its top level employees have become the victims of cyber-smear. Dozens of messages have appeared in the highly visible Yahoo Financial Bulletin Board that make the following unsubstantiated accusations:

- Synvisc (a product manufactured by Biomatrix) produces seriously harmful side effects
- Biomatrix has deceived its stockholders by suppressing negative financial and product information
- Biomatrix and its employees have connections to the mafia
- Company public releases that the merger between Biomatrix and Genzyme is friendly are false. In fact, the messages allege that the merger will never take place because of Biomatrix's terrible financial profile
- Biomatrix CEO is under investigation by famous Nazi hunter, Simon Wiesenthal, for crimes he allegedly committed in Germany during the Second World War
- Biomatrix Vice President requires sexual favors from employees under her supervision as a condition for promotion

None of these charges is true. But Balazas and Denlinger are devastated by the personal attacks made upon them. Biomatrix also stands to lose a great deal from the negative publicity. Allegations of side effects from using Synvisc, a promising new produce patented by the company, threaten to drive the product out of the market. The recently announced friendly merger between Biomatrix and Genzyme has produced modest gains in stock prices but the cyber slanderers seem determined to drive Biomatrix stock value down.

**You have been charged by Balazs and Denlinger, as publicist, with designing a rapid and effective campaign against this cyber-smear. Several issues have arisen that demand your immediate attention:**

1. The identity of the cyber-slanderers is unknown. What can you do, if anything, to find out who these individuals are?

2. One of the slanderers claims to have worked for Biomatrix in the past. He/she uses this to lend credence to the attacks made on the company and its managers. If true, is there anything that can be done to prevent future employees from resorting to slander as a way of retaliating against the company?

3. If the real identities of the individuals posting the Yahoo messages are revealed, should they be sued? What are the advantages of defamation lawsuits if those sued do not have the financial resources to compensate the victim for damages suffered?

4. Should the cyber-slanderers be attacked? If so, how? How, in general, should corporations and their managers respond to cyber-slander? By publicly refuting the messages? By ignoring these attacks? By ignoring them until they produce clear damage? Or by responding quickly and proactively before they produce damage?

### Decision Point Two: Defending Against Defamation:

The cat is out of the bag. The BXM Police, those self-styled whistle-blowers against the corporate greed of Biomatrix, have been revealed as Richard and Raymond Costanzo and Ephraim Morris. (Richard Costanzo and Ephraim Morris were former Biomatrix employees.) These are the real world names behind the 23 pseudonyms under which 16,000 anti-Biomatrix emails were posted on the Financial Bulletin Board of Yahoo between April 1999 and August 2000. These messages accused Biomatrix managers of sexual harassment and Nazi war crimes and Biomatrix of corporate greed.

**Biomatrix managers feel that the company has a problem if its former employees find the motivation to behave in this manner. You are a human resource official in the Biomatrix and it has fallen on you to design a strategy and program to prevent a reoccurrence of this cyber-smear disaster. What should you do?**

- Bring a defamatory lawsuit against the three? Would this help to recoup damages? What other benefits could a successful defamation lawsuit bring? What would be the downside of such an action?

- Alter the way in which employees are let go. (In other words develop procedures for firing or laying off employees that would defuse the desire to get even.) What could be done to sever a relation with an employee in as good a fashion as possible?

- What steps could be taken to reduce the possibility of a former employee taking a "short selling" strategy? For example, could steps be taken to restrict the ways in which former employees use the confidential information they have about the company? Could risk identification measures be taken to uncover those who could or are benefiting from short selling a company's stock?

- Could Human Resources develop an effective program to counter cyber smear by effective communication of true and accurate information? How can a good reputation be established that could serve as a basis for counter-acting defamation?

- In short, design a strategy for Biomatrix that could minimize the risk of future cyber-smear attacks and/or minimize the impact of these attacks. Defend your strategy in the Ethics Bowl debate.

### Decision Point Three: How far does free speech go?

You work with a public service organization devoted to the defense of free speech, both off and online. For this reason you immediately noticed a newspaper story that three individuals, Richard Costanzo, Raymond Costanzo, and Ephraim Morris, were found guilty in a summary judgment of defamation. It seems they published, under 23 psuedonyms, some 16,000 messages that made negative claims against Biomatrix and its managers that they were unable to substantiate.

**The claims made by these individuals in their emails were pretty strong:**

- Biomatrix's most popular product, Synvisc, has produced significant harmful side effects and the company has taken wrongful measures to suppress this information. Synvisc is a manufactured substance that resembles the natural fluids that lubricate knee movements. These fluids disappear with age producing a condition called osteoarthritis. Synvisc has been presented as a highly promising treatment for this problem.

- They also accuse Biomatrix of covering up that fact that they are targets of potentially damaging lawsuits.
- These three individuals, who style themselves the BXM Police, also accuse the company of covering up negative, harmful information about their upcoming merger with Genzyme. The messages claim that inside information reveals that the merger will never take place.
- The BXM police also accuse Biomatrix top management of having committed war crimes and acts of sexual harassment.

During pre-trial depositions, the accused were unable to substantiate any of these claims. While the motives for posting these messages have never been made clear three stand out: revenge, short selling, and the perception that rules of defamation did not apply in cyber space. You have been asked by your organization to contact the BXM Police and propose that they appeal this decision. You and your organization think that there are strong legal and ethical arguments, based on the right to free speech, that need to be put forth in this case. Your job in this decision point is to set forth these legal and moral arguments. In other words, construct a comprehensive defense for the BXM Police.

**Important Considerations**

- EPIC (Electric Privacy Information Center) and the ACLU (American Civil Liberties Union) present an amici curiae (friend of the court brief) outlining their concerns about the use of John Doe lawsuits to pierce online anonymity. This brief is summarized in the Biomatrix case materials.
- Perhaps the strongest case for Free Speech is made by John Stuart Mill in On Liberty. Consult this book and find his argument in the first chapter. The summary of this argument in the Biomatrix case materials will help. Do defamation lawsuits suppress free speech. Why does Mill think that it is wrong to suppress even completely false speech?
- Did Biomatrix and its management team suffer damages as a result of the Yahoo messages? What is this damage? What evidence proves that the damage was caused by the negative speech and not something else? Who bore the burden of proof in the summary judgment against the BXM Police?
- What is the strongest argument that Biomatrix made against the speech of the BXM three? How can you and organization counter this argument?
- The strongest argument the BXM Police offer for their actions is that they are not bound by rules of veracity and defamation while operating pseudonymously online. Should we be held responsible for what we say online? In the same way that we are held responsible off line? Doesn't Yahoo's disclaimer to readers that they should not assume that what they read is true suffice to exculpate those who post false speech?
- It has been suggested that the BXM Police were motivated by greed. Their speech was designed to lower the price of Biomatrix stock so they could profit from short selling it. Does this change you defense? There is also inconclusive evidence that they were not acting alone? Does this change your defense?

## 5.1.3 What you will do ...

In this section, you will learn about this module's exercises. The required links above provide information on the frameworks used in each section. For example, the Socio-Technical System module provides background information on socio-technical analysis. The "Three Frameworks" module provides a further description of the ethics tests, their pitfalls, and the feasibility test. These exercises will provide step by step instructions on how to work through the decision points presented above.

## 5.1.4 Exercise One: Problem Specification

In this exercise, you will specify the problem using socio-technical analysis. The STS section of the Biomatrix Case narrative (found at Computing Cases) provides a good starting point. In the first table, enter the information from the Biomatrix case materials pertinent to the general components of a STS, its hardware, software, physical surroundings, people/groups/roles, procedures, laws, data. Some examples taken from the STS description at Computing Cases are provided to get you started. Then, using the second table, identify the values that are embedded in the different components of the STS. For example, PICS (platforms for internet content selection) embody the values of security and privacy. Finally, using the data from your socio-technical analysis, formulate a concise problem statement.

**Exercise 1a:**

Read the socio-technical system analysis of the Biomatrix case at http://computingcases.org. Fill in the table below with elements from this analysis that pertain to your decision point.

### Socio-Technical System Table

| Hardware | Software | Physical Surroundings | People/Groups/Roles | Procedures | Laws, Codes, Regulations | Data and Data Structures |
|---|---|---|---|---|---|---|
| Plant manufacturing Synvisc | Yahoo software | cyber vs real space | Biomatrix, Genzyme, Yahoo | Getting a Yahoo account | John Doe Lawsuits | OSP user information |

**Table 5.2**

**Instructions for Table 1:**

1. Go to http://computingcases.org and review the STS description provided for the Biomatrix case.
2. Pull out the elements of the STS description that are relevant to your decision point. List them under the appropriate STS component in the above table.
3. Think about possible ways in which these components of the Biomatrix STS interact. For example, what kinds of legal restrictions govern the way data is collected, stored, and disseminated?
4. Develop your STS table with an eye to documenting possible ethical conflicts that can arise and are relevant to your decision point.

**Exercise 1b**

Examine the values embedded in the STS surrounding this decision point. Locate your values under the appropriate component in the Biomatrix STS. For example, according to the STS description for Biomatrix found at Computing Cases, the Yahoo software that structures the architecture of the bulletin boards embody certain values like free speech. Should this be changed given the threat of defamation? What are Yahoo responsibilities in the context of defamation?

### Value Table

| Hardware | Software | Physical Surroundings | People/Groups/Roles | Procedures | Laws/Codes/Regulations | Data/Data Structures |
|---|---|---|---|---|---|---|
| Security | | | | | | |
| Privacy | | | | | | |
| *continued on next page* | | | | | | |

| Property | | | | | | |
|---|---|---|---|---|---|---|
| Justice (Equity/Access) | | | | | | |
| Free Speecy | | | | | | |

Table 5.3

**Instructions for Table 2:**

1. This module links to another Connexions module, Socio-Technical Systems in Professional Decision-Making. There you will find short profiles of the values listed in the above table: security, privacy, property, justice, and free speech. These profiles will help you to characterize the values listed in the above table.
2. Look for value conflicts or mismatches. For example, free speech in the Yahoo discussion space could conflict with laws that protect against defamation. How are these laws transferred online?
3. Identify those components of the Biomatrix STS that embody or embed value. For example, list the values realized and frustrated by the software components discussed in the Biomatrix case in the STS description.
4. Look for ways in which different elements of the STS that embed value can interact and produce value conflicts. These conflicts are likely sources for problems that you should discuss in your problem statement and address in your solution.

**Exercise 1c:**

Write out the requirements (ethical and practical) for a good solution. Identify the parts of the STS that need changing. Then, develop a concise summary statement of the central problem your decision point raises. As you design solutions to this problem, you may want to revise this problem statement. Be sure to experiment with different ways of framing this problem.
**Harris, Pritchard, and Rabins provide a useful approach to problem specification. See references below.**

## 5.1.5 Exercise Two: Solution Generation

**Generate solutions to the problem(s) you have specified in Exercise 1. This requires that...**

- each member of your group develop a list of solutions,
- the group combines these individual lists into a group list, and...
- the group reduces this preliminary list to a manageable number of refined and clarified solutions for testing in the next stage.

**Helpful Hints for Solution Generation**

**1. Solution generation requires proficiency in the skills of moral imagination and moral creativity.**
Moral imagination is the ability to open up avenues of solution by framing a problem in different ways. Toysmart could be framed as a technical problem requiring problem-solving skills that integrate ethical considerations into innovative designs. Moral creativity is the ability to formulate non-obvious solutions that integrate ethical considerations over various situational constraints.

**2. Problems can be formulated as interest conflicts. In this case different solution options are available.**

- **Gather Information.** Many disagreements can be resolved by gathering more information. Because this is the easiest and least painful way of reaching consensus, it is almost always best to start here.

Gathering information may not be possible because of different constraints: there may not be enough time, the facts may be too expensive to gather, or the information required goes beyond scientific or technical knowledge. Sometimes gathering more information does not solve the problem but allows for a new, more fruitful formulation of the problem. Harris, Pritchard, and Rabins in Engineering Ethics: Concepts and Cases show how solving a factual disagreement allows a more profound conceptual disagreement to emerge.

- **Nolo Contendere.** Nolo Contendere is latin for not opposing or contending. Your interests may conflict with your supervisor but he or she may be too powerful to reason with or oppose. So your only choice here is to give in to his or her interests. The problem with nolo contendere is that non-opposition is often taken as agreement. You may need to document (e.g., through memos) that you disagree with a course of action and that your choosing not to oppose does not indicate agreement.
- **Negotiate.** Good communication and diplomatic skills may make it possible to negotiate a solution that respects the different interests. Value integrative solutions are designed to integrate conflicting values. Compromises allow for partial realization of the conflicting interests. (See the module, **The Ethics of Team Work,** for compromise strategies such as logrolling or bridging.) Sometimes it may be necessary to set aside one's interests for the present with the understanding that these will be taken care of at a later time. This requires trust.
- **Oppose.** If nolo contendere and negotiation are not possible, then opposition may be necessary. Opposition requires marshalling evidence to document one's position persuasively and impartially. It makes use of strategies such as leading an "organizational charge" or "blowing the whistle." For more on whistle-blowing consult the discussion of whistle blowing in the Hughes case that can be found at computing cases.
- **Exit.** Opposition may not be possible if one lacks organizational power or documented evidence. Nolo contendere will not suffice if non-opposition implicates one in wrongdoing. Negotiation will not succeed without a necessary basis of trust or a serious value integrative solution. **As a last resort,** one may have to exit from the situation by asking for reassignment or resigning.

**3. Solutions can be generated by readjusting different components of the STS.**

- **Technical Puzzle.** If the problem is framed as a technical puzzle, then solutions would revolve around developing designs that optimize both ethical and technical specifications, that is, resolve the technical issues and realize ethical value. In this instance, the problem-solver must concentrate on the hardware and software components of the STS.
- **Social Problem.** If the problem is framed as a social problem, then solutions would revolve around changing laws or bringing about systemic reform through political action. This would lead one to focus on the people/groups/roles component (working to social practices) or the legal component.
- **Stakeholder Conflict.** If the problem is framed as a conflict between different stakeholder interests, then the solution would concentrate on getting stakeholders (both individuals and groups) to agree on integrative or interest compromising solutions. This requires concentrating on the people/group/role component of the STS. (Note: A stakeholder is any group or individual with a vital interest at play in the situation.)
- **Management Problem.** Finally, if the problem is framed as a management problem, then the solution would revolve around changing an organization's procedures. Along these lines, it would address the (1) fundamental goals, (2) decision recognition procedures, (3) organizational roles, or (4) decision-making hierarchy of the organization. These are the four components of the CID (corporate internal decision) structure described in the "Ethical Reflections" section of the Toysmart case.
- **Nota Bene:** Financial issues are covered by the feasibility test in the solution implementation stage. As such, they pose side issues or constraints that do not enter into the solution generation phase but the solution implementation phase.

**4. Brainstorming. Moral creativity, which involves designing non-obvious solutions, forms an essential part of solution generation. Here are some guidelines to get you started.**

- Individually make out a list of solutions before the group meeting. Work quickly to realize a pre-established quota of five to ten solutions. After composing a quick first draft, revise the list for clarity only; make no substantial changes.
- Start the group brainstorming process by having the group review and assemble all the individual solutions. Do this quickly and without criticism. Beginning criticism at this stage will kill the creativity necessary for brainstorming and shut down the more timid (but creative) members of the group.
- Review the list and identify solutions that are identical or overlap. Begin the refining process by combining these solutions.
- Having reviewed all the brainstormed solutions, it is now time to bring in criticism. Begin by eliminating solutions with major ethical problems such as those that violate rights, produce injustices, or cause extensive harm.
- Identify but do not eliminate solutions that are ethical but raise serious practical problems. Do not initially eliminate an ethical solution because there are obstacles standing in the way of its implementation. Be descriptive. Identify and impartially describe the obstacles. Later, in the solution implementation stage, you may be able to design creative responses to these obstacles.
- Identify solutions that do not "fit" your problem statement. These require a decision. You can throw out the solution because it does not solve the problem or you can change the problem. If a solution does not fit the problem but, intuitively, seems good, this is a sign that you need to take another look at your problem statement.
- Don't automatically reject partial solutions. For example, sending memos through email rather than printing them out and wasting paper may not solve the entire recycling problem for your company. But it represents a good, partial solution that can be combined with other partial solutions to address the bigger problem.
- Through these different measures, you will gradually integrate criticism into your brainstorming process. This will facilitate working toward a manageable, refined list of solutions for testing in the next stage.

### Exercise 3: Develop a Solution List

- Have each member of your team prepare a solution list and bring it to the next group meeting. Set a quota for this individual list, say, 5 to 10 solutions.
- Prepare a group list out of the lists of the individual members. Work to combine similar solutions. Be sure to set aside criticism until the preliminary group list is complete.
- Make use of the following table.
- Refine the group list into a manageable number of solutions for testing in the next stage. Combine overlapping solutions. Eliminate solutions that do not respond to the requirements and the problem statement that you prepared in the previous exercise. Eliminate solutions that violate important ethical considerations, i.e., solutions that violate rights, produce harms, etc.
- Check your refined solution list with your problem statement. If they do not match, eliminate the solution or redefine the problem

### Refined Brainstorm List

| Solution Ranking | Description of Solution | Justification (fits requirements, fits problem) |
| --- | --- | --- |
| Best Solution | | |
| Second Best Solution | | |
| Third Best Solution | | |
| Fourth Best Solution | | |
| Fifth Best Solution | | |

**Table 5.4**

**Anthony Weston provides an illuminating and useful discussion of creative problem solving in the reference provided below.**

## 5.1.6 Exercise Three: Solution Testing

In this section, you will test the solutions on the refined list your group produced in the previous exercise. Three ethics tests, described below, will help you to integrate ethical considerations in the problem-solving process. A global feasibility test will help to identify solutions with serious practical problems. Finally, a Solution Evaluation Matrix summarizes the results for class debriefings.

**Setting up for the test.**

- Identify the agent perspective from which the decision will be made
- Describe the action as concisely and clearly as possible.
- Identify the stakeholders surrounding the decision, i.e., those who will suffer strong impacts (positively or negatively) from the implementation of your decision. Stakeholders have a vital or essential interest (right, good, money, etc) in play with this decision.
- In the harm/beneficence test, identify the likely results of the action and sort these into harms and benefits.
- For the reversibility test, identify the stakeholders with whom you will reverse positions.
- For the public identification test, identify the values, virtues, or vices your action embodies. Associate these with the character of the agent.

**Harm/Beneficence Test**

1. **What are the harms your solution is likely to produce? What are its benefits? Does this solution produce the least harms and the most benefits when compared to the available alternatives?**
2. **Pitfall—Too much.** In this "Paralysis of Analysis" one factor in too many consequences. To avoid the fallacy restrict the analysis to the most likely consequences with the greatest magnitude (Magnitude indicates the range and severity of impact).
3. **Pitfall—Too Little.** A biased or incomplete analysis results when significant impacts are overlooked. Take time to uncover all the significant impacts, both in terms of likelihood and in terms of magnitude.
4. **Pitfall—Distribution of Impacts.** Consider, not only the overall balance of harms and benefits but also how harms and benefits are distributed among the stakeholders. If they are equally or fairly distributed, then this counts in the solution's favor. If they are unequally or unfairly distributed, then this counts against the solution. Be ready to redesign the solution to distribute better (=more equitably or fairly) the harmful and beneficial results.

**Reversibility Test**

1. **Would this solution alternative be acceptable to those who stand to be most affected by it? To answer this question, change places with those who are targeted by the action and ask if from this new perspective whether the action is still acceptable?**
2. **Pitfall—Too much.** When reversing with Hitler, a moral action appears immoral and an immoral action appears moral. The problem here is that the agent who projects into the immoral standpoint loses his or her moral bearings. The reversibility test requires viewing the action from the standpoint of its different targets. But understanding the action from different stakeholder views does not require that one abandon himself or herself to these views.
3. **Pitfall—Too little.** In this pitfall, moral imagination falls short, and the agent fails to view the action from another stakeholder standpoint. The key in the reversibility test is to find the middle ground between too much immersion in the viewpoint of another and too little.

4. **Pitfall—Reducing Reversibility to Harm/Beneficence.** The reversibility test requires that one assess the impacts of the action under consideration on others. But it is more than a simple listing of the consequences of the action. These are viewed from the standpoint of different stakeholders. The reversibility test also goes beyond considering impacts to considering whether the action treats different stakeholders respectfully. This especially holds when the agent disagrees with a stakeholder. In these disagreements, it is important to work out what it means to disagree with another respectfully.

5. **Pitfall—Incomplete survey of stakeholders.** Leaving out significant stakeholder perspectives skews the results of the reversibility test. Building an excellent death chamber works when one considers the action from the standpoint of Hitler; after all, it's what he wants. But treating an individual with respect does not require capitulating to his or her desires, especially when these are immoral. And considering the action from the standpoint of other stakeholders (say the possible victims of newer, more efficient gas chambers) brings out new and radically different information.

6. **Pitfall—Not Weighing and Balancing Stakeholder Positions.** This pitfall is continuous with the previous one. Different stakeholders have different interests and view events from unique perspectives. The reversibility test requires reviewing these interests and perspectives, weighing them against one another, and balancing out their differences and conflicts in an overall, global assessment.

### Publicity (or Public Identification) Test

1. **Would you want to be publicly associated or identified with this action? In other words, assume that you will be judged as a person by others in terms of the moral values expressed in the action under consideration. Does this accord with how you would want to or aspire to be judged?**

2. **Pitfall—Failure to association action with character of agent.** In the publicity test, the spotlight of analysis moves from the action to the agent. Successfully carrying out this test requires identifying the agent, describing the action, and associating the agent with the action. The moral qualities exhibited in the action are seen as expressing the moral character of the agent. The publicity test, thus, rests on the idea that an agent's responsible actions arise from and express his or her character.

3. **Pitfall—Failure to appreciate the moral color of the action.** The publicity test assumes that actions are colored by the ends or goods they pursue. This means that actions are morally colored. They can express responsibility or irresponsibility, courage or cowardice, reasonableness or unreasonableness, honesty or dishonesty, integrity or corruption, loyalty or betrayal, and so forth. An analysis can go astray by failing to bring out the moral quality (or qualities) that an action expresses.

4. **Pitfall—Reducing Publicity to Harm/Beneficence Test.** Instead of asking what the action says about the agent, many reduce this test to considering the consequences of publicizing the action. So one might argue that an action is wrong because it damages the reputation of the agent or some other stakeholder. But this doesn't go deep enough. The publicity test requires, not that one calculate the consequences of wide-spread knowledge of the action under consideration, but that one draws from the action the information it reveals about the character of the agent. The consequences of bad publicity are covered by the harm/beneficence test and do not need to be repeated in the public identification test. The publicity test provides new information by turning from the action to the agent. It focuses on what the action (its moral qualities and the goods it seeks) says about the agent.

### Comparing the Test Results: Meta-Tests

1. The ethics tests will not always converge on the same solution because each test (and the ethical theories it encapsulates) covers a different dimension of the action: (1) harm/beneficence looks at the outcomes or consequences of the action, (2) reversibility focuses on the formal characteristics of the action, and (3) publicity zeros in on the moral character of the agent.

2. The meta-tests turn this surface disagreement into an advantage. The convergence or divergence between the ethics tests become indicators of solution strength and weakness.

3. **Convergence.** When the ethics tests converge on a given solution, this indicates solution strength and robustness.

4. **Divergence.** When tests diverge on a solution—a solution does well under one test but poorly under another—this signifies that it needs further development and revision. Test divergence is not a sign that one test is relevant while the others are not. Divergence indicates solution weakness and is a call to modify the solution to make it stronger.

**Exercise 3: Summarize your results in a Solution Evaluation Matrix**

1. Place test results in the appropriate cell.
2. Add a verbal explanation to the SEM table.
3. Conclude with a global feasibility test that asks, simply, whether or not there exist significant obstacles to the implementation of the solution in the real world.
4. Finish by looking at how the tests converge on a given solution. Convergence indicates solution strength; divergence signals solution weakness.

**Solution Evaluation Matrix**

| Solution/Test | Harm/Beneficence | Reversibility | Publicity (public identification) | Feasibility |
|---|---|---|---|---|
| First Solution | | | | |
| Second Solution | | | | |
| Third Solution | | | | |
| Fourth Solution | | | | |
| Fifth Solution | | | | |

**Table 5.5**

**The ethics tests are discussed in Cruz and Davis. See references below. Wike and Brincat also discuss value based approaches in the two references below.**

## 5.1.7 Exercise Four: Solution Implementation

In this section, you will trouble-shoot the solution implementation process by uncovering and defusing potential obstacles. These can be identified by looking at the constraints that border the action. Although constraints specify limits to what can be realized in a given situation, they are more flexible than generally thought. Promptly identifying these constraints allows for proactive planning that can push back obstacles to solution implementation and allow for realization of at least some of the value embodied in the solution.

A **Feasibility Test** focuses on these situational constraints and poses useful questions early on in the implementation process. What conditions could arise that would hinder the implementation of a solution? Should the solution be modified to ease implementation under these constraints? Can the constraints be removed or modified through activities such as negotiation, compromise, or education? Can solution implementation be facilitated by modifying both the solution and the constraints?

**Feasibility Constraints**

| Category | Sub-Category | | |
|----------|--------------|--|--|
| | | | |
| Resource | Money/Cost | Time/Deadlines | Materials |
| Interest | Organizational(Supervisor) | Legal (laws, regulations) | Political/Social |
| Technical | Technology does not exist | Technology patented | Technology needs modification |

**Table 5.6**

## Resource Constraints:

- **Does the situation pose limits on resources that could limit the realization of the solution under consideration?**
- **Time.** Is there a deadline within which the solution has to be enacted? Is this deadline fixed or negotiable?
- **Financial.** Are there cost constraints on implementing the ethical solution? Can these be extended by raising more funds? Can they be extended by cutting existing costs? Can agents negotiate for more money for implementation?
- **Resource.** Are necessary resources available? Is it necessary to plan ahead to identify and procure resources? If key resources are not available, is it possible to substitute other, more available resources? Would any significant moral or non-moral value be lost in this substitution?

## Interest Constraints

- **Does the solution threaten stakeholder interests? Could it be perceived as so threatening to a stakeholder's interests that the stakeholder would oppose its implementation?**
- **Individual Interests.** Does the solution threaten the interests of supervisors? Would they take measures to block its realization? For example, a supervisor might perceive the solution as undermining his or her authority. Or, conflicting sub-group interests could generate opposition to the implementation of the solution even though it would promote broader organizational objectives.
- **Organizational Interests.** Does the solution go against an organization's SOPs (standard operating procedures), formal objectives, or informal objectives? Could acting on this solution disrupt organization power structures? (Perhaps it is necessary to enlist the support of an individual higher up in the organizational hierarchy in order to realize a solution that threatens a supervisor or a powerful sub-group.)
- **Legal Interests.** Are there laws, statutes, regulations, or common law traditions that oppose the implementation of the solution? Is it necessary to write an impact statement, develop a legal compliance plan, or receive regulatory approval in order to implement the solution?
- **Political/Social/Historical Constraints.** Would the solution threaten or appear to threaten the status of a political party? Could it generate social opposition by threatening or appearing to threaten the interests of a public action group such as an environmental group? Are there historical traditions that conflict with the values embedded in the solution?

## Technical Constraints

- **Technology does not yet exist.** Would the implementation of the solution require breaking new technological ground?
- **Technology Protected by Patent.** The technology exists but is inaccessible because it is still under a patent held by a competitor.
- **Technology Requires Modification.** The technology required to implement solution exists but needs to be modified to fit the context of the solution. Important considerations to factor in would be the extent of the modification, its cost, and how long it would take to bring about the modification.

## 5.1.8 What did you learn?

This section provides closure to the module for students. It may consist of a formal conclusion that summarizes the module and outlines its learning objectives. It could provide questions to help students debrief and reflect on what they have learned. Assessment forms (e.g., the "Muddiest Point" Form) could be used to evaluate the quality of the learning experience. In short, this section specifies the strategy for bringing the module to a close.

**In this module, you have...**

- studied a real world case that raised serious problems with intellectual property, privacy, security, and free speech. Working with these problems has helped you to develop a better "working" understanding of these key concepts,
- studied and practiced using four decision-making frameworks: (1) using socio-technical analysis to specify the problem in a complex, real world case, (2) practiced brainstorming techniques to develop and refine solutions that respond to your problem, (3) employed three ethics tests to integrate ethical considerations into your solutions and to test these solutions in terms of their ethics, and (4) applied a feasibility analysis to your solutions to identify and trouble-shoot obstacles to the implementation of your ethical solution,
- explored the analogy between solving ethical and design problems,
- practiced the skills of moral imagination, moral creativity, reasonableness, and perseverance, and...
- experienced, through key participant perspectives, the challenges of ethics advocacy "under the gun."

**Debrief on your group work before the rest of the class**

1. Provide a concise statement and justification of the problem your group specified
2. Present the refined solution generation list your group developed in exercise 2.
3. Present and provide a quick summary explanation of the results of your group's solution evaluation matrix.
4. Show your group's feasibility matrix and summarize your assessment of the feasibility of implementing the solution alternatives you tested in exercise three.

**Group Debriefing**

1. Were there any problem you group had working together to carry out this case analysis? What were the problems and how did you go about solving them?
2. What problems did you have with understanding and practicing the four frameworks for solving problems? How did you go about solving these problems? Does your group have any outstanding questions or doubts?
3. Now that you have heard the other groups present their results, what differences emerged between your group's analysis and those of the other groups? Have you modified your analysis in light of the analyses of the other groups? If so how? Do the other groups need to take into account any aspects of your group's debriefing?

## 5.1.9 Appendix

This optional section contains additional or supplementary information related to this module. It could include: assessment, background such as supporting ethical theories and frameworks, technical information, discipline specific information, and references or links.

**References**

1. More references on the Biomatrix case (in addition to the links provided above) will be added at a later date.

2. Brincat, Cynthia A. and Wike, Victoria S. (2000) Morality and the Professional Life: Values at Work. Upper Saddle River, NJ: Prentice Hall.

3. Cruz, J. A., Frey, W. J. (2003) An Effective Strategy for Integration Ethics Across the Curriculum in Engineering: An ABET 2000 Challenge, **Science and Engineering Ethics**, 9(4): 543-568.

4. Davis, M., **Ethics and the University**, Routledge, London and New York, 1999: 166-167.

5. Richard T. De George, "Ethical Responsibilities of Engineers in Large Organizations: The Pinto Case," in Ethical Issues in Engineering, ed. Deborah G. Johnson (1991) New Jersey: Prentice-Hall: 175-186.

6. Charles Harris, Michael Pritchard and Michael Rabins (2005) **Engineering Ethics: Concepts and Cases**, 3rd Ed. Belmont, CA: Thomson/Wadsworth: 203-206.

7. Huff, Chuck and Jawer, Bruce, "Toward a Design Ethics for Computing Professionals in Social Issues in **Computing: Putting Computing in its Place**, Huff, Chuck and Finholt, Thomas Eds. (1994) New York: McGraw-Hill, Inc.

8. Solomon, Robert C. (1999) **A Better Way to Think About Business: How Personal Intgrity Leads to Corporate Success**. Oxford, UK: Oxford University Press.

9. Anthony Weston. (2001) **A Practical Companion to Ethics**, 2nd ed. USA: Oxford University Press, 2001, Chapter 3.

10. Carolyn Whitbeck (1998) **Ethics in Engineering Practice and Research**. U.K. Cambridge University Press: 55-72 and 176-181.

11. Wike, Victoria S. (2001) "Professional Engineering Ethics Bahavior: A Values-based Approach," **Proceedings of the 2001 American Society for Engineering Education Annual Conference and Exposition, Session 2461**.

## 5.1.10 EAC ToolKit Project

**5.1.10.1 This module is a WORK-IN-PROGRESS; the author(s) may update the content as needed. Others are welcome to use this module or create a new derived module. You can COLLABORATE to improve this module by providing suggestions and/or feedback on your experiences with this module.**

Please see the Creative Commons License[2] regarding permission to reuse this material.

**5.1.10.2 Funded by the National Science Foundation: "Collaborative Development of Ethics Across the Curriculum Resources and Sharing of Best Practices," NSF-SES-0551779**

# 5.2 Gray Matters for the Hughes Aircraft Case[3]

## 5.2.1 Introduction

**I. Introduction**

The Hughes Aircraft Case involves a group of employees in charge of testing chips for weapons systems. Because of the lengthy testing procedure required by the U.S. Defense Department, Hughes soon fell behind schedule in delivering chips to customers. To get chips out faster, some Hughes middle level managers began to put pressure on employees to pass chips that had failed tests or to pass them without testing. The scenarios below consist of narratives that stop at the point of decision. Your job is to complete the narrative by making a decision. Alternatives are provided to get the process started, but you may find it necessary to design your own solution. Ethics and feasibility tests help you to evaluate these alternatives and even design new ones more to your liking. This format superficially resembles the Gray Matters exercise used at Boeing Corporation. (More information on the history of Gray Matters can be found by consulting

---

[2]http://creativecommons.org/licenses/by/2.0/
[3]This content is available online at <http://cnx.org/content/m14036/1.7/>.

Carolyn Whitbeck, Ethics in Engineering Practice, 1998, 176-182.) This version differs in being more open-ended and more oriented toward giving you the opportunity to practice using ethical theory (which has been encapsulated into ethics tests).

## 5.2.2 Directions

**II. Directions**

- Read the following scenarios and the accompanying solutions
- Evaluate the alternatives in terms of the tests described below.
- Choose the one you think best or design your own solution if you believe you can do better.
- Summarize your results by filling in the solution evaluation matrix that appears on the page following the scenario. Notice that the first column repeats the solution alternatives.
- Be prepared to present your matrix to the class. You will also provide the other groups in the class with a copy of your matrix for their ethics portfolios

**Scenario One: Responding to Organizational Pressure**

Frank Saia has worked at Hughes Aircraft for a long time. Now he is faced with the most difficult decisions of his career. He has been having problems in the environmental testing phase of his microchip manufacturing plant; the detailed nature of these tests has caused Hughes to be consistently late in delivering the chips to customers. Because of the time pressure to deliver chips, Saia has been working to make the production of chips more efficient without losing the quality of the product. Chips are manufactured and then tested, and this provides two places where the process can bottle up. Even though you might have a perfectly fine chip on the floor of the plant, it cannot be shipped without testing. And, since there are several thousand other chips waiting to be tested, it can sit in line for a long time. Saia has devised a method that allows testers to put the important chips, the "hot parts," ahead of the others without disrupting the flow and without losing the chips in the shuffle. He has also added a "gross leak" test that quickly tells if a chip in a sealed container is actually sealed or not. Adding this test early in the testing sequence allows environmental testing to avoid wasting time by quickly eliminating chips that would fail a more fine-grained leak test later in the sequence. Because environmental testing is still falling behind, Saia's supervisors and Hughes customers are getting angry and have begun to apply pressure. Karl Reismueller, the director of the Division of Microelectronics at Hughes, has given Saia's telephone number to several customers, whose own production lines were shut down awaiting the parts that Saia has had trouble delivering. His customers are now calling him directly to say "we're dying out here" for need of parts. Frank Saia has discovered that an employee under his supervision, Donald LaRue, has been skipping tests on the computer chips. Since LaRue began this practice, they have certainly been more on time in their shipments. Besides, both LaRue and Saia know that many of the "hot" parts are actually for systems in the testing phase, rather than for ones that will be put into active use. So testing the chips for long-term durability that go into these systems seems unnecessary. Still, LaRue was caught by Quality Control skipping a test, and now Saia needs to make a decision. Upper management has provided no guidance; they simply told him to "handle it" and to keep the parts on time. He can't let LaRue continue skipping tests, or at least he shouldn't let this skipping go unsupervised. LaRue is a good employee, but he doesn't have the science background to know which tests would do the least damage if they were skipped. He could work with LaRue and help him figure out the best tests to skip so the least harm is done. But getting directly involved in skipping the tests would mean violating company policy and federal law.

**Alternatives**

1. Do nothing. LaRue has started skipping tests on his own initiative. If any problems arise, then LaRue will have to take responsibility, not Saia, because LaRue was acting independently of and even against Saia's orders.
2. Call LaRue in and tell him to stop skipping tests immediately. Then call the customers and explain that the parts cannot be shipped until the tests are carried out.
3. Consult with LaRue and identify non essential chips or chips that will not be used in systems critical to safety. Skipping tests on these chips will do the least damage.

4. Your solution....

## Scenario Two: Responding to Wrongdoing

Margaret Gooderal works in a supervisory position in the environmental testing group at Hughes Aircraft. Her supervisor, Donald LaRue, is also the current supervisor for environmental testing. The group that LaRue and Gooderal together oversee test the chips that Hughes makes in order to determine that they would survive under the drastic environmental conditions they will likely face. Rigorous testing of the chips is the ideal, but some chips (the hot chips) get in line ahead of others. Gooderal has found out that over the last several months, many of these tests are being skipped. The reason: Hughes has fallen behind in the production schedule and Hughes upper management and Hughes customers have been applying pressure to get chip production and testing back on schedule. Moreover, LaRue and others feel that skipping certain tests doesn't matter, since many of these chips are being used in systems that are in the testing phase, rather than ones that will be put into active use. A few months after Margaret Gooderal started her new position, she was presented with a difficult problem. One of the "girls" (the women and men in Environmental Testing at Hughes), Lisa Lightner, came to her desk crying. She was in tears and trembling because Donald LaRue had forcefully insisted that she pass a chip that she was sure had failed the test she was running. Lightner ran the hermeticity test on the chips. The chips are enclosed in a metal container, and one of the questions is whether the seal to that container leaks. From her test, she is sure that the chip is a "leaker"—the seal is not airtight so that water and corrosion will seep in over time and damage the chip. She has come to Gooderal for advice. Should she do what LaRue wants and pass a chip she knows is a leaker?

### Alternatives

1. Gooderal should advise Lightner to go along with LaRue. He is her supervisor. If he orders to pass the chip, then she should do so.
2. Gooderal should go to Human Resources with Lightner and file a harassment complaint against LaRue. Skipping tests is clearly illegal and ordering an employee to commit an illegal act is harassment.
3. Gooderal and Lightner should blow the whistle. They should go to the U.S. defense department and inform them of the fact that Hughes Aircraft is delivering chips that have either failed tests or have not been tested.
4. Your solution....

## Scenario 3: Goodearl, Ibarra, and the AMRAAM Incident

Now that Goodearl had few sympathizers among upper management, she increasingly turned to Ruth Ibarra in Quality assurance for support in her concerns about test skipping and the falsification of paperwork. One day, Goodearl noticed that some AMRAAM chips with leak stickers were left on her project desk in the environmental testing area. The leak stickers meant that the seal on the chips' supposedly airtight enclosure had failed a test to see if they leaked. AMRAAM meant that the chips were destined to be a part of an Advanced Medium Range Air-to-Air Missile. Goodearl knew that these parts could not be retested and needed to be simply thrown away. So why was someone keeping them? She also knew that these were officially "hot parts" and that the company was behind schedule in shipping these parts. After consulting with Ruth Ibarra, the two of them decided to do some sleuthing. They took the chips and their lot travelers to a photocopy machine and made copies of the travelers with "failed" noted on the leak test. They then replaced the chips and their travelers on the desk. Later that day, as Don LaRue passed the desk, Goodearl asked Don LaRue if he knew anything about the chips. "None of your business," he replied. The chips disappeared, and later the travelers showed up in company files with the "failed" altered to "passed." So, Goodearl and Ibarra had clear evidence (in their photocopy of the "failed" on the traveler) that someone was passing off failed chips to their customers. And these were important chips, part of the guidance system of an air-to-air missile.

### Alternatives: Since they have clear evidence, Gooderal and Ibarra should blow the whistle. Evaluate each of the following ways in which they could blow the whistle

1. Blow the whistle to Hughes' Board of Directors. In this way they can stop the test skipping but will also be able to keep the whole affair "in house."

2. Blow the whistle to the local news media. In this way they will shame Hughes into compliance with the testing requirements.

3. Take the evidence to the U.S. Department of Defense, since they are the client and are being negatively impacted by Hughes' illegal actions.

4. Some other mode of blowing the whistle....

### Solution Evaluation Matrix

| Alternatives/Tests | Reversibility/Rights Test | Harm/Benefits Test | Virtue/Value Test (Also Publicity) | Global Feasibility Test (Implementation Obstacles) |
|---|---|---|---|---|
| **Alternative One (Worst Alternative)** | Evaluate Alt 1 using reversibility/rights test | | | |
| **Alternative Two (Best among those given)** | | Weigh harms against benefits for alt 2 | | |
| **Alternative Three** | | | What values/disvalues are realized in alt 3? | |
| **Your Solution** | | | | What obstacles could hinder implementation of solution? |

**Table 5.7**

## 5.2.3 Ethics Tests: Set Up and Pitfalls

### III. Solution Evaluation Tests

- REVERSIBILITY: Would I think this is a good choice if I were among those affected by it?
- PUBILICITY: Would I want to be publicly associated with this action through, say, its publication in the newspaper?
- HARM/BENEFICENCE: Does this action do less harm than any of the available alternatives?
- FEASIBILITY: Can this solution be implemented given time, technical, economic, legal, and political constraints?

### Harm Test Set-Up

- Identify the agent (=the person who will perform the action). Describe the action (=what the agent is about to do).
- Identify the stakeholders (individuals who have a vital interest at risk) and their stakes.
- Identify, sort out, and weight the expected results or consequences.

### Harm Test Pitfalls

- Paralysis of Action–considering too many consequences.
- Incomplete analysis–considering too few results.

- Failure to weigh harms against benefits.
- Failure to compare different alternatives.
- Justice failures–ignoring the fairness of the distribution of harms and benefits.

## Reversibility Test Set-Up

- Identify the agent
- Describe the action
- Identify the stakeholders and their stakes
- Use the stakeholder analysis to select the relations to be reversed.
- Reverse roles between the agent (you) and each stakeholder: put them in your place (as the agent) and yourself in their place (as the target of the action
- If you were in their place, would you still find the action acceptable?

## Reversibility Pitfalls

- Leaving out a key stakeholder relation.
- Failing to recognize and address conflicts between stakeholders and their conflicting stakes.
- Confusing treating others with respect with capitulating to their demands (Reversing with Hitler).
- Failing to reach closure, i.e., an overall global reversal assessment that takes into account all the stakeholders the agent has reversed with.

## Public Identification Set-Up

- Set up the analysis by identifying the agent, describing the action under consideration, and listing the key values or virtues at play in the situation.
- Associate the action with the agent.
- Identify what the action says about the agent as a person. Does it reveal him or her as someone associated with a virtue/value or a vice?

## Public Identification Pitfalls

1. Action is not associated with the agent. The most common pitfall is failure to associate the agent and the action. The action may have bad consequences and it may treat individuals with disrespect but these points are not as important in the context of this test as what they imply about the agent as a person who deliberately performs such an action.
2. Failure to specify the moral quality, virtue, or value of the action that is imputed to the agent in the test. To say, for example, that willfully harming the public is bad fails to zero in on precisely what moral quality this attributes to the agent. Does it render him or her unjust, irresponsible, corrupt, dishonest, or unreasonable?

### Gray Matters in Hughes Exercises

This is an unsupported media type. To view, please see
http://cnx.org/content/m14036/latest/GM_Hughes_V2.doc

**Figure 5.2:** These exercises present three decision points from Hughes, solution alternatives, summaries of ethics and feasibility tests, and a solution evaluation matrix. Carry out the exercise by filling in the solution evaluation matrix.

This timeline is taken from the Computing Cases website developed and maintained by Dr. Charles Huff at St. Olaf College. Computing Cases is funded by the National Science Foundation, NSF DUE-9972280 and DUE 9980768.

## 5.2.4

**Time Line**

| 1979 | Ruth Ibarra beginsworking for Hughes Aircraft company's Microelectronic Circuit Division (Hughes MCD) in Newport Beach, CA |
|---|---|
| 1981 | Margaret Gooderal begins working for Hughes MCD as a supervisor for assembly on the hybrid production floor and as a supervisor in the hybrid engineering lab |
| 1984 | Ibarra becomes supervisor for hybrid quality assurance |
| 1985 | Goodearl asks Ibarra to look at errors in paperwork, Ibarra brings errors to the attention of her supervisors and was told to keep quiet. This begins time period where Goodearl/Ibarra become aware of problems in hybrid chip testing and paperwork. |
| 1986 | Goodearl becomes supervisor for seals processing in the environmental testing area. |
| 1986 | Faise Claims Act (31 U.S. C 3729-3733) becomes False Claims Reform Act of 1986 making it stronger and easier to apply. |
| Oct. 1986 | Goodearl/Ibarra report problems ot Hughes management, and, after the problems were not fixed, Goodearl/Ibarra reported the allegations of faulty testing to the United States Department of Defense. |
| Jan 9, 1987 | Earliest date that Hughes may have stopped neglecting environmental screening tests. |
| 1988 | Ibarra leaves Hughes feeling that her job had been stripped of all real responsibility. |
| March 1989 | Goodearl is laid off from Hughes. |
| 1995 | Goodearl and her husband are divorced. |

**Table 5.8**

**Civil Suit Timeline**

| 1990-1996 | United States of America, ex rel. Taxpayers Against Fraud, Ruth Aldred (was Ibarra), and Margaret Goodearl v. Hughes Aircraft Company, Inc. |
|---|---|
| | *continued on next page* |

*continued on next page*

| 1990 | Goodearl files wrongful discharge suit against Hughes and a number of individual managers, which was eventually dropped in favor of the civil suit. |
|---|---|
| May 29, 1990 | Thinking the government investigation was taking too much time, Goodearl/Aldred file civil suit against Hughes under False Claims Reform Act of 1986 with the help of Taxpayers Against Fraud and Washington law firm Phillips and Cohen. |
| December 1992 | Under provisions of the FCA, the U.S. Department of Justice Civil Division takes over the civil case. |
| Sep. 10, 1996 | Hughes found guilty in civil trial. Pays U.S. Government 4,050,00 dollars and each relator 891,000 dollars plus a separate payment of 450,000 dollars to cover attorney's fees, costs, and expenses. |

**Table 5.9**

**Criminal Suit Timeline**

| 1991-1993 | United States of America v. Hughes Aircraft Co., and Donald LaRue |
|---|---|
| December 13, 1991 | After a lengthy investigation, the U.S. Department of Defense charges Hughes and Donald A. LaRue with a 51-count indictment accusing it of falsifying tests of microelectronic circuits (criminal suit). |
| June 15, 1992 | Hughes found guilty of conspiring to defraud the U.S. Government in crminal case, co-defendent LaRUE acquitted following 4-week trial. Goodearl/Aldred called as witnesses in trial. Hughes appeals. |
| Oct. 29, 1992 | Hughes fined 3.5 million in criminal trial decision. |
| December 2, 1993 | Appellate court upholds 1992 criminal conviction and sentence. Hughes appeals. |

**Table 5.10**

**Hughes Socio Technical System**

| | Hardware/Software | Physical Surroundings | People, Roles, Structures | Procedures | Laws and Regulations | Data and Data Structures |
|---|---|---|---|---|---|---|
| Description | Hybrid Chips (circuitry hermetically sealed in metal or ceramic packages in inert gas atmosphere | Battle conditions under which chips might be used | Hughes Microelectric Circuit Division | Chip Testing: Temperature Cycle, Constant Acceleration, Mechanical Shock, Hermeticity (Fine and Gross Leak), P.I.N.D. | Legally Mandated Tests | Lot Travelors to document chips |
| | Analogue to Digital Conversion Chips | E-1000 at Hughes (Clean Room) | Department of Defense (Office of Inspector General) | Hughes Human Resources Procedures for Complaints | Whistle Blower Protection Legislation | |
| | Radar and Missile Guidance Systems | | Hughes Quality Control | Dissenting Professional Opinions | Qui Tam Lawsuit, Civil Suit, Criminal Suit | |
| | | | Individuals: Reismueller, Temple, Saia, LaRue, Goodearl, Ibarra/Aldren | | | |

**Table 5.11**

## 5.2.5 Blowing the Whistle

**Ethical Dissent**

1. Establish a clear technical foundation.
2. Keep your arguments on a high professional plane, as impersonal and objective as possible, avoiding extraneous issues and emotional outbursts.
3. Try to catch problems early, and keep the argument at the lowest managerial level possible.
4. Before going out on a limb, make sure that the issue is sufficiently important.
5. Use (and help estabish) organizational dispute resolution mechanisms.
6. Keep records and collect paper.
7. These items are taken from the IEEE website, link above.

**Before Going Public**

1. Make sure of your motivation.
2. Count your costs.
3. Obtain all the necessary background materials and evidence.
4. Organize to protect your own interests.
5. Choose the right avenue for your disclosure.
6. Make your disclosure in the right spirit.
7. These items come from the IEEE (see onlineethics link) and from the manuscript of **Good Computing** by Chuck Huff, William Frey, and Jose Cruz.

**Places to Go**

1. Government Agencies
2. Judicial Systems
3. Legislators
4. Advocacy Groups
5. News Media
6. In Puerto Rico, laws 14 and 426 have been passed to protect those who would blow the whistle on government corruption. The Oficina de Etica Gubernamental de Puerto Rico has a whistle blower's hotline. See link above.

**When to Blow the Whistle.**

1. Serious and Considerable Harm
2. Notification of immediate supervisor.
3. Exhaustion of internal channels of communication/appeal.
4. Documented Evidence.
5. Likelihood of successful resolution.

**References**

1. Richard T. De George, "Ethical Responsibilities of Engineers in Large Organizations: The Pinto Case," in **Ethical Issues in Engineering**, ed. Deborah G. Johnson (1991) New Jersey: Prentice-Hall: 175-186.
2. Carolyn Whitbeck (1998) Ethics in Engineering Practice and Research. U.K. Cambridge University Press: 55-72 and 176-181.
3. Charles Harris, Michael Pritchard and Michael Rabins (2005) Engineering Ethics: Concepts and Cases, 3rd Ed. Belmont, CA: Thomson/Wadsworth: 203-206.

# 5.3 Case Analysis Module: Therac-25[4]

Computer Ethics
    Case Module Template
    By William J. Frey
    Module Introduction:
    The Therac-25 case is what Huff and Frey call a thick, historical, evaluative, big news and bad news case. Tackling cases of this complexity requires both careful thought and considerable skill. Especially important is the ability to sift through the case details, documents, and conflicting narratives. The purpose of this module is to provide students with a structure to tackle big, long, and complicated cases. Students will receive frameworks to help them structure the case's ethical and social problems. They will also be provided with

---

[4]This content is available online at <http://cnx.org/content/m13765/1.1/>.

decision points that will help them to enter into the case and take up the standpoint of a participant. The module presented below can be linked to materials that can be found at www.computingcases.org. Nancy Leveson, in Safeware:System Safety and Computer (515-553), also provides an excellent and comprehensive account. Excellent advice on how to teach the case, updated information, and clear explanations of the programming errors are provided by Chuck Huff and Richard Brown in "Integrating Ethics into a Computing Curriculum: A Case Study of the Therac-25." The materials posted at Computing Cases were all developed through NSF projects DUE-9972280 and DUE 9980768.)

The module presents the case abstract and timeline. It then refers students to computingcases.org where they will find the case narrative, history, and supporting documents that provide background information necessary for analysis. The case abstract and timeline introduce students to the basic outlines of the case. The accompanying decision point taken from the case provides students with the necessary focus to carry out an in-depth analysis. Students respond to the decision-point by working through the four stages: problem specification, solution generation, solution testing, and solution implementation.

Module Activities:

1. Instructor introduces the case based on the abstract and timeline found at www.computingcases.org[5]

2. Students read case abstract, timeline, case decision point, and case analysis exercises.

3. Students do further research into the case by consulting ComputingCases materials which include narratives, histories, supporting documents, and ethical analyses.

4. Students carry out the activities outlined in the accompanying case exercises by (a) specifying the problem raised in the decision point, (b) generating solutions, (c) testing solutions using ethics tests, and (d) developing plans for implementing the solution over situational constraints.

5. Students prepare their case analyses working in small groups.

6. These groups present their completed analysis to the class in a case-debriefing session.

7. The instructor concludes by discussing the problem-solving issues and intermediate moral concepts raised by the case.

### 5.3.1 Therac-25 Abstract

Therac-25[6] was a new generation medical linear accelerator[7] for treating cancer. It incorporated the most recent computer control equipment. Therac-25's computerization made the laborious process of machine setup much easier for operators, and thus allowed them to spend minimal time in setting up the equipment. In addition to making setup easier, the computer also monitored the machine for safety. With the advent of computer control, hardware based safety mechanisms were transferred to the software. Hospitals were told that the Therac-25 medical linear accelerator had "so many safety mechanisms" that it was "virtually impossible" to overdose a patient. Normally, when a patient is scheduled to have radiation therapy for cancer, he or she is scheduled for several sessions over a few weeks and told to expect some minor skin discomfort from the treatment. The discomfort is described as being like a mild sunburn over the treated area. But in this case on safety critical software, you will find that some patients received much more radiation than prescribed

Therac -25 Timeline

---

[5]http://www.computingcases.org/

[6]http://www.computingcases.org/case_materials/therac/teaching/therac/supporting_docs/Therac%20Glossary.html#tr25

[7]http://www.computingcases.org/case_materials/therac/teaching/therac/supporting_docs/Therac%20Glossary.html#tr13

| | |
|---|---|
| Early1970's | AECL and a French Company (CGR) collaborate to build Medical Linear Accelerators (linacs). They develop Therac-6, and Therac-20. (AECL and CGR end their working relationship in 1981.) |
| 1976 | AECL developes the revolutionary "double pass" accelerator which leads to the development of Therac-25. |
| March, 1983 | AECL performs a safety analysis of Therac-25 which apparently excludes an analysis of software. |
| July 29,1983 | In a PR Newswire the Canadian Consulate General announces the introduction of the new "Therac 25" Machine manufactured by AECL Medical, a division of Atomic Energy of Canada Limited. |
| ca. Dec. 1984 | Marietta Georgia, Kennestone Regional Oncology Center implements the new Therac-25 machine. |
| June 3, 1985 | Marietta Georgia, Kennestone Regional Oncology CenterKatherine (Katy) Yarbrough, a 61-year-old woman is overdosed during a follow-up radiation treatment after removal of a malignant breast tumor. Tim Still, Kennestone Physicist calls AECL asking if overdose is possible; three days later he is informed it is not. |
| July 26, 1985 | Hamilton, Ontario, Canada. Frances Hill, a 40-year-old patient is overdosed during treatment for cervical carcinoma. AECL is informed of the injury and sends a service engineer to investigate. |
| | |
| November 3, 1985 | Hamilton Ontario patient dies of cancer, but it is noted on her autopsy that had she not died, a full hip replacement would have been necessary as a result of the radiation overdose. |
| November 8, 1985 | Letter from CRPB to AECL requesting additional hardware interlocks and changes in software. Letter also requested treatment terminated in the event of a malfunction with no option to proceed with single key-stroke. (under Canada's Radiation Emitting Devices Act.) |
| | |
| November 18, 1985 | Katy Yarbrough files suit against AECL and Kennestone Regional Oncology Center. AECL informed officially of Lawsuit. |
| December 1985 | Yakima Valley Memorial Hospital, Yakima Washington. A woman being treated with Therac-25 develops erythema on her hip after one of the treatments. |
| January 31, 1986 | Staff at Yakima sends letter to AECL and speak on the phone with AECL technical support supervisor. |
| February 24, 1986 | AECL technical support supervisor sends a written response to Yakima claiming that Therac-25 could not have been responsible for the injuries to the female patient. |

**Table 5.12**

Scenario: You are an engineer working for AECL sent to investigate an alleged overdosing incident at the Ontario Cancer Foundation in Hamilton. Ontario. The following is the description provided to you of what happened:

On July 26, 1985, a forty-year old patient came to the clinic for her twenty-fourth Therac-25 treatment for carcinoma of the cervix. The operator activated the machine, but the Therac shut down after five seconds with an HTILT error message. The Therac-25's console display read NO DOSE and indicated a TREATMENT PAUSE

Since the machine did not suspend and the control display indicated no dose was delivered to the patient, the operator went ahead with a second attempt at a treatment by pressing the Proceed Command Key, expecting the machine to deliver the proper dose this time. This was standard operating procedure, and Therac-25 operators had become accustomed to frequent malfunctions that had no untoward [bad] consequences for the patient. Again the machine shut down in the same manner. The operator repeated this process four times after the original attempt—the display showing NO DOSE delivered to the patient each time. After the fifth pause, the machine went into treatment suspend, and a hospital service technician was called. The technician found nothing wrong with the machine. According to a Therac-25 operator, this scenario also was not unusual.

After treatment, the patient complained of a burning sensation, described as an "electric tingling shock" to the treatment area in her hip....She came back for further treatment on July 29 and complained of burning, hip pain, and excessive swelling in the region of treatment. The patient was hospitalized for the condition on July 30, and the machine was taken out of service. (Description taken from Nancy Leveson, Safeware, pp 523-4)

You give the unit a thorough examination and are able to find nothing wrong. Working with the operator, you try to duplicate the treatment procedure of July 26. Nothing out of the ordinary happens. Your responsibility is to make a recommendation to AECL and to the Ontario Cancer Foundation. What will it be?

1. Identify key components of the STS

| Part/Level of Analysis | Hardware | Software | Physical Surroundings | People, Groups, & Roles | Procedures | Laws & Regulations | Data & Data Structures |
|---|---|---|---|---|---|---|---|
|  |  |  |  |  |  |  |  |
|  |  |  |  |  |  |  |  |
|  |  |  |  |  |  |  |  |

**Table 5.13**

2. Specify the problem:

2a. Is the problem a disagreement on facts? What are the facts? What are cost and time constraints on uncovering and communicating these facts?

2b. Is the problem a disagreement on a critical concept? What is the concept? Can agreement be reached by consulting legal or regulatory information on the concept? (For example, if the concept in question is safety, can disputants consult engineering codes, legal precedents, or ethical literature that helps provide consensus? Can disputants agree on positive and negative paradigm cases so the concept disagreement can be resolved through line-drawing methods?

2c. Use the table to identify and locate value conflicts within the STS. Can the problem be specified as a mismatch between a technology and the existing STS, a mismatch within the STS exacerbated by the introduction of the technology, or by overlooked results?

| STS/Value | Safety (freedom from harm) | Justice (Equity & Access) | Privacy | Property | Free Speech |
|---|---|---|---|---|---|
| Hardware/software | | | | | |
| Physical Surroundings | | | | | |
| People, Groups, & Roles | | | | | |
| Procedures | | | | | |
| Laws | | | | | |
| Data & Data Structures | | | | | |

**Table 5.14**

3. Develop a general solution strategy and then brainstorm specific solutions:

| Problem / Solution Strategy | Disagreement | | Value Conflict | | Situational Constraints |
|---|---|---|---|---|---|
| | Factual | Conceptual | Integrate? | Tradeoff? | Resource?Technical?Interest |

**Table 5.15**

3a. Is problem one of integrating values, resolving disagreements, or responding to situational constraints?

3b. If the conflict comes from a value mismatch, then can it be solved by modifying one or more of the components of the STS? Which one?

4. Test solutions:

| Alternative / Test | Reversibility | Value: Justice | Value: Responsibility | Value: Respect | Harm | Code |
|---|---|---|---|---|---|---|
| A #1 | | | | | | |
| A #2 | | | | | | |
| A #3 | | | | | | |

**Table 5.16**

5. Implement solution over feasibility constraints

| Alternative Constraint | Resource | Interest | Technical |
|---|---|---|---|
| | | *continued on next page* | |

*continued on next page*

|        | Time | Cost | Individual | Organization | Legal/ Social | Available Technology | Manufacturability |
|--------|------|------|------------|--------------|---------------|----------------------|-------------------|
| #1     |      |      |            |              |               |                      |                   |
| #2     |      |      |            |              |               |                      |                   |
| #3     |      |      |            |              |               |                      |                   |

**Table 5.17**

## 5.4 Toysmart Case Exercises - Student Module[8]

NOTE:  Write your module for a student audience.  To complete or edit the sections below erase the provided textual commentaries then add your own content using one or more of the following strategies:

```
    - Type or paste the content directly into the appropriate section

  - Link to a published CNX module or an external online resource
    using the ''Links'' tabs (see example on the right)

  - Link to a document or multimedia file within the content after
    uploading the file using the ''Files'' tab (see example below)

  - Cite content not available online
```

---

**Word Version of this Template**

---

This is an unsupported media type. To view, please see http://cnx.org/content/m14789/latest/ EAC TK STD TEMPLATE.doc

---

**Figure 5.3:** This is an example of an embedded link. (Go to "Files" tab to delete this file and replace it with your own files.)

---

### 5.4.1 Introduction

In this module you will study a real world ethical problem, the Toysmart case, and employ frameworks based on the software development cycle to (1) specify ethical and technical problems, (2) generate solutions that integrate ethical value, (3) test these solutions, and (4) implement them over situation-based constraints. This module will provide you with an opportunity to practice integrating ethical considerations into real

---

[8]This content is available online at <http://cnx.org/content/m14789/1.1/>.

world decision-making and problem-solving in business and computing. This whole approach is based on an analogy between ethics and design (Whitbeck).

Large real world cases like Toysmart pivot around crucial decision points. You will take on the role of one of the participants in the Toysmart case and problem-solve in teams from one of three decision points. Problem-solving in the real world requires perseverance, moral creativity, moral imagination, and reasonableness; one appropriates these skills through practice in different contexts. Designing and implementing solutions requires identifying conflicting values and interests, balancing them in creative and dynamic solutions, overcoming technical limits, and responding creatively to real world constraints.

Each decision point requires that you take up the position of a participant in the case and work through decision-making frameworks from his or her perspective. You may be tempted to back out and adopt an evaluative posture from which to judge the participants. Resist this temptation. This module is specifically designed to give you practice in making real world decisions. These skills emerge when you role play from one of the standpoints within the case. You will learn that decision-making requires taking stock of one's situation from within a clearly defined standpoint and then accepting responsibility for what arises from within that standpoint.

Cases such as Toysmart are challenging because of the large amount of information gathering and sorting they require. Moral imagination responds to this challenge by providing different framings that help to filter out irrelevant data and structure what remains. Framing plays a central role in problem specification. For example, Toysmart could be framed as the need to develop more effective software to help negotiate the exchange of information online. In this case, a software programming expert would be brought in to improve P3P programs. Or it could be framed as a legal problem that requires ammending the Bankruptcy Code. What is important at this stage is that you and your group experiment with multiple framings of the case around your decision point. This makes it possible to open up avenues of solution that would not be possible under one framing.

Tackling large cases in small teams also helps develop the communication and collaboration skills that are required for group work. Take time to develop strategies for dividing the work load among your team members. The trick is to distribute equally but, at the same time, to assign tasks according the different abilities of your team members. Some individuals are better at research while others excell in interviewing or writing. Also, make sure to set aside time when you finish for integrating your work with that of your teammates. Start by quickly reviewing the information available on the case. This is called "scoping the case." Then formulate specific questions to focus further research on information relevant to your problem solving efforts. This includes information pertinent to constructing a socio-technical analysis, identifying key "embedded" ethical issues, and uncovering existing best and worst practices.

A case narrative, STS (socio-technical system) description, and two ethical reflections have been published at http://computingcases.org. This module also links to websites on bankruptcy and privacy law, the Model Business Corporation Act, consumer privacy information, and the TRUSTe website.

## 5.4.2 What you need to know ...

### 5.4.2.1 What you need to know about socio-technical systems

**1. STS have seven broad components: hardware, software, physical surroundings, people/groups/roles, procedures, laws, and data/data structures.**

**2. Socio-technical systems embody values**

- These include moral values like safety, privacy, property, free speech, equity and access, and security. Non-moral values can also be realized in and through Socio Technical Systems such as efficiency, cost-effectiveness, control, sustainability, reliability, and stability.
- Moral values present in Socio Technical Systems can conflict with other embedded moral values; for example, privacy often conflicts with free speech. Non-moral values can conflict with moral values; developing a safe system requires time and money. And, non-moral values can conflict; reliability undermines efficiency and cost effectiveness. This leads to three problems that come from different

value conflicts within Socio Technical Systems and between these systems and the technologies that are being integrated into them.

- Mismatches often arise between the values embedded in technologies and the Socio Technical Systems into which they are being integrated. As UNIX was integrated into the University of California Academic Computing STS (see Machado case at Computing Cases), the values of openness and transparency designed into UNIX clashed with the needs of students in the Academic Computing STS at UCI for privacy.

- Technologies being integrated into Socio Technical Systems can magnify, exaggerate, or exacerbate existing value mismatches in the STS. The use of P2P software combined with the ease of digital copying has magnified existing conflicts concerning music and picture copyrights.

- Integrating technologies into STSs produces both immediate and remote consequences and impacts.

**3. Socio-technical systems change**

- These changes are bought about, in part, by the value mismatches described above. At other times, they result from competing needs and interests brought forth by different stakeholders. For example, bicycle designs, the configuration of typewriter keys, and the design and uses of cellular phones have changed as different users have adapted these technologies to their special requirements.

- These changes also exhibit what sociologists call a "trajectory", that is, a path of development. Trajectories themselves are subject to normative analysis. For example, some STSs and the technologies integrated into them display a line of development where the STS and the integrated technology are changed and redesigned to support certain social interests. The informating capacities of computing systems, for example, provide information which can be used to improve a manufacturing processes can or to monitor workers for enhancing management power. (See Shoshanna Zuboff, **The Age of the Smart Machine**

- Trajectories, thus, outline the development of STSs and technologies as these are influenced by internal and external social forces.

In this section, you will learn about this module's exercises. The required links above provide information on the frameworks used in each section. For example, the Socio-Technical System module provides background information on socio-technical analysis. The "Three Frameworks" module provides a further description of the ethics tests, their pitfalls, and the feasibility test. These exercises will provide step by step instructions on how to work through the decision points presented above.

**For more information see Huff and Jawer below.**

**Decision Point One:**

You are David Lord, a former employee of Holt Educational Outlet, a manufacturer of educational toys located in Waltham, Mass. Recently, you have joined with Stan Fung of Zero Stage Capital, a venture capital firm to buy out Holt Educational Outline. After changing its name to Toysmart, you and Fung plan to transform this brick and mortar manufacturer of educational toys into an online firm that will link customers to a vast catalogue of educational, high quality toys. Designing a website to draw in toy customers, linking to information on available toys, setting up a toy distribution and shipping system, and implementing features that allow for safe and secure online toy purchases will require considerable financing. But, riding the crest of the dot-com boom, you have two promising options. First, a venture capital firm has offered you $20,000,000 for website development, publicity, and other services. Second, Disney has offered the same amount for financing, but has added to it an additional $25,000,000 in advertising support. Disney has a formidable reputation in this market, a reputation which you can use to trampoline Toysmart into prominence in the growing market in educational toys. However, Disney also has a reputation of micro-managing its partners. Develop a plan for financing your new dot-com.

**Things to consider in your decision-making:**

1. What are Toysmart values? What are Disney values? Would Disney respect Toysmart's values?
2. What synergies could result from working with Disney? For example, could you share information on customers? You could feed your customer profiles to Disney in exchange for their customer profiles.

What kind of data managing technology would be required for this? What ethical problems could arise from transferring customer identifying information to third parties?

3. What kind of commitment would you be willing to make to Disney in terms of product and sales? How should Disney reciprocate? For example, how long should they stick with you through sales that fall short of projections?

## Decision Point Two:

You work for Blackstone, "an 18-person software business." You have been asked by Toysmart to provide software the following functions: (1) designing a webpage that would attract customers and communicate Toysmart Values, (2) advise Toysmart on its privacy and data security policy including whether to register with an online trust, security measures to protect customer data during online transactions, and measures to prevent unauthorized access to customer data while stored, and (3) a comprehensive online catalogue that would provide customers with access to educational toys from a variety of small busines manufacturers. An example of small toy manufacturers to which Toysmart should be linked is Brio Corporation which manufactures wooden toys such as blocks, trains, and trucks. Develop general recommendations for Toysmart around these three areas.

Information for this scenario comes from Laura Lorek, "When Toysmart Broke," http://www.zdnet.com/eweek/stories/general/0,1101,2612962,00.html. Accessed July 16, 2001.

### Things to consider in your decision-making

- Toysmart is a fairly new dot-com. While it is supported by Disney, it is still a risky venture. Should you ask them for advance payment for whatever services you render? What kind of policies does your company have for identifying and assessing financial risk?

- What kind of privacy and data security policy should you recommend to Toysmart? What kind of values come into conflict when a company like Toysmart develops and implements privacy and data security measures? (Use your STS description to answer this question.)

- Should Toysmart become bankrupt, their data base would turn into a valuable asset. What recommendations should you make to help Toysmart plan around this possibility? What values come into conflict when planning to dispose of assets during bankruptcy proceedings? What kind of obligations does a company take on during its operation that continue even after it has become bankrupt?

- Using the link provided with this module, visit the TRUSTe website and find its white paper on developing a privacy policy. Evaluate this privacy policy for Toysmart. What benefits can a strong privacy policy bring to a dot-com? Should Toysmart work to qualify to display the TRUSTe seal on its website? Examine TRUSTe procedures for transferring confidential customer PII to third parties? What obligations will this create? Would this over-constrain Toysmart?

## Decision Point Three:

You work for PAN Communications and have been providing advertising services for Toysmart. Now you find out that Toysmart has filed a Chapter 11 bankruptcy, and it has an outstanding debt to your company for $171,390. As a part of this filing procedure, Toysmart has reported its assets at $10,500,000 with debts of $29,000,000. Toysmart creditors, including PAN Communications, have petitioned the Office of the United States Trustee for a "Creditors' Committee Solicitation Form." This will allow for the formation of a committee composed of Toysmart creditors who decide on how the assets of the bankrupt firm will be distributed. You, because of your knowledge of bankruptcy and accounting procedures, have been asked to represent your company on this committee. This bleak situation is somewhat remedied by the customer data base that Toysmart compiled during its operation. It contains profiles of the PII (personal identifying information) of 260,000 individuals. Because selling educational toys is profitable, there is a good chance that this data base could be sold for up to $500 a profile to a third party. Should you recommend selling this data base? Should Toysmart customers be notified of the pending transfer of their PII and, if so, how should they be notified?

### Here are some constraints that outline your decision

- As a member of the Creditors' Committee, you have a fiduciary duty to Toysmart creditors in working to distribute fairly the remaining Toysmart assets. This would, all things being equal, lead to recommending selling the Toysmart customer data base
- There are some provisions in the bankruptcy code that may require or allow overriding fiduciary duties given prior legal commitments made by Toysmart. These commitments, in the form of strong privacy guarantees made to customers by Toysmart on its webpage, may constitute an "executory contract." See the Legal Trail table in the Toysmart case narrative and also Larren M. Nashelsky, "On-Line Privacy Collides With Bankruptcy Creditors," New York Law Journal, New York Law Publishing Company, August 28, 2000.
- Finally, Nashelsky makes an interesting argument. While deontological considerations would require setting aside creditor interests and honoring Toysmart privacy promises, a justice-based argument would recommend a compromise. Bankruptcy proceedings start from the fact that harm (financial) has been done. Consequently, the important justice consideration is to distribute fairly the harms involved among the harmed parties. Harm distributions are correlated with benefit distributions. Because Toysmart customers benefited from Toysmart offerings, they should also bear a share of the harms produced when the company goes bankrupt. This requires that they allow the distribution of their PII under certain conditions.

**Things to consider in your decision-making**

- How do you balance your obligations to PAN with those to other Toysmart creditors as a member of the Creditors' Committee?
- How should you approach the conflict between honoring Toysmart promises and carrying out Creditor Committee fiduciary duties? Do you agree with Nashelsky's argument characterized above?
- Should the Bankruptcy Code be changed to reflect issues such as these? Should privacy promises be considered an "executory contract" that overrides the duty to fairly and exhaustively distribute a company's assets?
- Finally, what do you think about the FTC's recommendation? The Bankruptcy Court's response? The final accommodation between Toysmart and Buena Vista Toy Company?

## 5.4.3 What you will do ...

In this section, you will learn about this module's exercises. The required links above provide information on the frameworks used in each section. For example, the Socio-Technical System module provides background information on socio-technical analysis. The "Three Frameworks" module provides a further description of the ethics tests, their pitfalls, and the feasibility test. These exercises will provide step by step instructions on how to work through the decision points presented above.

## 5.4.4 Exercise One: Problem Specification

In this exercise, you will specify the problem using socio-technical analysis. The STS section of the Toysmart Case narrative (found at Computing Cases) provides a good starting point. In the first table, enter the information from the Toysmart case materials pertinent to the general components of a STS, its hardware, software, physical surroundings, people/groups/roles, procedures, laws, data. Some examples taken from the STS description at Computing Cases are provided to get you started. Then, using the second table, identify the values that are embedded in the different components of the STS. For example, PICS (platforms for internet content selection) embody the values of security and privacy. Finally, using the data from your socio-technical analysis, formulate a concise problem statement.

**Exercise 1a:**

Read the socio-technical system analysis of the Toysmart case at http://computingcases.org. Fill in the table below with elements from this analysis that pertain to your decision point.

# Socio-Technical System Table

| Hardware | Software | Physical Surround-ings | People/Groups | Procedures | Laws, Codes, Regulations | Data and Data Struc-tures |
|---|---|---|---|---|---|---|
| Holt Educa-tion Outlet | Platforms for Internet Content Selection | Cyber Space | Toysmart the corpora-tion | Buying Toys Online | COPPA | Toysmart Customer Data Base |

**Table 5.18**

**Instructions for Table 1:**

1. Go to http://computingcases.org and review the STS description provided for the Toysmart case.
2. Pull out the elements of the STS description that are relevant to your decision point. List them under the appropriate STS component in the above table.
3. Think about possible ways in which these components of the Toysmart STS interact. For example, what kinds of legal restrictions govern the way data is collected, stored, and disseminated?
4. Develop your STS table with an eye to documenting possible ethical conflicts that can arise and are relevant to your decision point.

**Exercise 1b**

Examine the values embedded in the STS surrounding this decision point. Locate your values under the appropriate component in the Toysmart STS. For example, according to the STS description for Toysmart found at Computing Cases, the software programs prominent in this case embody certain values; SSLs embody security and privacy, P3P property, and PICS privacy. Next, look for areas where key values can come into conflict.

**Value Table**

| Hardware | Software | Physical Surround-ings | People/Groups | Procedures | Laws/Codes/Regulations | Data/Data Structures |
|---|---|---|---|---|---|---|
| Security | | | | | | |
| Privacy | | | | | | |
| Property | | | | | | |
| Justice (Eq-uity/Access) | | | | | | |
| Free Speecy | | | | | | |

**Table 5.19**

**Instructions for Table 2:**

1. This module links to another Connexions module, Socio-Technical Systems in Professional Decision-Making. There you will find short profiles of the values listed in the above table: security, privacy, property, justice, and free speech. These profiles will help you to characterize the values listed in the above table.
2. The second ethical reflection in the Toysmart case narrative (at Computing Cases) also contains a discussion of how property comes into conflict with privacy.
3. Identify those components of the Toysmart STS that embody or embed value. For example, list the values realized and frustrated by the software components discussed in the Toysmart case in the STS description.

4. Look for ways in which different elements of the STS that embed value can interact and produce value conflicts. These conflicts are likely sources for problems that you should discuss in your problem statement and address in your solution.

**Exercise 1c:**

Write out the requirements (ethical and practical) for a good solution. Identify the parts of the STS that need changing. Then, develop a concise summary statement of the central problem your decision point raises. As you design solutions to this problem, you may want to revise this problem statement. Be sure to experiment with different ways of framing this problem.

**Harris, Pritchard, and Rabins provide a useful approach to problem specification. See references below.**

## 5.4.5 Exercise Two: Solution Generation

**Generate solutions to the problem(s) you have specified in Exercise 1. This requires that...**

- each member of your group develop a list of solutions,
- the group combines these individual lists into a group list, and...
- the group reduces this preliminary list to a manageable number of refined and clarified solutions for testing in the next stage.

**Helpful Hints for Solution Generation**

**1. Solution generation requires proficiency in the skills of moral imagination and moral creativity.**

Moral imagination is the ability to open up avenues of solution by framing a problem in different ways. Toysmart could be framed as a technical problem requiring problem-solving skills that integrate ethical considerations into innovative designs. Moral creativity is the ability to formulate non-obvious solutions that integrate ethical considerations over various situational constraints.

**2. Problems can be formulated as interest conflicts. In this case different solution options are available.**

- **Gather Information.** Many disagreements can be resolved by gathering more information. Because this is the easiest and least painful way of reaching consensus, it is almost always best to start here. Gathering information may not be possible because of different constraints: there may not be enough time, the facts may be too expensive to gather, or the information required goes beyond scientific or technical knowledge. Sometimes gathering more information does not solve the problem but allows for a new, more fruitful formulation of the problem. Harris, Pritchard, and Rabins in Engineering Ethics: Concepts and Cases show how solving a factual disagreement allows a more profound conceptual disagreement to emerge.
- **Nolo Contendere.** Nolo Contendere is latin for not opposing or contending. Your interests may conflict with your supervisor but he or she may be too powerful to reason with or oppose. So your only choice here is to give in to his or her interests. The problem with nolo contendere is that non-opposition is often taken as agreement. You may need to document (e.g., through memos) that you disagree with a course of action and that your choosing not to oppose does not indicate agreement.
- **Negotiate.** Good communication and diplomatic skills may make it possible to negotiate a solution that respects the different interests. Value integrative solutions are designed to integrate conflicting values. Compromises allow for partial realization of the conflicting interests. (See the module, **The Ethics of Team Work**, for compromise strategies such as logrolling or bridging.) Sometimes it may be necessary to set aside one's interests for the present with the understanding that these will be taken care of at a later time. This requires trust.

- **Oppose.** If nolo contendere and negotiation are not possible, then opposition may be necessary. Opposition requires marshalling evidence to document one's position persuasively and impartially. It makes use of strategies such as leading an "organizational charge" or "blowing the whistle." For more on whistle-blowing consult the discussion of whistle blowing in the Hughes case that can be found at computing cases.

- **Exit.** Opposition may not be possible if one lacks organizational power or documented evidence. Nolo contendere will not suffice if non-opposition implicates one in wrongdoing. Negotiation will not succeed without a necessary basis of trust or a serious value integrative solution. **As a last resort,** one may have to exit from the situation by asking for reassignment or resigning.

**3. Solutions can be generated by readjusting different components of the STS.**

- **Technical Puzzle.** If the problem is framed as a technical puzzle, then solutions would revolve around developing designs that optimize both ethical and technical specifications, that is, resolve the technical issues and realize ethical value. In this instance, the problem-solver must concentrate on the hardware and software components of the STS.

- **Social Problem.** If the problem is framed as a social problem, then solutions would revolve around changing laws or bringing about systemic reform through political action. This would lead one to focus on the people/groups/roles component (working to social practices) or the legal component.

- **Stakeholder Conflict.** If the problem is framed as a conflict between different stakeholder interests, then the solution would concentrate on getting stakeholders (both individuals and groups) to agree on integrative or interest compromising solutions. This requires concentrating on the people/group/role component of the STS. (Note: A stakeholder is any group or individual with a vital interest at play in the situation.)

- **Management Problem.** Finally, if the problem is framed as a management problem, then the solution would revolve around changing an organization's procedures. Along these lines, it would address the (1) fundamental goals, (2) decision recognition procedures, (3) organizational roles, or (4) decision-making hierarchy of the organization. These are the four components of the CID (corporate internal decision) structure described in the "Ethical Reflections" section of the Toysmart case.

- **Nota Bene:** Financial issues are covered by the feasibility test in the solution implementation stage. As such, they pose side issues or constraints that do not enter into the solution generation phase but the solution implementation phase.

**4. Brainstorming. Moral creativity, which involves designing non-obvious solutions, forms an essential part of solution generation. Here are some guidelines to get you started.**

- Individually make out a list of solutions before the group meeting. Work quickly to realize a pre-established quota of five to ten solutions. After composing a quick first draft, revise the list for clarity only; make no substantial changes.

- Start the group brainstorming process by having the group review and assemble all the individual solutions. Do this quickly and without criticism. Beginning criticism at this stage will kill the creativity necessary for brainstorming and shut down the more timid (but creative) members of the group.

- Review the list and identify solutions that are identical or overlap. Begin the refining process by combining these solutions.

- Having reviewed all the brainstormed solutions, it is now time to bring in criticism. Begin by eliminating solutions with major ethical problems such as those that violate rights, produce injustices, or cause extensive harm.

- Identify but do not eliminate solutions that are ethical but raise serious practical problems. Do not initially eliminate an ethical solution because there are obstacles standing in the way of its implementation. Be descriptive. Identify and impartially describe the obstacles. Later, in the solution implementation stage, you may be able to design creative responses to these obstacles.

- Identify solutions that do not "fit" your problem statement. These require a decision. You can throw out the solution because it does not solve the problem or you can change the problem. If a solution does not fit the problem but, intuitively, seems good, this is a sign that you need to take another look at your problem statement.

- Don't automatically reject partial solutions. For example, sending memos through email rather than printing them out and wasting paper may not solve the entire recycling problem for your company. But it represents a good, partial solution that can be combined with other partial solutions to address the bigger problem.
- Through these different measures, you will gradually integrate criticism into your brainstorming process. This will facilitate working toward a manageable, refined list of solutions for testing in the next stage.

### Exercise 3: Develop a Solution List

- Have each member of your team prepare a solution list and bring it to the next group meeting. Set a quota for this individual list, say, 5 to 10 solutions.
- Prepare a group list out of the lists of the individual members. Work to combine similar solutions. Be sure to set aside criticism until the preliminary group list is complete.
- Make use of the following table.
- Refine the group list into a manageable number of solutions for testing in the next stage. Combine overlapping solutions. Eliminate solutions that do not respond to the requirements and the problem statement that you prepared in the previous exercise. Eliminate solutions that violate important ethical considerations, i.e., solutions that violate rights, produce harms, etc.
- Check your refined solution list with your problem statement. If they do not match, eliminate the solution or redefine the problem

#### Refined Brainstorm List

| Solution Ranking | Description of Solution | Justification (fits requirements, fits problem) |
|---|---|---|
| Best Solution | | |
| Second Best Solution | | |
| Third Best Solution | | |
| Fourth Best Solution | | |
| Fifth Best Solution | | |

**Table 5.20**

**Anthony Weston provides an illuminating and useful discussion of creative problem solving in the reference provided below.**

### 5.4.6 Exercise Three: Solution Testing

In this section, you will test the solutions on the refined list your group produced in the previous exercise. Three ethics tests, described below, will help you to integrate ethical considerations in the problem-solving process. A global feasibility test will help to identify solutions with serious practical problems. Finally, a Solution Evaluation Matrix summarizes the results for class debriefings.

**Setting up for the test.**

- Identify the agent perspective from which the decision will be made
- Describe the action as concisely and clearly as possible.
- Identify the stakeholders surrounding the decision, i.e., those who will suffer strong impacts (positively or negatively) from the implementation of your decision. Stakeholders have a vital or essential interest (right, good, money, etc) in play with this decision.

- In the harm/beneficence test, identify the likely results of the action and sort these into harms and benefits.
- For the reversibility test, identify the stakeholders with whom you will reverse positions.
- For the public identification test, identify the values, virtues, or vices your action embodies. Associate these with the character of the agent.

### Harm/Beneficence Test

1. **What are the harms your solution is likely to produce? What are its benefits? Does this solution produce the least harms and the most benefits when compared to the available alternatives?**

2. **Pitfall—Too much.** In this "Paralysis of Analysis" one factor in too many consequences. To avoid the fallacy restrict the analysis to the most likely consequences with the greatest magnitude (Magnitude indicates the range and severity of impact).

3. **Pitfall—Too Little.** A biased or incomplete analysis results when significant impacts are overlooked. Take time to uncover all the significant impacts, both in terms of likelihood and in terms of magnitude.

4. **Pitfall—Distribution of Impacts.** Consider, not only the overall balance of harms and benefits but also how harms and benefits are distributed among the stakeholders. If they are equally or fairly distributed, then this counts in the solution's favor. If they are unequally or unfairly distributed, then this counts against the solution. Be ready to redesign the solution to distribute better (=more equitably or fairly) the harmful and beneficial results.

### Reversibility Test

1. **Would this solution alternative be acceptable to those who stand to be most affected by it? To answer this question, change places with those who are targeted by the action and ask if from this new perspective whether the action is still acceptable?**

2. **Pitfall—Too much.** When reversing with Hitler, a moral action appears immoral and an immoral action appears moral. The problem here is that the agent who projects into the immoral standpoint loses his or her moral bearings. The reversibility test requires viewing the action from the standpoint of its different targets. But understanding the action from different stakeholder views does not require that one abandon himself or herself to these views.

3. **Pitfall—Too little.** In this pitfall, moral imagination falls short, and the agent fails to view the action from another stakeholder standpoint. The key in the reversibility test is to find the middle ground between too much immersion in the viewpoint of another and too little.

4. **Pitfall—Reducing Reversibility to Harm/Beneficence.** The reversibility test requires that one assess the impacts of the action under consideration on others. But it is more than a simple listing of the consequences of the action. These are viewed from the standpoint of different stakeholders. The reversibility test also goes beyond considering impacts to considering whether the action treats different stakeholders respectfully. This especially holds when the agent disagrees with a stakeholder. In these disagreements, it is important to work out what it means to disagree with another respectfully.

5. **Pitfall—Incomplete survey of stakeholders.** Leaving out significant stakeholder perspectives skews the results of the reversibility test. Building an excellent death chamber works when one considers the action from the standpoint of Hitler; after all, it's what he wants. But treating an individual with respect does not require capitulating to his or her desires, especially when these are immoral. And considering the action from the standpoint of other stakeholders (say the possible victims of newer, more efficient gas chambers) brings out new and radically different information.

6. **Pitfall—Not Weighing and Balancing Stakeholder Positions.** This pitfall is continuous with the previous one. Different stakeholders have different interests and view events from unique perspectives. The reversibility test requires reviewing these interests and perspectives, weighing them against one another, and balancing out their differences and conflicts in an overall, global assessment.

### Publicity (or Public Identification) Test

1. **Would you want to be publicly associated or identified with this action? In other words, assume that you will be judged as a person by others in terms of the moral values expressed in the action under consideration. Does this accord with how you would want to or aspire to be judged?**

2. **Pitfall—Failure to association action with character of agent.** In the publicity test, the spotlight of analysis moves from the action to the agent. Successfully carrying out this test requires identifying the agent, describing the action, and associating the agent with the action. The moral qualities exhibited in the action are seen as expressing the moral character of the agent. The publicity test, thus, rests on the idea that an agent's responsible actions arise from and express his or her character.

3. **Pitfall—Failure to appreciate the moral color of the action.** The publicity test assumes that actions are colored by the ends or goods they pursue. This means that actions are morally colored. They can express responsibility or irresponsibility, courage or cowardice, reasonableness or unreasonableness, honesty or dishonesty, integrity or corrpution, loyalty or betrayal, and so forth. An analysis can go astray by failing to bring out the moral quality (or qualities) that an action expresses.

4. **Pitfall—Reducing Publicity to Harm/Beneficence Test.** Instead of asking what the action says about the agent, many reduce this test to considering the consequences of publicizing the action. So one might argue that an action is wrong because it damages the reputation of the agent or some other stakeholder. But this doesn't go deep enough. The publicity test requires, not that one calculate the consequences of wide-spread knowledge of the action under consideration, but that one draws from the action the information it reveals about the character of the agent. The consequences of bad publicity are covered by the harm/beneficence test and do not need to be repeated in the public identification test. The publicity test provides new information by turning from the action to the agent. It focuses on what the action (its moral qualities and the goods it seeks) says about the agent.

## Comparing the Test Results: Meta-Tests

1. The ethics tests will not always converge on the same solution because each test (and the ethical theories it encapsulates) covers a different dimension of the action: (1) harm/beneficence looks at the outcomes or consequences of the action, (2) reversibility focuses on the formal characteristics of the action, and (3) publicity zeros in on the moral character of the agent.

2. The meta-tests turn this surface disagreement into an advantage. The convergence or divergence between the ethics tests become indicators of solution strength and weakness.

3. **Convergence.** When the ethics tests converge on a given solution, this indicates solution strength and robustness.

4. **Divergence.** When tests diverge on a solution—a solution does well under one test but poorly under another—this signifies that it needs further development and revision. Test divergence is not a sign that one test is relevant while the others are not. Divergence indicates solution weakness and is a call to modify the solution to make it stronger.

## Exercise 3: Summarize your results in a Solution Evaluation Matrix

1. Place test results in the appropriate cell.
2. Add a verbal explanation to the SEM table.
3. Conclude with a global feasibility test that asks, simply, whether or not there exist significant obstacles to the implementation of the solution in the real world.
4. Finish by looking at how the tests converge on a given solution. Convergence indicates solution strength; divergence signals solution weakness.

**Solution Evaluation Matrix**

| Solution/Test | Harm/Beneficence | Reversibility | Publicity (public identification) | Feasibility |
|---|---|---|---|---|
| First Solution | | | | |
| Second Solution | | | | |
| Third Solution | | | | |
| Fourth Solution | | | | |
| Fifth Solution | | | | |

**Table 5.21**

**The ethics tests are discussed in Cruz and Davis. See references below. Wike and Brincat also discuss value based approaches in the two references below.**

## 5.4.7 Exercise Four: Solution Implementation

In this section, you will trouble-shoot the solution implementation process by uncovering and defusing potential obstacles. These can be identified by looking at the constraints that border the action. Although constraints specify limits to what can be realized in a given situation, they are more flexible than generally thought. Promptly identifying these constraints allows for proactive planning that can push back obstacles to solution implementation and allow for realization of at least some of the value embodied in the solution.

A **Feasibility Test** focuses on these situational constraints and poses useful questions early on in the implementation process. What conditions could arise that would hinder the implementation of a solution? Should the solution be modified to ease implementation under these constraints? Can the constraints be removed or modified through activities such as negotiation, compromise, or education? Can solution implementation be facilitated by modifying both the solution and the constraints?

**Feasibility Constraints**

| Category | Sub-Category | | |
|---|---|---|---|
| Resource | Money/Cost | Time/Deadlines | Materials |
| Interest | Organizational(Supervisor) | Legal (laws, regulations) | Political/Social |
| Technical | Technology does not exist | Technology patented | Technology needs modification |

**Table 5.22**

**Resource Constraints:**

- **Does the situation pose limits on resources that could limit the realization of the solution under consideration?**
- **Time.** Is there a deadline within which the solution has to be enacted? Is this deadline fixed or negotiable?
- **Financial.** Are there cost constraints on implementing the ethical solution? Can these be extended by raising more funds? Can they be extended by cutting existing costs? Can agents negotiate for more money for implementation?

- **Resource.** Are necessary resources available? Is it necessary to plan ahead to identify and procure resources? If key resources are not available, is it possible to substitute other, more available resources? Would any significant moral or non-moral value be lost in this substitution?

## Interest Constraints

- **Does the solution threaten stakeholder interests? Could it be perceived as so threatening to a stakeholder's interests that the stakeholder would oppose its implementation?**
- **Individual Interests.** Does the solution threaten the interests of supervisors? Would they take measures to block its realization? For example, a supervisor might perceive the solution as undermining his or her authority. Or, conflicting sub-group interests could generate opposition to the implementation of the solution even though it would promote broader organizational objectives.
- **Organizational Interests.** Does the solution go against an organization's SOPs (standard operating procedures), formal objectives, or informal objectives? Could acting on this solution disrupt organization power structures? (Perhaps it is necessary to enlist the support of an individual higher up in the organizational hierarchy in order to realize a solution that threatens a supervisor or a powerful sub-group.)
- **Legal Interests.** Are there laws, statutes, regulations, or common law traditions that oppose the implementation of the solution? Is it necessary to write an impact statement, develop a legal compliance plan, or receive regulatory approval in order to implement the solution?
- **Political/Social/Historical Constraints.** Would the solution threaten or appear to threaten the status of a political party? Could it generate social opposition by threatening or appearing to threaten the interests of a public action group such as an environmental group? Are there historical traditions that conflict with the values embedded in the solution?

## Technical Constraints

- **Technology does not yet exist.** Would the implementation of the solution require breaking new technological ground?
- **Technology Protected by Patent.** The technology exists but is inaccessible because it is still under a patent held by a competitor.
- **Technology Requires Modification.** The technology required to implement solution exists but needs to be modified to fit the context of the solution. Important considerations to factor in would be the extent of the modification, its cost, and how long it would take to bring about the modification.

### 5.4.8 What did you learn?

This section provides closure to the module for students. It may consist of a formal conclusion that summarizes the module and outlines its learning objectives. It could provide questions to help students debrief and reflect on what they have learned. Assessment forms (e.g., the "Muddiest Point" Form) could be used to evaluate the quality of the learning experience. In short, this section specifies the strategy for bringing the module to a close.

**In this module, you have...**

- studied a real world case that raised serious problems with intellectual property, privacy, security, and free speech. Working with these problems has helped you to develop a better "working" understanding of these key concepts,
- studied and practiced using four decision-making frameworks: (1) using socio-technical analysis to specify the problem in a complex, real world case, (2) practiced brainstorming techniques to develop and refine solutions that respond to your problem, (3) employed three ethics tests to integrate ethical considerations into your solutions and to test these solutions in terms of their ethics, and (4) applied a feasibility analysis to your solutions to identify and trouble-shoot obstacles to the implementation of your ethical solution,

- explored the analogy between solving ethical and design problems,
- practiced the skills of moral imagination, moral creativity, reasonableness, and perseverance, and...
- experienced, through key participant perspectives, the challenges of ethics advocacy "under the gun."

**Debrief on your group work before the rest of the class**

1. Provide a concise statement and justification of the problem your group specified
2. Present the refined solution generation list your group developed in exercise 2.
3. Present and provide a quick summary explanation of the results of your group's solution evaluation matrix.
4. Show your group's feasibility matrix and summarize your assessment of the feasibility of implementing the solution alternatives you tested in exercise three.

**Group Debriefing**

1. Were there any problem you group had working together to carry out this case analysis? What were the problems and how did you go about solving them?
2. What problems did you have with understanding and practicing the four frameworks for solving problems? How did you go about solving these problems? Does your group have any outstanding questions or doubts?
3. Now that you have heard the other groups present their results, what differences emerged between your group's analysis and those of the other groups? Have you modified your analysis in light of the analyses of the other groups? If so how? Do the other groups need to take into account any aspects of your group's debriefing?

## 5.4.9 Appendix

This optional section contains additional or supplementary information related to this module. It could include: assessment, background such as supporting ethical theories and frameworks, technical information, discipline specific information, and references or links.

**References**

1. Brincat, Cynthia A. and Wike, Victoria S. (2000) Morality and the Professional Life: Values at Work. Upper Saddle River, NJ: Prentice Hall.
2. Cruz, J. A., Frey, W. J. (2003) An Effective Strategy for Integration Ethics Across the Curriculum in Engineering: An ABET 2000 Challenge, **Science and Engineering Ethics**, 9(4): 543-568.
3. Davis, M., **Ethics and the University**, Routledge, London and New York, 1999: 166-167.
4. Richard T. De George, "Ethical Responsibilities of Engineers in Large Organizations: The Pinto Case," in Ethical Issues in Engineering, ed. Deborah G. Johnson (1991) New Jersey: Prentice-Hall: 175-186.
5. Charles Harris, Michael Pritchard and Michael Rabins (2005) **Engineering Ethics: Concepts and Cases**, 3rd Ed. Belmont, CA: Thomson/Wadsworth: 203-206.
6. Huff, Chuck and Jawer, Bruce, "Toward a Design Ethics for Computing Professionals in Social Issues in **Computing: Putting Computing in its Place**, Huff, Chuck and Finholt, Thomas Eds. (1994) New York: McGraw-Hill, Inc.
7. Solomon, Robert C. (1999) **A Better Way to Think About Business: How Personal Intgrity Leads to Corporate Success**. Oxford, UK: Oxford University Press.
8. Anthony Weston. (2001) **A Practical Companion to Ethics**, 2nd ed. USA: Oxford University Press, 2001, Chapter 3.
9. Carolyn Whitbeck (1998) **Ethics in Engineering Practice and Research**. U.K. Cambridge University Press: 55-72 and 176-181.
10. Wike, Victoria S. (2001) "Professional Engineering Ethics Bahavior: A Values-based Approach," **Proceedings of the 2001 American Society for Engineering Education Annual Conference and Exposition, Session 2461**.

### 5.4.10 EAC ToolKit Project

**5.4.10.1 This module is a WORK-IN-PROGRESS; the author(s) may update the content as needed. Others are welcome to use this module or create a new derived module. You can COLLABORATE to improve this module by providing suggestions and/or feedback on your experiences with this module.**

Please see the Creative Commons License[9] regarding permission to reuse this material.

**5.4.10.2 Funded by the National Science Foundation: "Collaborative Development of Ethics Across the Curriculum Resources and Sharing of Best Practices," NSF-SES-0551779**

## 5.5 Ethics and Laptops: Identifying Social Responsibility Issues in Puerto Rico[10]

**Module Introduction**

While social responsibility has been recognized as one of the key areas of business ethics, much more needs to be done to develop frameworks and tools to clarify the concept itself and to implement it in business and professional practice on a day-to-day basis. This module will give students the opportunity to practice using frameworks and techniques that address these two needs.

Developing socio-technical system analyses provides an effective means to highlight issues of social responsibility. Since socio-technical systems embody values, building their descriptions allows us to read off potential problems due to harmful impacts and value conflicts. To facilitate this, you will be building socio-technical system descriptions using a grid or matrix that provides the components of socio-technical systems, levels under which they can be analyzed, and the values that they tend to embody. Building socio-technical system descriptions also requires using methods of participatory observation. These include constructing surveys and questionnaires, developing interviews, and building day-in-the-life scenarios. This module will help you frame and respond to social responsibility issues by providing a framework for socio-technical analysis and a set of methodological tools taken from participatory observation.

Module m14025 (Social-Technical Systems in Professional Decision Making) provides background information on STSs, their construction and their uses. Links to this module and to the website, Computing Cases, can be found in the upper left hand corner of this module. They provide useful background information. This module makes use of a case, Texas Laptops, that was developed by Chuck Huff and C. Nathan DeWall for NSF projects, DUE-9972280 and DUE-9980768.

**Texas Laptop Case**

1. In the late 1990's, the Texas State Board of Education proposed the ambitious plan of providing each of the state's four million public school students with their own laptop computer. This plan was devised to solve several problems confronting Texas public education.
2. Laptop computers could make educational resources more accessible to students who were faced with special challenges like deafness or blindness. Computers offer software options (such as audio books) that promise to reach more students than traditional printed textbooks.
3. Laptops also promised to solve the problem of obsolete textbooks. Texas purchased textbooks for their students at considerable costs. The purchasing cycle ran six years. By the end of this cycle, textbooks were out of date. For example, in the late 1990's when the laptop plan was proposed, history textbooks still referred to the Soviet Union and to the existence of the Berlin Wall. Laptops, on the other hand, would present textbook content in digital form which would eliminate printing and shipping costs and facilitate updates through online downloads.
4. Texas business leaders were concerned about the computer literacy of the upcoming generation of students. By employing laptops in more and more teaching activities, students would learn how to

---

[9]http://creativecommons.org/licenses/by/2.0/
[10]This content is available online at <http://cnx.org/content/m14257/1.3/>.

interact with computers while taking advantage of the new and more effective modes of presentation offered.

1. However, adopting laptops also presented problems that critics quickly brought forth.
2. Teachers would need to learn how to use laptop computers and would have to change their teaching to accomodate them in the classroom.
3. Apparent cost savings disappeared upon further, closer examination. For example, it became clear that textbook publishers would not so easily give up the revenues they had come to depend upon that came from textbook purchases for public school students. Updates from downloads could turn out to be more expensive and eductional software could be coded to restrict access and dissemination.
4. Further studies indicated that technical support costs would run two to three times initial outlays. Keeping laptop hardware and software up and running required technical support and continued investment.
5. Texas found that while some school districts–the richer ones–had already begun projects to integrate computing technology, the poorer school districts would require considerable financial support.

To deal with these problems, Texas carried out several pilot projects that examined the effectiveness of laptop integration in select school districts. While several successes were reported a series of problems arose that led Texas Board of Educaton officials to postpone the laptop project. First, pilot projects depended on donations from private computing vendors. While some were forthcoming, others failed to deliver hardware on time and provided only minimal technical support. Second, teachers resisted laptop integration due to the extensive investment of time required to appropriate computing skills and the difficulty of modifying existing curricula and teaching styles to accomodate laptop hardware and software. Third, at that time the available educational software, such as digitalized textbooks, was expensive, inadequately developed, and narrowly focused on curricular areas such as writing and math practice. Teachers also began to develop more comprehensive and philosophical criticisms of laptop use. Education specialist, Larry Cuban, argued that while laptops provided good support for a vocational education, they failed to deliver on other educational goals such as teaching children how to interact with their peers and teachers and teaching children the civic virtues necessary to become active participants in a democratic form of government. Studies began to appear that argued that skills developed through computer use came at the expense of other, more social skills.

The Texas Laptop plan was never formally implemented beyond the pilot project phase. However, several computer integration projects have been carried out in other parts of the country. For example, Larry Cuban reports on computer integration projects carried out in Silicon Valley in California. MIT has developed a cheap laptop computer for use in developing nations. You can find a link to computer integration projects that have been implemented in Philadelphia public schools through the support of the Microsoft Foundation.

Students in computer ethics classes at the University of Puerto Rico at Mayaguez have looked into the feasibility of integrating laptops in the public school socio-technical system in Puerto Rico. They began by looking at the project to provide public school teachers with laptops that was carried out in the late 1990's under the Pedro Rossello administration. The student research projects came to focus on three problem areas. First, they examined whether there were structures in laptop design that made computers unfit for use by children. Second, they studied whether social or ethical problems would arise from disposal of spent laptops. Third, they investigated the impact on copyright law and intellectual property practices that digitalizing printed textbooks would have.

### Exercise 1: Prepare a STS Grid

- Construct a socio-technical system (STS) grid for public schools in Puerto Rico
- Using the templates found at m14025 (Socio-Technical Systems in Professional Decision Making) identify the key constituents such as hardware, software, physical surroundings, etc.
- Select key levels for analysis. For example, you may want to look at the STS from the standpoint of individuals (students and teachers), small groups (public school systems), and institutions (education and business).

- Starting with a short list of values, identify the values embedded in the public school STS and, if possible, the specific components in which these values are embedded. A good place to start is to see how different physical arrangements of the classroom embody different approaches to education.

### Values in STSs

Values that can be used for exercise 1 include Justice (equity and access), Property, Privacy, Free Speech, Responsibility (Safety). More on these values can be found by clicking on the Computing Cases link provided in this module. Several of these values are defined in the Ethics of Team Work module, m13769.

### Exercise 2: Identifying Potential or Latent Problems in STSs

- Choose one of the following three problem areas to help focus your work: (1) value problems that may arise when laptops with their current design are integrated in the PR STS; (2) value problems that may arise by the digitalization of textbooks and other educational materials; (3) value problems and potential harms that may arise during the disposal of spent laptops.
- Compare values embodied in current laptop design with those embodied in the Puerto Rican public school STS. Are there any conflicts? What are these?
- Look more closely at the Puerto Rican public school STS. Are there any conflicts that will be highlighted, exaggerated, or increased by the integration of laptop computers.
- Finally, look for potential harms that could occur in the short, middle, and long term future.

### Exercise 3: Develop Counter-Measures to Problems

- Generate 5 to 10 options to respond to the problems you have identified. Make sure that you include the status quo among your options.
- Check each option against the problems you have identified. Does the option solve the problems identified in your STS analysis? Does it integrate the conflicting values and avoid untoward results? Does it give rise to new problems?
- Prepare a short presentation for the class (5 to 10 minutes) where you outline your problem, set forth the range of solutions you have identified, and describe and justify your solution. Be sure to address issues that may arise when you turn to implementing your solution.
- Provide a one or two sentence argument that your solution is best for delivering on social responsibility.

### Exercise 4: Evaluate the Microsoft Philadelphia Public Schools Project

- Listen to/read the news report on the Microsoft Foundation's project to integrate computing technology in Philadelphia. (You can find it by clicking on the link in this module.)
- Is this an example of a corporation carrying out its social responsibility to the surrounding community?.
- Evaluate Microsoft generally in terms of its social responsibility.

## 5.6 Case Analysis and Presentation: Machado[11]

Computer Ethics
    Case Module Template: Machado Case
    By William J. Frey
    Module Abstract:
    This module, designed for the EAC Toolkit (NSF SES 0551779), will test the Toolkit and Connexion's ability to network different online and offline sources for ethics across the curriculum. It consists of four components designed to provide tools for an in-depth analysis of the cases found at www.computingcases.org[12] ; it also makes substantial references to the draft manuscript of a textbook in computer ethics entitled

---

[11]This content is available online at <http://cnx.org/content/m13818/1.2/>.
[12]http://www.computingcases.org/

Good Computing: A Virtue Approach to Computer Ethics under contract with Jones and Bartlett Publishing Company. (This book will consist of the cases displayed at Computing Cases—Therac-25, Machado, and Hughes Aircraft—and 7 additional cases all developed through NSF projects DUE-9972280 and DUE 9980768.)

Module Introduction:

This module as displayed in Connexions presents the case abstract and timeline both taken from Computing Cases. It then refers to the website where the following can be found by browsing:

- case narrative,
- case history,
- a teaching introduction which also provides a useful overview,
- an ethical analysis that can be accessed by clicking on the appropriate concept in the table displayed (clicking on safety will open a short document that discusses the safety implications of the case)
- a Socio-Technical Analysis which spells out the different components of the cases socio-technical system such as hardware, software, physical surroundings, people/groups/roles, procedures, laws, and data/data structures.
- supporting documents such as three RFCs (Request for Comments) on the Unix finger command, a profile of students at UCI, and an interview with Allen Schiano from the University of California at Irvine's Office of Academic Computing.

These materials all posted at www.computingcases.org[13] provide the background information necessary for a detailed and exhaustive case analysis. (A suggestion: since you will be working in groups, divide these readings among your group members and take advantage of class time to report to one another on the contents of the links you have individually explored. Be sure to triangulate by assigning more than one member to each link. This will help to identify and solve problems in interpretation.)

The case abstract and timeline in this module outline the case. The following decision point taken from the Machado case will provide the focus for an in-depth case analysis. You will respond to the decision-point by working through a four stage decision making procedure inspired by the standard Software Development cycle:

- problem specification,
- solution generation,
- solution testing, and...
- solution implementation.

Module Activities:

1. Instructor introduces the case based on the abstract and timeline found at www.computingcases.org[14]

2. Students read case abstract, timeline, case decision point, and case analysis exercises.

3. Students do further research into the case by consulting ComputingCases materials which include narratives, histories, supporting documents, and ethical analyses.

4. Students carry out the activities outlined in the accompanying case exercises by (a) specifying the problem raised in the decision point, (b) generating solutions, (c) testing solutions using ethics tests, and (d) developing plans for implementing the solution over situational constraints.

5. Students prepare their case analyses working in small groups.

6. These groups present their completed analysis to the class in a case-debriefing session.

7. The instructor concludes by discussing the problem-solving issues and intermediate moral concepts raised by the case.

Machado Abstract:

In September of 1996, 19 year-old Richard Machado sent email to 59 Asian students at his public college, threatening them with phrases like "I will personally make it my life's career to hunt you down and kill you"

---

[13]http://www.computingcases.org/

[14]http://www.computingcases.org/

and signed by "Asian Hater." Several of these individuals reported this incident to the Office of Academic computing (OAC). One of the recipients was a student employee of the OAC. The administrators of the OAC were faced with a decision about how to respond to harassing and threatening email sent over their system to students of their University, using their facilities.

Machado Timeline

| 11/16/95 | Machado sends email threat to New University paper (UCI) via his roommate's computer.The email is traced to the roommate's computer.Roommate later said Machado had access to the computerMachado identified as sender. |
|---|---|
| 11/21/95 | Warrant for arrest is filed against Machado, issued by Irvine Police Department—the warrant is a "no bail felony warrant."Machado consents to a property search.Case given up shortly after—Machado's roommate took the blame so he "wouldn't be bothered anymore." |
| (Between 1/1/96 and 9/20/96) | Machado's older brother murdered in armed robbery prior to following incident;Machado is doing poorly in school, getting pressure from family to uphold high expectations. |
| 9/20/96(Friday, 10:54 am) | Machado sends hate Asians/threat email to about 59 UCI studentsMachado sent message a second time shortly after, when he did not receive replies to the first email.Incident brought to the attention of Assoc. Director of The Academic Computing Center, by her employees.Machado identified in computer lab and was asked to leave by Core Services manager. |
| 9/21/96 | Director of OAC reads Machado's email and decides that it is a police matter. |
| 9/24/96(Monday) | The incident is reported to University Police DepartmentAn officer is assigned to the case. |
| 9/26/96 | Retrieval of surveillance video confirmed Machado as the sender.Irving City Police notified and involved in case. |
| | *continued on next page* |

| 9/27/96 | Registrar's office helps police locate Machado's address and phone number. |
|---|---|
| 9/28/96 | An officer phones Machado's residence and leaves messageMachado calls back and agrees to meet with an officer that afternoon at 5pm.Two charges filed after meeting: Machado (1) knowingly and without permission uses computer services and (2) makes telephone calls with intent to annoy. |
| 11/14/96 | A stolen vehicle report is filed for Machado's second roommate's car.Machado had told one roommate he was borrowing his other roommate's car.Machado did not have permission to borrow car. |
| 11/18/96 | FBI attempts investigation.An agent goes to Machado's residence; Machado is not there and hasn't been seen there since 11/13.Machado allegedly left with Young's keys on 11/14.Other suspicions: $80 missing from roommate's coin jar; $154 visa charges to roommate's card, $54 of which were unauthorized; calls on 11/10, 11, and 12. |
| 11/21/96 | FBI agent phones Machado's roommate for confirmation of stolen car/info on Machado's disappearance. |
| 11/22/96 | Roommate interviewed. |
| 11/23/96 | Tammy Machado (Machado's sister) interviewed and said Machado had disappeared on the day his brother called him to inquire about Machado's name appearing in newspaper regarding Asian hate mails.Machado denied the reports in the paper to his brother; claimed it to be someone else.Tammy is informed that court date is set for 11/25 and if Richard doesn't show, they would issue a warrant for his arrest. |

*continued on next page*

| | |
|---|---|
| 2/6/97 | Machado is arrested when attempting to enter US from Mexico—caught by US Immigration Inspector.Machado is reported as looking homeless, having no possessions, looking for construction work in Mexico. |
| 9/16/97 | Machado is charged with 10 counts of interfering with a federally protected activity—in this case, students attending a university.Machado is told he will face up to 10 years if convicted. |
| 11/12/97 | Trial takes place and on this date a recess is granted when new information is uncovered/presented.Questionnaires were revealed in which 9 of the students who got the messages said they were not overtly bothered by Machado's email. |
| 11/18/97 | Jury deadlocked 9 to 3 in favor of acquittal.Case said to have national importance by federal prosecutors, so a second trial was set for 1/27/98. |
| 2/13/98 | Richard Machado is found guilty on 2 counts of civil rights violations.Took only 3 weeks of trial to reach verdict.Following conviction, Machado is released on a $10,000 bond from custody but is turned over to Irvine police on impending auto theft charges.Sentencing is postponed until 4/10/98.Possible maximum time Machado could serve would be 1 yr.Machado has already spent 1 yr. in jail awaiting trials, tec.Machado is recommended for anger & racial tolerance counseling, not allowed on UCI campus, and prohibited from having any contact with victims. |
| | *continued on next page* |

|  |  |
|--|--|
|  |  |

**Table 5.23**

Scenario #1:

You are a systems administrator at the Office of Academic Computing at the University of California at Irvine and have been asked to modify the Unix system to prevent the reoccurrence of the Machado incident

Scenario #2:

You are a systems administrator at the Office of Academic Computing at the University of California at Irvine and have been asked to develop an orientation program for students who will use university computing laboratories and facilities. Special emphasis is put on preventing a reoccurrence of the Machado incident.

1. Identify key components of the STS

| Part/Level of Analysis | Hardware | Software | Physical Surroundings | People, Groups, & Roles | Procedures | Laws & Regulations | Data & Data Structures |
|---|---|---|---|---|---|---|---|
|  |  |  |  |  |  |  |  |
|  |  |  |  |  |  |  |  |
|  |  |  |  |  |  |  |  |

**Table 5.24**

2. Specify the problem:

2a. Is the problem a disagreement on facts? What are the facts? What are cost and time constraints on uncovering and communicating these facts?

2b. Is the problem a disagreement on a critical concept? What is the concept? Can agreement be reached by consulting legal or regulatory information on the concept? (For example, if the concept in question is safety, can disputants consult engineering codes, legal precedents, or ethical literature that helps provide consensus? Can disputants agree on positive and negative paradigm cases so the concept disagreement can be resolved through line-drawing methods?

2c. Use the table to identify and locate value conflicts within the STS. Can the problem be specified as a mismatch between a technology and the existing STS, a mismatch within the STS exacerbated by the introduction of the technology, or by overlooked results?

| STS/Value | Safety (freedom from harm) | Justice (Equity & Access) | Privacy | Property | Free Speech |
|---|---|---|---|---|---|
| Hardware/software |  |  |  |  |  |
| Physical Surroundings |  |  |  |  |  |
| | | | | continued on next page | |

| People, Groups, & Roles | | | | | |
|---|---|---|---|---|---|
| Procedures | | | | | |
| Laws | | | | | |
| Data & Data Structures | | | | | |

**Table 5.25**

3. Develop a general solution strategy and then brainstorm specific solutions:

| Problem / Solution Strategy | Disagreement | | Value Conflict | | Situational Constraints |
|---|---|---|---|---|---|
| | Factual | Conceptual | Integrate? | Tradeoff? | Resource?Technical?Interest |

**Table 5.26**

3a. Is problem one of integrating values, resolving disagreements, or responding to situational constraints?

3b. If the conflict comes from a value mismatch, then can it be solved by modifying one or more of the components of the STS? Which one?

4. Test solutions:

| Alternative / Test | Reversibility | Value: Justice | Value: Responsibility | Value: Respect | Harm | Code |
|---|---|---|---|---|---|---|
| A #1 | | | | | | |
| A #2 | | | | | | |
| A #3 | | | | | | |

**Table 5.27**

5. Implement solution over feasibility constraints

| Alternative Constraint | Resource | | Interest | | | Technical | |
|---|---|---|---|---|---|---|---|
| | Time | Cost | Individual | Organization | Legal/ Social | Available Technology | Manufacturability |
| *continued on next page* | | | | | | | |

| #1 | | | | | | | |
|----|----|----|----|----|----|----|----|
| #2 | | | | | | | |
| #3 | | | | | | | |

**Table 5.28**

---

**Machado Summary**

---

This is an unsupported media type. To view, please see
http://cnx.org/content/m13818/latest/Machado_F06.ppt

---

**Figure 5.4:** PowerPoint File.

---

# Chapter 6

# Business Ethics Bowl

## 6.1 Practical and Professional Ethics Bowl Activity: Follow-Up In-Depth Case Analysis[1]

### 6.1.1 Module Introduction

This module provides students with a structure for preparing an in-depth case study analysis based on feedback they have received through their participation in an **Ethics Bowl** competition as part of the requirements for courses in Practical and Professional Ethics taught at the University of Puerto Rico at Mayaguez. Students viewing this module will find formats for analyzing decision making cases and position cases such as the decisions published by the National Society of Professional Engineers **Board of Ethical Review**. They will receive information pertinent to preparing in-depth case analyses, short summaries of the case pool for the Ethics Bowl competition, and a summary of procedures for carrying out a group self-evaluation. More information on the Engineering Ethics Bowl carried out at UPRM can be found in Jose A Cruz-Cruz, William J. Frey, and Halley D. Sanchez, "The Ethics Bowl in Engineering Ethics at the University of Puerto Rico - Mayaguez" in Teaching Ethics 4(3): 15-32.

### 6.1.2 Choosing Your Case

1. You must choose one of the two cases you presented on in the Ethics Bowl. (This means the case on which you gave your initial presentation.
2. You may choose either the first round decision-making case or the NSPE Board of Ethical Review Case

How should you choose your case?

1. Which case did you find the most interesting, challenging, or fruitful?
2. On which case did you receive the most interesting feedback from the other team and the judges?
3. Do you want to make, defend, and implement a decision or analyze a BER decision?

Once you choose your case, you need to analyze it according to the following steps:
Decision-Making Cases

---

[1]This content is available online at <http://cnx.org/content/m13759/1.12/>.

| Worksheets | Decision-Making Case |
|---|---|
| | Identify and state the (ethically) relevant facts |
| STS Table (Table + Verbal Explanation) | Prepare a Socio-Technical Analysis. Fill in the STS table (see below) and then verbally describe each component. |
| Value Table (Table + Written Problem Statement) | Fill out a Value Table (see below) Use it to identify the ethical problem or problems. Summarize this by providing a concise problem statement that is explicitly tied to the Value Table. |
| Brainstorm Lists (initial and refined lists) | 4. Brainstorm solution to the problem or problems. Be sure to discuss how list was generated and how it was refined. Describe value integration and interest negotiating strategies used. |
| Solution Evaluation Matrix (Matrix + Verbal Explanation and Justification) | 5. Compare, evaluate, and rank the solutions |
| | 6. Choose the best available solution. Provide a justification summarizing ethical and feasibility considerations highlighted in Solution Evaluation Matrix. |
| Feasibility Matrix (Matrix + Verbal Explanation) | 7. Develop a plan for implementing your solution. Discuss and justify this plan explicitly in terms of the specific feasibility considerations in the Feasibility Matrix. |
| | Develop and discuss preventive measures (if applicable) |

**Table 6.1**

NSPE-BER Case

| Worksheets | |
|---|---|
| | 1. Identify and state the (ethically) relevant facts |
| Stakeholders (Matrix + Verbal Explanation) | 2. Identify the stakeholders and their stakes. |
| Problem Classification (Matrix + Concise Verbal Problem Statement) | 3. Identify the ethical problem or problems |
| | 4. State the BER decision and summarize their code-based justification (cite code provisions, summarize principles, and list relevant precedents) |
| | *continued on next page* |

| Solution Evaluation (Matrix + detailed verbal explanation and justification) | 5. Evaluate the BER decision using the three ethics tests, code test, and global feasibility test. |
|---|---|
| | 6. Construct a strong counter-position and counter-argument to the BER decision |
| Solution Evaluation (Matrix + detailed verbal explanation and justification) | 7. Evaluate counter-position and counter-argument using the 3 ethics tests, feasibility test, and code test |
| Solution Implementation (Feasibility Matrix + Verbal Explanation) | 8. Evaluate counter-position and counter-argument in terms of relevant feasibility considerations. Provide a matrix/table + verbal explanation. |

**Table 6.2**

## 6.1.3 In-Depth Analysis: Step by Step

Description of In-Depth Case Analysis

Title of Assignment: "In-Depth Case Analysis"

Due Date for Written Projects:One week after the last class of the semester.

What is required?

1. Participation in at two ethics bowl competitions.

2. Each group will choose from the two cases it debated in the Ethics Bowl a case for a more extended analysis carrying out the seven-step decision making framework. They will prepare an extended analysis of this case (10 to 20 pages).

3. Each group will prepare summaries of the 15 cases assigned for the ethics bowl. These summaries (a minimum of one page for each case) will be handed in with the extended case study analysis. These summaries should include a problem statement, a solution evaluation matrix, and a feasibility matrix.

4. Each final submission will also include a group self-evaluation. This evaluation will include:

- _____a list of the goals each group set for itself
- _____a careful, justified and documented assessment of your success in reaching these goals
- _____a careful assessment of what you did and did not learn in this activity
- _____a discussion of obstacles you encountered and measures your group took to overcome these.
- _____a discussion of member participation and contribution including the member contribution forms
- _____in general what worked and what didn't work for you and your group in this activity

5. A group portfolio consisting of the materials prepared by your group during the group class activities:

- _____Virtue Chart (Responsibility)
- _____Gray Matters Solution Evaluation Matrix
- _____Rights Chart: Free & Informed Consent
- _____Group Code of Ethics

### Structure of Written Analysis

1. A brief summary of the case focusing on the ethically relevant facts.
2. A Socio-Technical System Table + Short paragraph on each of the seven categories.
3. A Value Table + a short paragraph on the embedded values you have identified and where they occur in the STS. Then state whether you have found any value mismatches, magnified existing value conflicts, and remote/harmful consequences.

4. On the basis of your STS analysis and value conflict analysis, provide a short, concise problem statement. Make sure your the problem you have identified is grounded in your STS and value analysis. If not, one or the other (or both) needs to be changed.

5. A brainstorm list in which you record the solutions your group has designed to solve the problem stated above. The rough unrefined list should include around 10 solutions. Then refine this list into three. Spend time detailing how you reached your refined list. Did you synthesize rough solutions? On what basis did you leave a solution out all together? Did you find other ways of relating or combining solutions? Spend time documenting your brainstorming and refining process. Show in detail how you came up with the refined list.

6. Do a comparative evaluation of three of the refined solutions you developed in the previous step. First, prepare a solution evaluation matrix that summarizes your comparative evaluation. Use the table provided below. Second, provide a verbal account of the solution evaluation and comparison process you present in the solution evaluation matrix.

7. Reach a final decision. Defend your decision using the ethics and feasibility tests. If the decision situation in which you are working is a dynamic one, then proppose a series of solutions that you will pursue simultaneously, including how you would respond to contingencies that might arise. (You could express this in the form of a decision tree.)

8. Fill out a Feasibility Matrix. See matrix below

9. Present an implementation plan based on your Feasibility Matrix. This plan should list the obstacles that might arise and how you plan to overcome them. (For example, don't just say, "Blow the whistle." Discuss when, how, where, to whom, and in what manner. How would you deal with reprisals? Would your action seriously disrupt internal relations of trust and loyalty? How would you deal with this?) Work out a detailed plan to implement your decision using the feasibility constraints to "suggest" obstacles and impediments.

10. Finally, discuss preventive measures you can take to prevent this type of problem from arising again in the future.

## Socio-Technical System Table

| Hardware | Software | Physical Surround-ings | People, Groups, Roles | Procedures | Laws, Statutes, Regulations | Data and Data Struc-tures |
|---|---|---|---|---|---|---|
|  |  |  |  |  |  |  |
|  |  |  |  |  |  |  |
|  |  |  |  |  |  |  |

**Table 6.3**

## STS Value Table

|  | Hardware | Software | Physical Surround-ings | People, Groups, Roles | Procedures | Laws | Data and Data Structures |
|---|---|---|---|---|---|---|---|
| *continued on next page* | | | | | | | |

| Integrity | | | | | | | |
|---|---|---|---|---|---|---|---|
| Justice | | | | | | | |
| Respect | | | | | | | |
| Responsibility for Safety | | | | | | | |
| Free Speech | | | | | | | |
| Privacy | | | | | | | |
| Property | | | | | | | |

**Table 6.4**

## Solution Evaluation Matrix

| Solution/Test | Reversibility or Rights | Harms/Beneficence or Net Utility | Virtue | Value | Code | Global Feasibility |
|---|---|---|---|---|---|---|
| Description | Is the solution reversible with stakeholders? Does it honor basic rights? | Does the solution produce the best benefit/harm ratio? Does the solution maximize utility? | Does the solution express and integrate key virtues? | Moral values realized? Moral values frustrated? Value conflicts resolved or exacerbated? | Does the solution violate any code provisions? | What are the resource, technical, and interest constraints that could impede implementation? |
| Best solution | | | | | | |
| Best alternate solution | | | | | | |
| Worst solution | | | | | | |

**Table 6.5**

| Feasibility Matrix | | |
|---|---|---|
| Resource Constraints | Technical Constraints | Interest Constraints |
| | *continued on next page* | |

| Time | Cost | Available mate-rials, labor, etc | Applicable technol-ogy | Manufactur-ability | Per-son-alities | Organiza-tional | Legal | Social, Political, Cultural |
|------|------|------|------|------|------|------|------|------|
|      |      |      |      |      |      |      |      |      |

**Table 6.6**

### 6.1.4 Format

1. Group, team-written projects are to be 10-20 pages in length, double spaced, with standard 1-inch margins, and typewritten. This does not include documentation, appendices, and other notes.

2. It is essential that you carefully and fully document the resources that you have consulted. The most direct way to do this is to include numbered entries in a concluding section entitled, "Works Cited". These entries should provide complete bibliographical information according to standard form (Chicago Manual of Style or the MLA Manual of Style). Then insert the number of the entry in parenthesis in the text next to the passage that is based on it. (Example: "The self is a relation that relates itself to its own self...." (4) The number "4" refers to the forth item in the "Works Cited" section at the end of your paper.)

3. Practical norm 5j of the CIAPR code of ethics sets forth the obligation of the professional engineer to give others due credit for their work. For this reason, plagiarism will not be tolerated in any form. Possible forms of plagiarism include but are not limited to the following:

- Quoting directly from other sources without documenting (footnote or bibliography) and/or without using quotation marks. Claiming that this is an appendix will not excuse this action. Claiming ignorance will not excuse this action.

- Using the ideas or work of others without giving due credit or proper acknowledgment. "Proper acknowledgment"," in this context, requires a standard bibliographical reference and the use of quotation marks if the material is being directly quoted.

- If your paper relies exclusively or primarily on extensively quoted materials or materials closely para-phrased from the work of others, then it will not be credited as your work even if you document it. To make it your own, you have to summarize it in your own words, analyze it, justify it, or criticize it.

- You will not be credited for material that you translate from English to Spanish unless you add to it something substantial of your own.

- In general, what you appropriate from another source must be properly digested, analyzed, and ex-pressed in your own words. If you have any questions on this, please ask me.

- Any plagiarized document—one which violates the above rules—will be given a zero. You will be given a chance to make this up, and the grade on the make-up project will be averaged in with the zero given to the plagiarized document. Since this is a group grade, everyone in the group will be treated the same, even though the plagiarizer may be only one person. Each member of the group is responsible to assure that other members do not plagiarize in the name of the group. (Since the due date for the written project is late in the semester, this will probably require that I give the entire group, i.e., all members, an Incomplete.) Each member of the group will be held individually responsible in the above-described manner for the final content of the written report.

4. This is not a research project but an exercise in integrating ethics into real world cases. In Chapters 2 and 3 of Engineering Ethics: Concepts and Cases, the authors present a thorough discussion of the case study analysis/problem solving method discussed in class. You also have supporting handouts in your file folders from Magic Copy Center as well as materials I have presented directly in class. Engineering Ethics: Concepts and Cases also contains several sample case studies that can help guide you in constructing your own presentation. What I am looking for is a discussion of the case in terms of the ethical approaches and decision-making frameworks we have discussed this semester. You do not need to "wow" me with research

into other areas peripherally related to the case; you need to show me that you have practiced decision-making and made a serious effort to integrate ethical considerations into the practice of engineering.

5. The usual criteria concerning formal presentations apply when competing in the Ethics Bowl. Dress professionally.

6. You may write your group, team-written project in either Spanish or English.

7. All competitions will take place in the regular classroom.

## 6.1.5 Media Files Beginning Spring 2007

These media files provide information on the ethics bowl and the follow-up activities including individual decision point summaries, in-depth case analysis, and group self-evaluation. They have been integrated into the Business Ethics course during the Spring semester, 2008 and will apply from this date on into the future.

### Team Member Evaluation Form

This media object is a downloadable file. Please view or download it at
<TEAM MEMBER RATING SHEET.doc>

**Figure 6.1:** This file contains the team member rating sheet which each group member must fill out and turn in with his or her group project.

### Final Project and Group Self-Evaluation Rubrics

This media object is a downloadable file. Please view or download it at
<Be_Rubric_S07.doc>

**Figure 6.2:** This rubric will be used to grade the in-depth case analysis, the group self-evaluation, and the Ethics Bowl case summaries.

### Basic Moral Concepts for Ethics Bowl

This media object is a downloadable file. Please view or download it at
<BME_V2_97.doc>

**Figure 6.3:** Clicking on this figure will download the basic moral concepts that you will be integrating into the ethics bowl and your final in-depth case analysis. You will be asked to show how you worked to integrate these concepts in your group self-evaluation.

---

### Intermediate Moral Concepts for Ethics Bowl

This media object is a downloadable file. Please view or download it at
<IMC_V2_97.doc>

**Figure 6.4:** Clicking on this future will open a table that summarizes the intermediate moral concepts that are at play in the four cases that are being used in the Ethics Bowl: Hughes, Therac, Toysmart, and Biomatrix.

---

**Ethics Bowl Cases for ADMI 4016: Environment of the Organization**
[MEDIA OBJECT][2]

## 6.1.6 Check List

Breakdown of Project Grade:

**Group Team-Written Project: 200 points, group grade.**

- This is your group's in-depth case analysis
- It will analyze the decision scenario your group presented on in the ethics bowl
- Your task is to give a full and comprehensive analysis of a decision point using the tables presented above, accompanying verbal descriptions, and carrying out the four-stage problem-solving framework of specifying the problem, generating solutions, testing solutions in terms of their ethics, and implementing these solutions.

**Nota Bene**

- After the Ethics Bowl, I will provide the class with general feedback and presentations on how to prepare the final project. When you submit your final report, I will be looking for how you responded to my comments and suggestions and to the comments and suggestions of the judges and the class.
- Attendance is mandatory for all Ethics Bowl competitions. This is important because you will help one another by the comments and discussions that are generated by the presentations. Students not competing need to listen actively and respectfully to the presenting group. Keep in mind the twin standards of respect and professionalism. I will deduct points from the grades of groups and/or individuals who do not listen courteously to the presentations of others or who do not attend class during the presentation cycle.

Nota Bene:

**Check List**

- **Each group will turn in this checklist, fully filled out and signed. Checking signifies that your group has completed and turned in the item checked. Failure to submit this form will cost your group 20 points**
- _ _ _ _ One page summaries of the 10 Ethics Bowl decision points taken from the Therac-25, Biomatrix, Toysmart, and Hughes cases.
- _ _ _ _ Group, in-depth analysis of the case your team presented on in the Ethics Bowl.
- _ _ _ _ List of Ethically Relevant Facts
- _ _ _ _ Socio-Technical System Table + Verbal Explanation

---

[2]This media object is a downloadable file. Please view or download it at
<Ethics Bowl Cases.docx>

- _ _ _ _ Value Table + Problem Statement + Justification
- _ _ _ _ List of Brainstormed Solutions + Descriptin of Refining Process + Refined list
- _ _ _ _ Solution Evaluation Matrix + Verbal Comparison of Three Alternatives from refined solution list
- _ _ _ _ Chosen Solution + Verbal Justification
- _ _ _ _ Feasibility Matrix + Solution Implementation Plan concretely described and based on feasibility matrix
- _ _ _ _ Preventive Measures (if applicable)

## Materials Required from Ethics Bowl

- _ _ _ _ _Ethics Bowl Score Sheets
- _ _ _ _ _The decision point your team **presented** on in the competition
- _ _ _ _ _The decision point your team **commented** on in the competition

## _ _ _ _ Group Self-Evaluation Form including...

- _ _ _ _ a list of the goals your group set for itself
- _ _ _ _ a carefully prepared, justified, and documented assessment of your group's success in reaching these goals
- _ _ _ _ a careful assessment of what you did and did not learn in this activity
- _ _ _ _ a discussion of obstacles you encountered and the measures your group took to overcome these
- _ _ _ _ a discussion of member participation and contribution including the member contriution forms
- _ _ _ _ a general discussion of what worked and what did not work for you and your group in this activity

_ _ _ _ _ _Each member will turn in a filled out Team Member Evaluation Form. This form can be accessed through the media file listed above. It is suggested that you do this anonomously by turning in your Team Member Evaluation Form in a sealed envelop with the rest of these materials. You are to evaluate yourself along with your teammates on the criteria mentioned in the form. Use the scale suggested in the form.

## Group Portfolios Include...

- _ _ _ _ _ _Virtue Tables including the moral exemplar profile your group prepared and presented.
- _ _ _ _ _ _The justification using the rights framework of the right assigned to your group. This was one of the rights asserted by engineers against their corporate employers.
- _ _ _ _ _ _A one page summary of how you developed your role in the Incident at Morales **"Vista Publica."**
- _ _ _ _ _ _The code or statement of values summary prepared by your group as a part of the Pirate Code of Ethics module. This summary focused on one of six organizations: East Texas Cancer Center, Biomatrix, Toysmart, Hughes Aircraft, CIAPR, or AECL (in the Therac case).

Copy-paste this checklist, examine the assembled materials prepared by your group, and check the items your group has completed. Then read, copy-paste, and sign the following pledge.

## Group Pledge

- **I certify that these materials have been prepared by those who have signed below, and no one else. I certify that the above items have been checked and that those items with checkmarks indicate materials that we have turned in. I also certify that we have not plagiarized any material but have given due acknowledgment to all sources used. All who sign below and whose names are included on the title page of this report have participated fully in the preparation of this project and are equally and fully responsible for its results.**
- Member signature here _ _ _ _ _ _ _ _ _ _ _ _ _ _ _ _ _ _ _ _ _ _ _ _ _ _ _ _
- Member signature here _ _ _ _ _ _ _ _ _ _ _ _ _ _ _ _ _ _ _ _ _ _ _ _ _ _ _ _

- Member signature here _ _ _ _ _ _ _ _ _ _ _ _ _ _ _ _ _ _ _ _ _ _ _ _ _ _ _
- Member signature here _ _ _ _ _ _ _ _ _ _ _ _ _ _ _ _ _ _ _ _ _ _ _ _ _ _ _
- Member signature here _ _ _ _ _ _ _ _ _ _ _ _ _ _ _ _ _ _ _ _ _ _ _ _ _ _ _
- Member signature here _ _ _ _ _ _ _ _ _ _ _ _ _ _ _ _ _ _ _ _ _ _ _ _ _ _ _

# 6.2 Ethics Bowl: Cases and Score Sheets[3]

## 6.2.1 Module Introduction

This module is designed to give you a brief orientation in the Ethics Bowl competition. It is designed to compliment and complete other modules concerning the ethics bowl that you will find in the Corporate Governance course.

## 6.2.2 Ethics Bowl Rules (briefly)

- The moderator will begin the competition by flipping a coin to determine which team will present first. If the team that calls wins the toss, they choose whether they or the other team go first.
- Monday: (1) Team 1 will have one minute to consult and seven minutes to give its initial presentation. The presentation must be tied to the question/task given to it by the moderator. (2) Team 2 has a minute to consult and seven minutes to make its Commentary on Team 1's presentation. Team 2 can close its commentary by posing a question to Team 1. (3) Team 1 then has a minute to consult and fiveminutes to respond to Team 2's Commentary. (4) Team 1 will then answer questions posed by the two peer review teams. Each peer review team will ask a question. A quick follow-up is allowed. The peer review question and answer session will go for 15 minutes. (5) The peer review teams will score the first half of the competition but not announce the results.
- Wednesday: The same procedure will occur while reversing the roles between Teams 1 and 2. Thus, team 2 will present, team 1 comment, team 2 respond, and then team 2 will answer questions from the peer review panels. The peer review panels will add the scores for the second part of the competition but will hold off on announcing the results until Friday's class.
- Friday: The two peer review teams will present and explain their scores. Peer Review teams will take note: you're objective is not to criticize or evaluate the debating teams but to provide them feedback in terms of the four categories.
- Debating teams may trade minutes from consulting to presenting. For example, Team 1 may decide to take two minutes to consult when given their case and task. This means that they will have 6 minutes, instead of 7, to present.
- Nota Bene: Debating teams and Peer Review teams are not allowed to bring notes into the competition. You will be provided with paper to take notes once the competition starts.
- Even though the national Ethics Bowl competition allows only one presenter, debating teams will be allowed to "pass the baton." When one person finishes speaking, another can step in his or her place. It is absolutely forbidden that more than one person speak at a time. Also, the competing team's speaking time is limited to its commentary. Once that is over, they are instructed to quitely listen. Infractions will be followed first by a warning. Second infractions will result in points being taken away.

## 6.2.3 Competition Time Line

1. Team 1 Presentation: One minute to consult, seven minutes to present.
2. Team 2 Commentary: One minute to consult, seven minutes to present.
3. Team 1 Response to Commentary: One minute to consult, five minutes to respond.

---

[3]This content is available online at <http://cnx.org/content/m13852/1.6/>.

4. The question and answer session between Team 1 and the Peer Review teams will last 15 minutes (running clock). The first peer review team will have 7 minutes 30 seconds for its questions and the second will have roughly the same time.
5. In the second round, the time line is the same while the debating teams change roles.

## 6.2.4 Advice to Debating Teams

- Tell us what you are going to do, do it, and then tell us what you have done. In other words, start your presentation with a summary, then launch into the main body of your presentation, and then conclude with another summary. This will help the listening audience understand what you are trying to do.
- Be professional, formal, and courteous. Address yourself to the other team and the peer review team. It is a good idea to stand when you are giving your initial presentation.
- Be sure to communicate your understanding of the scoring criteria. What do you and your team understand by intelligibility, ethical integration, feasibility, and moral imagination/creativity? Take time to listen to the other team and the peer review teams to gain insights into their understanding. During the commentary and the question and answer session you will get crucial clues into what others think you have achieved and where you need further work. Use this feedback.
- Be sure to thank the peer review teams, moderators, and your opponents during and after the competition. Such formalities make it possible to penetrate to the deeper practices that underlie the virtue of reasonableness.
- Relax and have fun! You may not have the opportunity to say everything you want to say. One of the purposes behind this competition is to help you see just how hard it is to advocate for ethical positions. We almost always have to do so under serious constraints such as time limits. Also, remember that you have other forums for "getting it said," namely, your group self evaluation and your in-depth case analysis. In these places you will be able to discuss these issues in the kind of depth you think necessary.

## 6.2.5 Advice to the Peer Review Teams on Scoring

- Remember that all three scoring events of the competition are worth 20 points. The initial presentation, the response to the commentary and questions, and the commentary on the other team's presentation all count for the same 20 points.
- Although you have the complete rubric only for the initial presentation, you will score the other parts of the presentation based on the four criteria: intelligibility, ethical integration, feasibility and moral imagination/creativity. You will score 1 to 5 on each criteria for a total of 20.
- Three is the middle of the road score. In other words, three is a good, average score. It is not a C–don't think of scoring as grading. Start each team off from a default of three. Then move off that default only when something exceptionally good or not so good happens. If your scores deviate much from straight twelves (36), then you are scoring too high or too low.

## 6.2.6 Ethics Bowl Scoring Criteria

1. **Intelligibility** includes three skills or abilities: (1) the ability to construct and compare multiple arguments representing multiple viewpoints; (2) the ability to construct arguments and provide reasons that are clear, coherent, and factually correct; (3) evidence of realizing the virtue of reasonableness by formulating and presenting value integrative solutions?
2. **Integrating Ethical Concerns** includes three skills: (1) presenting positions that are clearly reversible between stakeholders; (2) identifying and weighing key consequences of positions considered; (3) developing positions that integrate values like integrity, responsibility, reasonableness, honesty, humility, and justice.

3. **Feasibility** implies that the positions taken and the arguments formulated demonstrate full recognition and integration of interest, resource, and technical constraints. While solutions are designed with constraints in mind, these do not serve to trump ethical considerations.

4. **Moral Imagination and Creativity** demonstrate four skill sets: (1) ability to clearly formulate and frame ethical issues and problems; (2) ability to provide multiple framings of a given situation; (3) ability to identify and integrate conflicting stakeholders and stakes; (4) ability to generate solutions and positions that are non-obvious, i.e., go beyond what is given in the situation.

### 6.2.7 Peer Review Team Responsibilities

- Attend the debate sessions and the feedback session on Friday after the competition. Remember this is the capstone event of the course. It looks bad if you do not bother to attend.

- You team will ask questions during the debate. This will constitute, at a minimum, one question and a quick follow up if necessary. You are not to debate with the presenting team. So your questions should not be designed to trap them. Rather, seek through your questions to explore seeming weak points, unclear statements, and incomplete thoughts. Use your questions to help you line up the debating team against the four criteria.

- Fill out the score sheet and assess the debating teams in terms of intelligibility, integrating ethics, feasibility and moral imagination/creativity.

- Lead, with the other Peer Review team, the feedback sessions. This requires that you prepare a short, informal presentation that shows your scoring and then explains it.

- Always, always, always be courteous in your feedback comments. Try to present things positively and proactively. This is difficult but practice now will serve you well later when you are trying to explaibn to a supervisor how he or she has made a mistake.

### 6.2.8 Media Files with Cases and Score Sheets

---

**Engineering Ethics Bowl**

---

This is an unsupported media type. To view, please see
http://cnx.org/content/m13852/latest/Revised_ScoreSheet_T1_V2.doc

---

**Figure 6.5:** Score Sheet Team One.

## Engineering Ethics Bowl

This is an unsupported media type. To view, please see
http://cnx.org/content/m13852/latest/Revised_ScoreSheet_T2_V2.doc

**Figure 6.6:** Score Sheet Team Two.

## Ethics Bowl Cases

This is an unsupported media type. To view, please see http://cnx.org/content/m13852/latest/Ethics
Bowl Cases for Spring 2007.doc

**Figure 6.7:** Click here to open the word file containing the 12 Ethics Bowl classes for Business Ethics
Apring 2007.

## Ethics Bowl Cases for Fall 2007

This is an unsupported media type. To view, please see http://cnx.org/content/m13852/latest/EB_
Fall07_W97.doc

**Figure 6.8:** These are the cases for the Ethics Bowl Competition for the Fall Semester in the year 2007.
These scenarios or decision points are taken from Incident at Morales, Hughes Aircraft Case, Biomatrix
Case, and Toysmart Case.

**Debriefing for Ethics Bowl, Round Two**

This is an unsupported media type. To view, please see
http://cnx.org/content/m13852/latest/Debriefing_Round_2.ppt

**Figure 6.9:** This presentation was given Friday, April 27 to the Ethics Bowl teams that debated on the Therac-25 case and the Inkjet case.

# Chapter 7

# Course Procedures

## 7.1 Rubrics for Exams and Group Projects in Ethics[1]

Module Introduction

This module provides a range of assessment rubrics used in classes on engineering and computer ethics. Rubrics will help you understand the standards that will be used to assess your writing in essay exams and group projects. They also help your instructor stay focused on the same set of standards when assessing the work of the class. Each rubric describes what counts as exceptional writing, writing that meets expectations, and writing that falls short of expectations in a series of explicit ways. The midterm rubrics break this down for each question. The final project rubrics describe the major parts of the assignment and then break down each part according to exceptional, adequate, and less than adequate. These rubrics will help you to understand what is expected of you as you carry out the assignment, provide a useful study guide for the activity, and familiarize you with how your instructor has assessed your work.

---

**Business Ethics Course Syllabus**

---

This is an unsupported media type. To view, please see http://cnx.org/content/m14059/latest/Business Ethics Spring 2007.doc

---

Figure 7.1: Course Requirements, Timeline, and Links

---

[1]This content is available online at <http://cnx.org/content/m14059/1.7/>.

**Business Ethics Syllabus, Spring 2008**

This is an unsupported media type. To view, please see
http://cnx.org/content/m14059/latest/Syllabus_S08_W97.doc

**Figure 7.2:** This figure contains the course syllabus for business ethics for spring semester 2008.

**Business Ethics Syllabus Presentation**

This is an unsupported media type. To view, please see
http://cnx.org/content/m14059/latest/BE_Intro_F07.ppt

**Figure 7.3:** Clicking on this figure will open the presentation given on the first day of class in Business Ethics, Fall 2007. It summarizes the course objectives, grading events, and also provides a PowerPoint slide of the College of Business Administration's Statement of Values.

Ethical Theory Rubric

This first rubric assesses essays that seek to integrate ethical theory into problem solving. It looks at a rights based approach consistent with deontology, a consequentialist approach consistent with utilitarianism, and virtue ethics. The overall context is a question presenting a decision scenario followed by possible solutions. The point of the essay is to evaluate a solution in terms of a given ethical theory.

**Ethical Theory Integration Rubric**

This is an unsupported media type. To view, please see
http://cnx.org/content/m14059/latest/EE_Midterm_S05_Rubric.doc

**Figure 7.4:** This rubric breaks down the assessment of an essay designed to integrate the ethical theories of deontology, utilitarianism, and virtue into a decision-making scenario.

This next rubric assess essays that integrate ethical considerations into decision making by means of three tests, reversibility, harm/beneficence, and public identification. The tests can be used as guides in designing ethical solutions or they can be used to evaluate decision alternatives to the problem raised in an ethics case or scenario. Each theory partially encapsulates an ethical approach: reversibility encapsulates deontology, harm/beneficence utilitarianism, and public identification virtue ethics. The rubric provides students with pitfalls associated with using each test and also assesses their set up of the test, i.e., how well they build a context for analysis.

---

### Integrating Ethics into Decision-Making through Ethics Tests

---

This is an unsupported media type. To view, please see
http://cnx.org/content/m14059/latest/CE_Rubric_S06.doc

---

**Figure 7.5:** Attached is a rubric in MSWord that assesses essays that seek to integrate ethical considerations into decision-making by means of the ethics tests of reversibility, harm/beneficence, and public identification.

---

Student teams in Engineering Ethics at UPRM compete in two Ethics Bowls where they are required to make a decision or defend an ethical stance evoked by a case study. Following the Ethics Bowl, each group is responsible for preparing an in-depth case analysis on one of the two cases they debated in the competition. The following rubric identifies ten components of this assignment, assigns points to each, and provides feedback on what is less than adequate, adequate, and exceptional. This rubric has been used for several years to evaluate these group projects

---

### In-Depth Case Analysis Rubric

---

This is an unsupported media type. To view, please see
http://cnx.org/content/m14059/latest/EE_FinalRubric_S06.doc

---

**Figure 7.6:** This rubric will be used to assess a final, group written, in-depth case analysis. It includes the three frameworks referenced in the supplemental link provided above.

---

This rubric provides assessment criteria for the Good Computing Report activity that is based on the Social Impact Statement Analysis described by Chuck Huff at www.computingcases.org. (See link) Students take a major computing system, construct the socio-technical system which forms its context, and look for potential problems that stem from value mismatches between the computing system and its surrounding socio-technical context. The rubric characterizes less than adequate, adequate, and exceptional student Good Computing Reports.

**Good Computing Report Rubric**

This is an unsupported media type. To view, please see
http://cnx.org/content/m14059/latest/CE_FinalRubric_S06.doc

**Figure 7.7:** This figure provides the rubric used to assess Good Computing Reports in Computer Ethics classes.

Computing Cases provides a description of a Social Impact Statement report that is closely related to the Good Computing Report. Value material can be accessed by looking at the components of a Socio-Technical System and how to construct a Socio-Technical System Analysis.[2]

**Business Ethics Midterm Rubric Spring 2008**

This is an unsupported media type. To view, please see http://cnx.org/content/m14059/latest/Midterm Rubric Spring 2008.doc

**Figure 7.8:** Clicking on this link will open the rubric for the business ethics midterm exam for spring 2008.

## 7.2 Integrating the Values of Responsibility and Honesty Into Class Attendance Module[3]

### 7.2.1 Module Introduction

Class Absence Module

Module Introduction

According to the course syllabus, "Class attendance is compulsory. The University of Puerto Rico, Mayagüez Campus, reserves the right to deal at any time with individual cases of non-attendance. Professors are expected to record the absences of their students. Frequent absences affect the final grade and may even result in total loss of credits. Arranging to make up work missed because of legitimate class absence is the responsibility of the student. (Bulletin of Information Undergraduate Studies, pp 39 1995/6.)"

In this class (Computer and Engineering Ethics) students can miss three classes without losing points. After this, each further absence will result in four points being subtracted from the student's semester point total. This module does not in any way affect the university policy or this syllabus policy; both

---

[2]http://www.computingcases.org
[3]This content is available online at <http://cnx.org/content/m13788/1.3/>.

stand as stated above. However, above and beyond University and syllabus policy, this module uses class attendance as the occasion to reflect upon and realize two important ethical values, responsibility and honesty. Students will print and fill out the form given below and turn it in to the class instructor upon each absence. Emphasis under responsibility will be on missing class only for morally legitimate purposes and on the student's demonstrating a responsible attitude for the class missed by developing a corrective action plan. Under honesty, the student will make an affirmation that the reasons provided are, in reality, the reasons underlying the absence. Honesty will also come into play as the student commits to attending class in the future.

## 7.2.2 Exercise One

**Understanding Morally Legitimate Excuses**

- The table below lists characteristics of what ethicists call "capacity responsibility." These conditions–presented by F.H. Bradley–describe when we can associate an agent with an action for the purposes of moral evaluation. They consist of (1) self-sameness, (2) moral sense, and (3) ownership. Only the last applies in the case of absences. Here excuses arise from compulsion or ignorance. Conflicting obligations,compelling circumstances, and ignorance serve as the basis of morally legitimate excuses.
- The table above correlates general excuses with the conditions of capacity responsibility that they deny. For example, since you are not morally responsible for actions performed under compulsion, and your car breaking down on the road is compulsion, then you are not morally responsible for missing class when your car breaks down.
- But you are responsible for falling under compulsion or ignorance if these present states have resulted from your past negligence. Aristotle, for example, allows for excusing actions performed out of compulsion and because of compulsion. But actions performed out of compulsion but due to past negligence fall under the umbrella of responsibility. So if your car broke down because you failed to check it for foreseeable mechanical failure, then the untoward action is due to your negligence, not to circumstances beyond your control.

### Retroactive Responsibility Table

| Retroactive Responsibility | Excuse | Excuse Statement (Some Examples) |
|---|---|---|
| | 1. Conflicts within a role responsibility and between different role responsibilities. | I have a special project due in another class and finishing it conflicts with attending your class. |
| | 2. Overly determining situational constraints: conflicting interests. | I am interviewing for a position after I graduate, and I must be off the island for a few days. |
| | 3. Overly determining situational constraints: resource constraints | My car had a flat tire. My babysitter couldn't come so I had to stay home with my child. My alarm clock didn't go off because of a power outage. |
| | | *continued on next page* |

| | 4. Knowledge limitations | Class was rescheduled, and I was unaware of the change. |
|---|---|---|
| | 5. Knowledge limitations | I didn't know the assignment for class so I cam unprepared. (Not an excuse for missing class) |

**Table 7.1**

**Exercise 1:  Provide a Morally Justifiable Excuse for Missing Class**

- Offer an honest and responsible ethical assessment of the reason you were unable to carry out your role responsibility for coming to class. Note that the default here is attending class and any departure from the default (i.e., missing class) requires a moral justification.
- Begin by examining whether your action can be classified as an excuse arising out of compulsion or ignorance.
- Your absence may not be morally excusable. In this case, you cannot **excuse** your absence but still must **explain** it.
- Remember that, following Aristotle, you must show that your action was done under and because of compulsion or under and because of ignorance. In other words, you must show that it did not arise from past negligence or recklessness.

## 7.2.3 Proactive/Prospective Responsibility

- In this class, it is not enough to offer a moral excuse to get "off the hook" for your absence. Expressing remorse, guilt, and regret help you to disassociate yourself from moral harms or wrongs. But it is also necessary to take measures to prevent the problem from reoccurring in the future.
- This can be put even more forcefully. According to the "Principle of Responsive Adjustment" (or PRA), failure to take measures to prevent past excusable wrongs from reoccuring leads us to reevaluate these past actions as no longer excusable but culpable. Showing an unwillingness to "learn from the past" reveals past negligence or recklessness as–if not intended–at least not unintended. (See Peter A. French, **Corporate and Collective Responsibility**)
- Responsibility as a virtue originates in the project of converting our moral weaknesses into strengths. If past wrongs occurred because of compulsion, future prevention requires extending control and power. If past wrongs occurred because of ignorance, future prevention requires extending and maintaining necessary knowledge.
- The table below describes the characteristics of a preventive stance where we begin by identifying potential wrongs and harms. Once we identify these then we take serious measures to prevent them from occurring.
- Finally, responsibility as a virtue opens up the horizon of the exemplary. Pursuing excellence requires our identifying opportunities to go beyond preventing harm to realizing value.
- Your job here is to go beyond attending class to outlining and realizing exemplary participation. Think of what this entails, first within your group, and then within the class as a whole.

| Responsibility as a Virtue or Proactive Responsibility | Characteristic | Proactive Response |
|---|---|---|
| | Diffuse blame avoidance strategies | Avoid trying to diffuse the blame for missing class on some other person or situation. For example, "I couldn't come to class because I had a project due in another class" is not a morally legitimate excuse because it places the blame on the other class. You have not taken responsibility for your absence. |
| | Design responsibilities with overlapping domains | If you fail to participate in a group activity, describe the group's "Plan B," i.e., how they worked around your absence. |
| | Extend the scope and depth of knowledge. | Describe how you found out what was covered in class and document how you have learned this material |
| | Extend power and control | Describe the measures you have taken to eliminate the "responsibility gap" between you and your work group. For example, how did you "make up" for not participating in the activity held in the class you missed. |
| | Adopt a proactive problem solving/preventive approach for the future | Describe what measures you have taken to avoid missing classes in the future. |

**Table 7.2**

**Exercise 2: Getting Proactive about your absence**

- Develop a plan for "getting back into the loop." What are you going to do to cover the material and activities you have missed?
- Get Preventive. Describe what you are going to do now to avoid absences in the future.
- Shoot for the ideal. What can you do–above and beyond class attendance–to realize exemplary participation in your ethics class.

## 7.2.4 Conclusion

### Exercise #3: Getting and Staying Honest

- Below is a template that you need to duplicate, fill out, and place in the class attendance file that will be on the desk in front of class.
- Duplicate and sign the honesty pledge at the end of this module.
- Students often wish to provide evidence documenting their claims regarding their absences. You may do this, but remember that this is neither required nor in the spirit of prospective responsibility.
- Furthermore, be aware that you are not to provide confidential information such as personal health information or student id numbers or social security numbers. Health issues are to be referred to generically by saying something like, "I was unable to come to class Tuesday because of health reasons."

1. Class Missed (Day of week and date):
   2. Material covered during class:
   3. Reason for missing class (please do not provide confidential information):
   4. Action Plan for Absence: How you intend to take responsibility for the material covered while you were absent; How you intend to make reparations to your group for not participating in group learning activities for the class you missed;
   5. How do you plan to avoid absences in the future:

### Honesty Pledge

- To realize the value of honesty, you will make the following affirmation:
- **The information I have provided above is truthful, the excuses I have ennumerated rigorously examined from a moral point of view, and the responsive commitments I have made above are serious, and I will take active and realistic efforts to carry them out.**

   Signature:_____

# Index of Keywords and Terms

**Keywords** are listed by the section with that keyword (page numbers are in parentheses). Keywords do not necessarily appear in the text of the page. They are merely associated with that section. *Ex.* apples, § 1.1 (1) **Terms** are referenced by the page they appear on. *Ex.* apples, 1

# Attributions

## Business Ethics

Business Ethics is a derived copy from the Corporate Governance course previously published in Connexions. While many courses using this title place emphasis on applying classical philosophical and ethical theory, this course's approach is decidedly interdisciplinary and practical. It is not designed as a socio-humanistic elective, a service philosophy course, or even an applied philosophical ethics course but as a laboratory, skills-based course where students develop, practice, and refine decision-making and problem-solving strategies that they will carry with them into the world of business practice. Emphasis has been placed on responding to the four ethical themes identified by the AACSB ethics task force: Ethical Leadership, Ethical Decision-Making, Social Responsibility, and Corporate Governance. Modules include (1) theory building activities (responsibility, rights, virtue), (2) problem specification frameworks emphasizing socio-technical system building and analogies with design, (3) specific modules responding to AACSB ethics themes (moral ecologies, corporate social responsibility, corporate governance, and a history of the modern corporation) and (4) modules that provide the course with a capstone, integrative experience (Business Ethics Bowl, Social Impact Statement Reports, and Corporate Ethics Compliance Officer Reports). While a quick glance shows that this collection holds more modules than can possibly be covered in a single semester, this approach gives the user flexibility as to the method used for integrating ethics into the business administration curriculum. Modules can be recombined into different standalone courses such as business ethics, business/government/society, or environment of organizations. Since each module can be covered independently, they can be integrated into the business administration curriculum as specific interventions in mainstream business courses in areas like accounting, finance, management, information systems, human resources or office administration. (In fact many have been written for and tested in these circumstances.) Business Ethics has been developed through the NSF-funded project, "Collaborative Development of Ethics Across the Curriculum Resources and Sharing of Best Practices," NSF SES 0551779.

## About Connexions

Since 1999, Connexions has been pioneering a global system where anyone can create course materials and make them fully accessible and easily reusable free of charge. We are a Web-based authoring, teaching and learning environment open to anyone interested in education, including students, teachers, professors and lifelong learners. We connect ideas and facilitate educational communities.

Connexions's modular, interactive courses are in use worldwide by universities, community colleges, K-12 schools, distance learners, and lifelong learners. Connexions materials are in many languages, including English, Spanish, Chinese, Japanese, Italian, Vietnamese, French, Portuguese, and Thai. Connexions is part of an exciting new information distribution system that allows for **Print on Demand Books**. Connexions has partnered with innovative on-demand publisher QOOP to accelerate the delivery of printed course materials and textbooks into classrooms worldwide at lower prices than traditional academic publishers.